ETHICAL PATTERNS IN EARLY CHRISTIAN THOUGHT

Previous works by the same author

Justin Martyr (J C. B. Mohr (Paul Siebeck), 1973)

The Philosophy of Clement of Alexandria (C.U.P., 1957)

ETHICAL PATTERNS IN EARLY CHRISTIAN THOUGHT

ERIC OSBORN

PROFESSOR OF NEW TESTAMENT AND
EARLY CHRISTIANITY
QUEEN'S COLLEGE
UNIVERSITY OF MELBOURNE

CAMBRIDGE UNIVERSITY PRESS

CAMBRIDGE

LONDON · NEW YORK · MELBOURNE

Published by the Syndics of the Cambridge University Press
The Pitt Building, Trumpington Street, Cambridge CB2 1RP
Bentley House, 200 Euston Road, London NW1 2DB
32 East 57th Street, New York, NY 10022, USA
296 Beaconsfield Parade, Middle Park, Melbourne 3206, Australia

First published 1976

Printed in Great Britain by
Western Printing Services Ltd
Bristol

Library of Congress Cataloguing in Publication data

Osborn, Eric Francis
Ethical patterns in early Christian thought

Bibliography: p. 221
Includes index
1. Christian ethics – Early church, ca. 30–600. I. Title

BJ1212.08   241   75–10040

ISBN 0 521 20835 1

CONTENTS

TO
WILLIAM ELLIS
AND
IN MEMORY OF
WILLIAM J. HUNKIN

PREFACE

At the end of '*Christian Ethics and Contemporary Philosophy*', the editor, I. T. Ramsey, stressed the urgent need for 'such a thorough biblical and patristic study, including a study of Christian moral theology down the ages, as enables us both to formulate the most reliable Christian principles and the moral obligations they express, relating this understanding to some key-phrase in terms of which the full Christian commitment is given'. This book springs from a sense of the same need. It begins with an account of the function of ethical patterns. After the historical background and New Testament beginnings, the ethics of Clement of Alexandria, Basil, John Chrysostom and Augustine are examined. The four patterns of righteousness, discipleship, faith and love are seen in the distinctive thought of each writer. Exposition is tied to text because ethical terms are either ambiguous or meaningless when lifted out of context. Two necessary features of any Christian ethic emerge – a respect for the contingent and a challenge to perfection.

The obstacles to a work of this scope are considerable; there is too much material. The New Testament possesses an ethical complexity which has been carefully explored. Clement's writings are oriented to ethics and intricate in content. Basil poses questions to which there are no answers. Suidas said that it was for God, not man, to know all that John Chrysostom had written; Isidore of Seville confidently asserted that anyone who claimed to have read all of Augustine was a liar.

The wider one's bounds are set, the greater is the need for discussion and criticism. It would be impossible to name all who have helped in this way. In scholarship as in all things, 'Wir sind Bettler' and no man can list his creditors. Some debts stand out. The late A. Boyce Gibson helped me to see the issues, while Ernst Käsemann and C. F. D. Moule pointed the way through the New Testament. Maurice Wiles read and commented on an earlier draft. Study leave in Cambridge provided the opportunity to complete the work in conversation with G. W. H. Lampe and other scholars. In the checking of references and manuscript, William Ellis, Andrew Lenox-Conyngham and Robin Wood have been of great assistance. To all these and others I am deeply grateful for the friendship Augustine prized as 'cocta fervore parilium studiorum'. Finally, I wish to thank the University Press who have once again showed me a competence and a care which are beyond praise.

Queen's College   ERIC OSBORN
University of Melbourne
30 September 1974

ABBREVIATIONS

ABR	Australian Biblical Review
ATR	Anglican Theological Review
BHT	Beiträge zur historischen Theologie
CQ	Classical Quarterly
CR	The Classical Review
CSEL	Corpus Scriptorum Ecclesiasticorum Latinorum
DCB	Dictionary of Christian Biography
DR	Downside Review
GCS	Die griechischen christlichen Schriftsteller
JBL	Journal of Biblical Literature
JR	The Journal of Religion
JTS	Journal of Theological Studies
MSR	Mélanges de Science Religieuse
NTS	New Testament Studies
POC	Le Proche-Orient Chrétien
RA	Recherches augustiniennes
RAC	Reallexikon für Antike und Christentum
RAM	Revue d'Ascétique et Mystique
RB	Revue Biblique
REA	Revue des Études Augustiniennes
REG	Revue des Études Grecques
RHPR	Revue d'Histoire et Philosophie Religieuses
RP	Historia Philosophiae Graecae, H. Ritter et L. Preller (8th edition, 1898)
RSR	Recherches de Science Religieuse
RevSR	Revue des Sciences Religieuses
SA	Studia Anselmiana
SC	Sources Chrétiennes
SVF	Stoicorum Veterum Fragmenta, von Arnim
TU	Texte und Untersuchungen
TWNT	Theologisches Wörterbuch zum Neuen Testament, Kittel
VC	Vigiliae Christianae
ZAM	Zeitschrift für Aszese und Mystik
ZNW	Zeitschrift für die Neutestamentliche Wissenschaft

INTRODUCTION

An examination of early Christian ethics may begin with a brief appreciation of those contemporary factors which make this enterprise appropriate now. The study of ethics has, in the last thirty years, moved towards a wider recognition of the complexity and diversity of ethical problems. If moral philosophy is a practical science concerned with questions of the form 'What shall I do?' then, one writer insists, 'no general answer can be given to this type of question. The most a moral philosopher can do is to paint a picture of various types of life in the manner of Plato and ask which type of life you really want to lead.'[1] Another sees the function of moral philosophy as 'that of helping us to think better about moral questions by exposing the logical structure of the language in which this thought is expressed'.[2] For him moral judgements are prescriptive, can be universalised,[3] are descriptive and may be logically interrelated.[4] Reason, good reason for acting in one way rather than in another, provides another way of looking at ethical inquiry or moral judgements.[5] The crucial thing is that we should have moral points of reference which we have deliberately adopted. 'To become morally adult is...to learn to use "ought"-sentences in the realisation that they can only be verified by reference to a standard or set of principles which we have by our own decision accepted and made our own.'[6]

Still more recently has come a criticism of this prescriptivism, which finds it, like the intuitionism and emotivism which preceded it, barren and restrictive. There is urgent need to identify the subject-matter of ethics and to see it as 'a subject in which there is still almost everything to be done'.[7]

[1] P. H. Nowell Smith, *Ethics* (Oxford, 1957), pp. 277f.
[2] R. M. Hare, *Freedom and Reason* (Oxford, 1963), p.v.
[3] *Ibid.*, p. 4.
[4] *Ibid.*, p. 16.
[5] R. M. Hare, *The Language of Morals* (Oxford, 2 ed. 1961), p. 197; cf. K. Baier, *The Moral Point of View* (Cornell, 1958), p.v.
[6] R. M. Hare, *The Language of Morals*, p. 196.
[7] G. J. Warnock, *Contemporary Moral Philosophy* (London, 1967), p. 77.

Under the promising title *The Varieties of Goodness*[8] another writer has shown the breadth of ethical questions. In particular the neglect of any consideration of virtue or virtues has been remedied. Virtues are neither value-terms like good and bad nor are they normative terms like right and wrong.[9] A distinct category, virtues are states or traits of character. They are relevant to choice-situations in which the good of some being is at stake. They enable a choice to be made without the obscuring or blurring effects of passion.[10] The reinstatement of virtue and virtues, or the study of 'aretaics' as it was once called,[11] is an encouragement for the study of early Christian ethics. Much of the material may be considered under this head; but something more remains. The determining ideas in ethics are never simply ethical and this is clearly the case in early Christian writings. The concepts which give coherence and vitality to ethical thought may be called patterns or pictures. Moral judgements are only a part of morals. What holds them together? Aesthetic or quasi-aesthetic concepts like 'patterns', 'myth' and 'picture' play an important part.[12] Moral life is not just the record of the choices which one makes nor even the record of what one does.

> When we apprehend and assess other people we do not consider only their solutions to specifiable practical problems, we consider something more elusive which may be called their total vision of life, as shown in their mode of speech or silence, their choice of words, their assessments of others, their conception of their own lives, what they think attractive or praiseworthy, what they think funny: in short, the configurations of their thought which show continually in their reactions and conversation.[13]

One may go further and insist that there are positive and radical moral conceptions which stand over against universal rules. These are concerned with the infinite variety of the world, 'the importance of not assuming that one has got individuals and situations "taped", the connection of knowledge with love and of spiritual insight with apprehension of the unique'.[14] A morality is a complex, a ramification of

---

[8] G. H. von Wright, *The Varieties of Goodness* (London, 1963).

[9] *Ibid.*, p. 136.

[10] *Ibid.*, p. 147.

[11] J. Laird, *An Enquiry into Moral Notions* (London, 1935), pp. 13–98.

[12] R. W. Hepburn, 'Vision and Choice in Morality', in *Christian Ethics and Contemporary Philosophy* (ed. I. T. Ramsey, London, 1966), pp. 181ff.

[13] Iris Murdoch, 'Vision and Choice in Morality', in *Christian Ethics and Contemporary Philosophy*, p. 202.

[14] Iris Murdoch, *op. cit.*, pp. 208ff. L. Wittgenstein, *Philosophical Investigations*, 226e.

concepts. What appear to be single judgements owe their apparent simplicity to the number of suppressed premisses which we all employ. Further, important moral values are visions, inspirations or powers which have to be explored rather than analysed. Wittgenstein was concerned to safeguard diversity when he said, 'What has to be accepted, the given is – so one could say – *forms of life*.' One must accept the givenness of the various forms of moral life and not try to find a single form behind them.

The third encouraging element in contemporary ethics is a deepening seriousness. On the one hand it has been shown 'that moral virtues must be connected with human good and harm, and that it is quite impossible to call anything you like good or harm'.[15] On the other hand the urbanity of much twentieth-century ethics has worn thin. An unconscious behaviourism may be discerned behind it. Moral concepts are not merely factual statements plus recommendations, and moral judgements need not be universal. The inner life cannot be reduced to overt choices. Nor is man as free as he sometimes thinks.[16]

In this context a restatement of Platonism has been put forward.[17] To this view we shall return since it offers a contemporary expression of the mind of the early fathers. For while the detail of their ethics is frequently Stoic, the shape is predominantly Platonist. It would be hard to exaggerate the importance for Christian ethics of this recent account of the sovereignty of Good.

The movement from the banal has been continued by another concise work.[18] The amoralist is shown to have moral sensibility as soon as he thinks in terms of others' need and interests.[19] Disagreement in moral matters does not indicate subjectivism but rather that 'you cannot pass the moral buck on to how the world is'.[20] Consideration of human nature does not lead to a unique moral ideal for there are too many things which may claim to be distinctively human.[21] A swift, negative critique of utilitarianism rounds off the work.[22]

[15] P. Foot, 'Moral Beliefs', in *Theories of Ethics* (ed. P. Foot, Oxford, 1967), p. 92.

[16] Iris Murdoch, 'Vision and Choice in Morality', pp. 217 and 198.

[17] Iris Murdoch, *The Sovereignty of Good* (London, 1970).

[18] Bernard Williams, *Morality* (Penguin Books, 1973).

[19] *Ibid.*, p. 25.

[20] *Ibid.*, p. 47. 'The fact that men of equal intelligence, factual knowledge and so forth, confronted with the same situation, may morally disagree shows something about morality – that (roughly) you cannot pass the moral buck on to how the world is. But that does not show (as subjectivism originally seemed to insinuate) that there is something *wrong* with it.'

[21] *Ibid.*, p. 76.

[22] This is further developed in J. J. C. Smart and Bernard Williams, *Utilitarianism* (Cambridge, 1973).

The new depth of ethical study makes it easier to approach the ethics of early Christian writers for their concern with moral issues was intense. Dread of evil and enthusiasm for good were always with them. Today the obvious evils of war and hunger, brought to wider notice by new means of communication, ensure that some moral issues will be taken seriously.

A final feature of contemporary thought is a thoughtful rejection of Christian claims. Morality cannot depend on religion because of 'the impossibility of thinking coherently about God'. Religious motives need not invalidate the autonomy of morals but they cannot help because religion is incurably unintelligible.[23] An increasing number of people believe Christian moral judgements to be wrong in fundamental ways.[24] Christians need to recognise that the universe is far from sympathetic to milder aspects of their morality,[25] and that the harsher aspects (intransigence, unfairness, rigour and neglect of human concerns) are far from attractive.[26] Artists and lovers, parents and patriots are just as able as Christians to forget themselves.[27] The record of Christian morality does not evoke confidence. Time and again Christians have stood to conserve what was bad and to hinder reform. The character of God in the Christian story of redemption seems repugnant. Too much in the ascetic tradition is plainly morbid. Inequality of sexes and psychological terror have come from the same authoritarian source. Intolerance has discouraged intellectual honesty.[28]

The need for exploration in this area is therefore urgent. It is not merely a matter of better understanding but a question of integrity. Christians have no grounds for holding to moral standards which are plainly inferior or impenetrably obscure. Four things, then, diversity of material, patterns which give coherence, a new seriousness and current criticism, point to the work of reassessing early Christian ethics. The second factor is most important for it provides a method.

Patterns or pictures indicate a necessary element in ethical analysis. 'Man is a creature who makes pictures of himself and then comes to resemble the picture. This is the process which moral philosophy must attempt to describe and analyse.'[29] The work which follows is descrip-

[23] Bernard Williams, *Morality*, p. 86.
[24] See H. Oppenheimer, *The Character of Christian Morality* (London, 1965), which begins, p. 11, 'Christian morality today needs to be defended, but it is not yet clear where the main battle is to be fought and what is to count as victory.'
[25] *Ibid.*, p. 38.   [26] *Ibid.*, p. 62.   [27] *Ibid.*, p. 72.
[28] D. Cupitt, *Crisis of Moral Authority* (London, 1972), p. 10. These theses are sustained in the course of Mr Cupitt's valuable book.
[29] Iris Murdoch, 'Metaphysics and Ethics', *The Nature of Metaphysics* (ed. D. F. Pears, London, 1957), p. 122.

tion and analysis of patterns or pictures which persist through the first centuries of Christianity and which have two continuing characteristics: *a respect for the contingent and an awareness of perfection.* Unlike moral codes, patterns or pictures can deal with the contingent and the perfect at the same time. Patterns must respect contingency and variety. Some pictures seem simple and unambiguous; but this simplicity must either be transformed or discarded.[30] Clement valued symbolic language because it could say more than one thing at a time, like 'shapes seen through veils which add more allusions to them'.[31] The variety of human experience forces pictures to produce related galleries. We cannot hope to catalogue but we can show the creativity. Patterns are not exclusive and often come together to produce subordinate creations. There will always be untidiness. 'Reality is not a given whole. An understanding of this, a respect for the contingent, is essential to imagination as opposed to fantasy.'[32]

Christianity, as a religion of divine incarnation, is committed to both a sense of perfection and a respect for the contingent. This leads to a second reason why Christian talk about ethics should be considered as picture or pattern. Christianity offers a challenge to perfection and, like true art, always looks beyond itself. It does not give a secular or commonsense morality. 'Be ye perfect as your Father in heaven is perfect' cannot be translated into a prudential code. It stands as far from any moral behaviourism of the last forty years as a great work of art stands from a television advertisement. 'While thus renewing our sense of distance we may remind ourselves that art too lives in a region where all human endeavour is failure.'[33] We turn now to the background of early Christianity and then to four great patterns which will show a respect for the contingent and a challenge to perfection.

GREECE

The glory of ancient Greece was an insistence that right and wrong, justice and injustice, were not matters of human opinion, but were fixed by an eternal pattern. Five hundred years before Christ was born, the obscure Heraclitus of Ephesus wrote, 'The people should fight for

---

[30] It has taken two millennia to modify the Greek athletic ideal to a recent account, 'The chaplain has a pleasant way of making you think that Jesus Christ once rowed for the college...and that even now he is the finest stroke that any crew could possibly have in the great Boat Race which is life', R. J. White, *Cambridge Life* (London, 1960), p. 75.

[31] *Stromateis* 5.9.56.5.

[32] Iris Murdoch, 'Against Dryness', *Encounter XVI* (1961), 20.

[33] *Ibid.* Cf. A. Boyce Gibson, *The Challenge of Perfection* (Melbourne, 1968).

the law as if for their city wall.' 'All human laws are nourished by one divine law.'[34] The story of Greek justice takes form around the figure of *Solon* who was responsible for the code of Athenian laws. Solon said of the law, 'Beneath her rule all things throughout the world are tuned to wisdom and to harmony.' He insisted that his laws were the same for rich and for poor, 'I wrote laws for the base-born and the noble alike, and fitted a rule of justice, straight and true to every man.' Solon foresaw the destruction of his city, not at the hands of an outside enemy, but at the hands of the people themselves, for they could not survive the day when they neglected 'the holy foundations of justice'.[35] Behind the affairs of men stood a pattern of right and justice which no one could alter or ignore.

Three great philosophies contributed to a deeper understanding of moral truth. Plato drew inspiration from the heroic figure of Socrates who was concerned to stand out against any values beside those of virtue and truth. There is an ultimate simplicity in morals.

> In the divine there is no shadow of unrighteousness, only the perfection of righteousness. Nothing is more like the divine than any one of us who becomes as righteous as possible. It is here that a man shows his true spirit and power or lack of spirit and nothingness. For to know this is wisdom and excellence of the genuine sort; not to know it is to be manifestly blind and base.[36]

Righteousness is the only thing that matters, and those who imagine that they are great because they ignore moral standards are poorest and weakest of all.

Plato devoted his longest dialogue to the question of justice or righteousness. He considered it in man and in the state, for the two must go together. It is a harmony of parts of the soul, 'binding together all these elements and moulding the many within into one temperate and harmonious whole'.[37] Other virtues like fortitude, wisdom and self-control are concerned with particular parts of the soul, while justice involves the agreement of all three parts. Virtues are connected for it is not possible to have one without others and virtue is the excellence or function of the soul, so that a bad soul will do bad things, and a good soul will do good things. Virtue is also health, vigour or harmony and fulfils man's excellence as a man.[38] Man is free and can only blame himself for his misdeeds. God is not responsible for what man has chosen. The blame is on the one who chooses.[39] Good and evil are

---

[34] Heraclitus, RP 43.
[35] Solon. See K. Freeman, *The Paths of Justice* (London, 1954), pp. 19–30.
[36] *Theaetetus* 176 (Cornford's translation is generally followed.)
[37] *Republic* 443.   [38] *Republic* 353.   [39] *Republic* 617.

mutually necessary in this world, so that the only way to avoid evil is to escape to a divine world. This flight is described as becoming like God as far as possible and likeness to God is achieved by becoming just with the help of wisdom.[40] The one goal of all actions is the good, and every man must distinguish between the good, the pleasant, and the bad.[41] Virtue is knowledge and can be taught. True virtue can be found in no one but the wise man or the philosopher. Unless such a man rules over a state it will not achieve justice. Morals find their fulfilment in politics.

Aristotle stresses even more firmly the importance of goal or end in morals and reaffirms the importance of politics. Man is a political animal.[42] All men seek for well-being, which is the supreme good, desired for its own sake and found when man fulfils his proper function by acting in accordance with reason. This function of man acts out the best and most complete virtue, and spreads over a complete life. The excellence of man is the excellence of his soul which has two parts, rational and irrational. To the rational part belong the intellectual excellences such as wisdom and prudence. Moral excellences are concerned with the emotional half of the irrational part of the soul. Virtue is chiefly taught and becomes habit. It is found in the mean between excess and deficiency. Virtue is a state of 'deliberate moral purpose, consisting in a mean which is relative to our souls, the mean being determined by reason or as a prudent man would determine it'. Courage lies between foolhardiness and cowardice, temperance between licence and insensibility, friendliness between cringing and quarrelsomeness. A man should try to avoid the extreme which seems to be further from the mean, and to pull himself in the direction which is opposite to his natural inclination. When he cannot find a mean he should choose the lesser of the evils which confront him. Moral purpose involves deliberate choice. Virtue and vice are freely chosen, and therefore may be rewarded or punished. Justice takes different forms, such as distributive justice which works by proportion to allot what is fair, and corrective justice which tries to balance what has been uneven. The mean is chosen by right reason, that part of the soul which is rational in obedience to truth. The highest form of human life passes beyond human limits to what is divine. God is the simple unmoved mover of all things, the highest good, an eternal, living being. Man achieves happiness by becoming like this pure being; 'If pure intellect as compared with human nature is divine, so too will the life in accordance with it be divine compared with man's ordinary life.'[43] Summing up,

[40] *Theaetetus* 176.   [41] *Gorgias* 499.
[42] Aristotle, *Nicomachean Ethics, passim,* and *Politics* 1253
[43] *Nic. Eth.* 1177.

the good is what man aims at, that is, his happiness or the performance
of his function as a man. Moral virtue is concerned with the rational
control of desires and is learnt by practice and the formation of habit.
Virtue is rational and in its obedience to reason it follows the mean
between excess and deficiency. The wise man becomes like God because
God's function is contemplation and thought and these things fulfil
man's highest excellence.

By the beginning of the Christian era, the dominant ethical teaching
was that of *Stoicism*. Plato and Aristotle continued to be important, and
indeed Stoicism absorbed much of what they had said. Morals became
the chief part of philosophy, and were centred upon the ideal of the
Stoic sage. Stoicism, now three hundred years old, had lost some of its
first rigour and made allowance for man's imperfections and development. The Stoics divided man into body and soul, or into body, mind
and soul. Marcus Aurelius said, 'You are made up of three parts – body,
breath, mind. The first two are yours insofar as they require your care;
only the third is properly your own.'[44] The body was a hindrance, or at
least a subordinate thing. Seneca went so far from Zeno's high estimate
as to call it a prison house, following an Orphic maxim. The soul contains reason, which is the ruling part, and guides man in his desire to
live agreeably with nature. The world is governed by necessity; the path
of virtue recognises what is and what is not within our power. The
things which are not in our power include wealth and position. 'For
if the essence of the good be in those things that are in our own power,
neither envy nor jealousy has any place, and you will not long to be a
general, a president or a consul, but you will long to be free. There is
only one path to freedom and that is to despise the things which are
not in our own power.'[45] Nothing external can harm man. Only he can
harm himself. There are no degrees in virtue or vice. A man is either
good or bad and it is as easy to drown in one foot of water as it is to
drown in ten. Virtue is its own reward and vice is its own punishment.
The worth of virtue is independent of our appreciation of it. Within the
wide sphere of things which are indifferent because they are not in our
power, there are things which are to be preferred and which have worth
over against things which are not to be preferred and which have no
worth. The wise man alone is free and reflects the image of the God
from whom all have sprung. Yet despite man's dignity his feelings must
not be recognised. 'If you love an earthen jar you must say "it is only
an earthen jar that I love," for when it is broken you will not be per-
turbed; when you kiss your little child or your wife, say that you are
kissing a human being, and then when either of them dies you will not

[44] Marcus Aurelius, *Meditations* 12.2.
[45] Epictetus *Encheir.* 19.

be shaken.'[46] Stoics stressed the importance of the training of the soul.
Plato had spoken of the philosopher's life as the practice of death, and
Epictetus wrote, 'The school of the philosophers, O men, is a surgery;
you should not go out of it pleased but in pain."[47]

Man strives to live according to nature or to reason. He achieves
happiness when the soul within him becomes like God and is self-
sufficient and autonomous. The wise man is free from passion, possessing the virtue of *apatheia*. The ideal of the wise man is always before the
Stoic as he spares no effort or sacrifice to reach the goal of wisdom and
independence. Men are bound together by the spermatic logos which is
in them all. The world is one city in which all men are citizens. Virtue
is a corporate thing. Men are members one of another, and the world
is the one parent of us all. The wise man bears the burden of government. Stoicism produced statesmen and rulers.

When we look at the broad scope of Greek ethics we may hazard
some general comments. The good life is a matter of virtue, excellence
or function. It should be lived according to nature or an order which is
basic to the world, and should pursue the final end toward which all
things point. The soul must be ruled by its rational rather than its
irrational part. Man is autonomous as an individual, and the goal of
the good life is to give him freedom and independence. External things
cannot make man good or bad. Wealth and position are irrelevant to
the virtue of the soul. Family life and marriage must not conflict with
the progress of the individual, and the moral significance of domestic
relations is not great. Education is important and the training of children is given a high place.

The general as well as some of the particular features of Platonic,
Aristotelian and Stoic ethics are found in early Christian ethical discourse. They mean something different because they are joined and
used in different ways. What this new and sometimes loose synthesis is,
cannot be predicted. There is no one general principle which will
explain what happens when the terms change their context. We have
seen what they mean in one context. We shall see later what they mean
in other contexts.

ISRAEL

The people of Israel are joined in common pursuit of a good life, for
the Hebrew speaks of his fellow Hebrew as neighbour or brother. To
this holy nation, God has spoken his will; ethics are bound to a personal
God. It is the Lord who requires that man should do justice, love mercy,

---

[46] Epictetus, *Encheir.* 3.   [47] Epictetus, *Diss.* 3, 23.

and walk humbly with his God. The covenant which binds Israel and God together, pledges Israel to be holy as the Lord God is holy. God has acted in the history of his people and made his ways known. In the golden days, God acted through his anointed king. The king led his people in battle, brought them before God in worship and dispensed justice. As God worked through his king, so God himself is a king to his people, bound to them by personal loyalty. The law of God tells man his place in God's world and guides him concerning his duties to God and to his neighbour. The study and practice of the law bring virtue and wisdom. God's people delight in his law.[48]

Simeon the Righteous maintains that the world rests on three foundations – the law, the worship of God and the doing of kindnesses.[49] The law embodies an unqualified demand for loyalty to God and respect for man. The worship of the temple governs the whole life of the Jew. His obligations in worship were as much his duty to God as was the fulfilment of the law. Acts of kindness or mercy point to the covenant relation between God and his people. The inward direction of the heart to God is all important and it is wrong to obey the law for selfish reasons; obedience must be directed to God himself.[50]

There is considerable variety in the Judaism of the first century; but certain things are general. Law, ethics and worship are held together, and righteousness is central in each. The consciousness of a covenant people remains, and Hellenising influence has been resisted in the Maccabean revolt and in the conscious promotion of independent Jewish culture. Intellectual resistance shows itself among the Pharisees and in sects which look to an imminent end in which God will vindicate his people. The Pharisees studied the detail of the law and elaborated its requirements. Their legalism was less rigorous and more humane and practical than has been thought. The sects, which we understand through Qumran, were inspired with fervent eschatological zeal. In preparation for the fiery day they turned from outward observance to inward piety and humility. The poor man of the Psalms was their ideal as they withdrew from the world.

Hellenistic Judaism is best seen in Philo, an eclectic Platonist who links the formula of man's assimilation to God with the biblical doctrine of man made in the image of God. He adds the Stoic theme that one should live in conformity with nature, identifying natural and Mosaic law, and tries to combine practical and contemplative lives, moderation of and freedom from passion. His highest virtue is faith, or piety. From

[48] For the following outline I am indebted in several parts to A. Dihle for his article in *RAC*, 6, 'Ethik', 646–796.

[49] Pirke Aboth 1.2 (ed. R. T. Herford, 1945).

[50] T. W. Manson, *Ethics and the Gospel* (London, 1960), chapters 1 and 2.

his many sources he builds no final system, but makes important initial moves. His acceptance of the Platonic formula of assimilation to God[51] marks a central point in the history of human thought, for it blends biblical and Platonic ethics.

Judaism shares with Hellenism a respect for political activity which does not come over into Christianity. A modern Jewish critique of Jesus' idea of God is interesting: 'However lofty a conception it may represent for the individual moral conscience, it stands for ruin and catastrophe for the general conscience, for the public, social, national and universal conscience.'[52]

Looking back over Greek ethics we observe two main patterns. The good is part of a rational order which stands in or beyond the world. All that man does is set against the order of a moral universe. In each case we also found that the order was related to a chief end or supreme good. In the case of Stoicism, order was more important than end. In the case of Plato, both are important, while for Aristotle the end dominates. When we turn to Christianity, the patterns of righteousness or order and of purpose or end are found again. Righteousness is a different thing but it remains a way and an order. The end has become a person. The end of Christian discipleship is to follow Jesus, who has little in common with the philosophers' god. Judaism has anticipated the service of a personal God and the zeal for righteousness.

Christianity goes further in two directions. Righteousness is modified by the account of faith, about which the Greeks had little to say. Faith recognises man's sin and is the way to freedom. The end is modified by love. To become like the Christian God means to love even more than Judaism had anticipated. Love shows what grace can do, and demands the love of enemies because Christ loved us first. In short, Christian ethics begins with the two basic patterns of Greek thought – order and end. It goes beyond these by speaking of both faith and love, because the understanding of justice and the understanding of purpose have been changed by the incarnation, death and resurrection of Jesus Christ. Faith works by love. Faith is the doer and love the deed.[53]

Christian ethics is built around the four patterns of righteousness, discipleship, faith and love. Like every part of Christianity it is subordinate to the gospel of the Word made flesh whence it draws both a respect for the contingent and a sense of perfection. When the tension

---

[51] Philo, *De migratione Abrahami*, 127ff.

[52] J. Klausner, *Jesus of Nazareth* (London, 1925), p. 380. This theme is further developed in the same work, pp. 381–97.

[53] Luther (Weimar edition), 17.2.98.5. Cited by G. Ebeling, *Luther* (Tübingen, 1964), p. 178; (ET, London, Fontana, 1972, p. 159).

between these two is lost, each pattern may degenerate in one of the two directions. It may drift to contingency or to perfection. The distortion towards contingency may be described as legalist or concrete. The perfectionist distortion may be called enthusiast or abstract. Righteousness may become concrete in new sets of rules or abstract in the general principle of natural law. Discipleship may become concrete in ecclesiastical office or undirected mortification. It may become abstract in mystic absorption. Faith may harden into a formal creed or may soften into libetarianism. Love may harden into a mutual benefit society or soften into abstract affection and amoral ecstasy.

How deeply the two poles of contingency and perfection are set in Christian ethics may be seen in a rapid glance at the Sermon on the Mount. The beatitudes offer perfection to those whose quality is contingent. The poor in spirit receive the kingdom and the meek inherit the earth. The hungry are filled and the persecuted have a heavenly reward. Salt must have its savour and light its good works. Love of friend links contingent with contingent but love of enemy links contingent with divine perfection. God shows care for evil and good men alike: that is his perfection. Secret prayer reaches the Father in heaven. The God whose will is done in earth and heaven is asked for a day's supply of bread. The contingent remains contingent but God knows man's daily needs. To those who seek the kingdom the other things are added day by day. Delusions of glory are to be unmasked. Only those who hear and do the sayings of Jesus will survive the storms and floods and be owned by their Lord at the last day.

A similar polarity may be discerned in later Judaism. The whole law can and must be fulfilled. Everyone is in a position to fulfil at least one hundred commandments each day. The drive for good in man can hold his evil tendencies down.[54] At the same time there is an obligation to fulfil the many works of love such as visiting the sick, sheltering the homeless and comforting the mourners. These acts of kindness are set out carefully.[55] In the end of the age all obligations become stronger.

The Qumran Manual of Discipline shows a heightening of concern for perfection and particularity. The members are to hold to all that God has commanded. Total separation from sinners and sinful things, total loyalty to the community and total obedience to God are to be shown in every detail of life.[56]

---

[54] Strack Billerbeck, *Kommentar zum NT aus Talmud und Midrasch* (Munich, 1965), 4, 1, p. 4. There is complete confidence 'dass der Mensch durchaus die volle sittliche Freiheit und Kraft besitze, die Gebote der Tora restlos zu erfüllen'.

[55] *Ibid*. 'Die altjüdischen Liebeswerke', pp. 559–610.

[56] Manual of Discipline 9.23. 'To be a man zealous for the ordinance and its

The Zadokite fragment shows how keeping the covenant means avoiding bad company, refusing dishonest gain, observing the sabbath in every detail and taking the hand of poor and needy.[57]

In his controversies on ethical matters Jesus always pushes the question still further towards contingency or to perfection.[58] Rules and laws break down for two reasons: because they do not allow for individuals who are hungry or ill on the sabbath day, and they are not demanding enough, for true righteousness goes beyond that of scribes and Pharisees. This polarity comes through the whole of the Bible from the Deuteronomic reform through dread of the glorious and fearful name of the Lord and the word that is very near in mouth and heart, to the Spirit who heals the broken hearted and proclaims the acceptable year, or from the divine friend of sinners to the wiping of tears in the New Jerusalem. The radical preaching of the kingdom of God is marked by the co-humanity of men. By different routes, interpreters of Christianity come upon this polarity: 'God the Father and the infinite value of the human soul'[59] or, 'he made co-humanity possible and demanded it. He did not do this on the strength of any human ideal, but connected it directly with the beginning of God's reign on earth.'[60]

What kind of criteria govern the probability of any analysis of ethical patterns? Critical deductive process may establish rule and end as a basic distinction and then see this distinction carried over first to righteousness and discipleship and then to faith and love. Simple empirical processes, like the observation of word frequency, will justify the selection of righteousness, discipleship, faith, love. Each pattern overlaps with other patterns; righteousness and faith must go together and discipleship is unthinkable without love. Each has at some time been regarded as adequate to cover the whole of New Testament ethics; a recognition of the claims of each allows greater sensitivity. To begin with, we spread our nets over the manifold, as Wittgenstein, and Wisdom put it, and allow them to illuminate and bring understanding as

time, for the day of vengeance, and to do God's will in all that he sets his hand to, and in all the exercise of his authority according as he has commanded'.

[57] Zadokite Fragment 6.11–7.6.

[58] A comparable assessment is found in J. C. Fenton, *What was Jesus' Message?* (London, 1971), p. 43: 'It went beyond the Law in two directions: on the one hand, God's demand is greater than that of the Law; on the other hand, God's mercy is wider than that involved in rewarding men according to their deeds. His teaching was offensive on both counts.'

[59] A. von Harnack, *What is Christianity?* (London, 1923), p. 55.

[60] E. Käsemann, *Der Ruf der Freiheit* (Tübingen, 1968), p. 57 (ET of 3 ed., 1969, *Jesus Means Freedom*, p. 40).

they are able. Time and prolonged reflection can judge their value. But such reflection must be critical.[61] What is the new testament or gospel to which these writings point? They are not, in the first place, ethical discourses. Any account of their ethical patterns must be related to the critical process of discerning what the New Testament writers and the fathers consider to be the gospel. Here we are on surer ground; no critical treatment of the documents could deny that, whatever the gospel is, it is constantly concerned with righteousness, discipleship, faith and love.

[61] See E. Käsemann, 'Thoughts on the Present Controversy about Scriptural Interpretation', *Exegetische Versuche und Besinnungen* (hereafter *EVB*), 2, 268–90; *New Testament Questions of Today* (hereafter NTQT), pp. 260–85. See E. F. Osborn, 'Historical-Critical Exegesis – Käsemann's Contribution', *ABR* (1971), pp. 17–35.

I

NEW TESTAMENT

Even if we like diversity, the task of sketching New Testament ethics at first seems formidable. As well as variety of expression there is variety of setting. Every part of the New Testament must be understood against its historical background and the framework of the book in which it is found. We cannot take statements of Matthew and blend them with verses of the Apocalypse. One work is written in the face of the challenge of Judaism redivivus and the other in the face of Nero redivivus. There is a difference of style but that is the smallest thing. The same could be said about the differences between the three Synoptics, Matthew's new law, Mark's mysterious son of man and Luke's world church, even before we move on to the Fourth Gospel with its lord of glory and its community under the word.[1] However, ethical patterns can guide us through this diversity. 'What then does the New Testament effectively provide, in ethics as in doctrine? It yields certain perspectives, patterns and priorities and it forms the Christian mind which then turns to the examination of contemporary issues.'[2] The four main patterns are righteousness (or justice), discipleship, faith and love. We glimpse their New Testament outlines before considering their later development.

RIGHTEOUSNESS

Righteousness[3] dominates two parts of the New Testament – the Epistle

[1] A good brief account is now available in J. L. Houlden, *Ethics and the New Testament* (Penguin Books, 1973). He sets out some distinctive approaches of various NT writers. Two studies by V. R. Furnish, *Theology and Ethics in Paul* (Nashville, 1962), and *The Love Command in the New Testament* (New York, 1972), cover a wide area of the NT with sound critical judgement.

[2] J. L. Houlden, *op. cit.*, pp. 119f.

[3] Human justice in the OT is linked with divine judgement. The just man fulfils his duties to God as a member of God's people. The Messiah will be the 'just man' because he will fulfil completely the will of God. In the

to the Romans and the Gospel according to Matthew. In the Epistle to the Romans, righteousness is the word used to describe the power of God which saves mankind. It is 'God's liberating justice'. The time has come in which this righteousness is being revealed. Jesus Christ, in his life, death and resurrection, is the righteousness of God. He is the decisive act by which God sets right what is wrong. Looking at the detailed use of this word in Romans, we notice that the righteousness of God is concerned for all the human race: 5:17–19. It is a power by which God makes man free: 1:17, 3:21–4. God's righteousness is localised in the cross: 3:25 and 5:9ff. God is just and shows his justice: 3:25f. God judges and gives grace in the one act, making man just. The legal idea of the righteousness of God is clear in 8:34, and forgiveness is seen as a present gift: 4.7. Righteousness is grasped by faith as man is part of the community which believes in Christ: 3:21f. And righteousness is something which looks forward to the future in hope: 8:19ff. To sum up, righteousness is a power by which God forgives, vindicates, and saves mankind. It is something by which man himself is brought to be righteous.[4]

The most illuminating recent treatment begins from the antitheses or dichotomies which recur in the study of righteousness in Paul. 'But our particular problem is to identify the unitary centre from which he managed to combine present and future eschatology, "declare righteous"

NT, three Romans, Pilate, his wife, and the centurion at the cross, all describe Jesus as 'just' (Matt. 27:24 and 19; Luke 23:47). The list of values in Phil. 4:8 includes just things among the proper objects of thought. The disciples and Jesus are just in the sense that they fulfil the law or will of God; but Paul denies the existence of just men (Rom. 3:10) before proceeding to show how man may be justified through faith. See Kittel, *TWNT*, 2, 187–93.

[4] J. Ziesler, *The Meaning of Righteousness in Paul* (Cambridge, 1972). This study of 'justify', 'righteousness' and 'righteous' claims (p. 212) 'the verb as essentially relational and forensic and the noun and adjective as describing behaviour within relationship'. N. M. Watson, in a review article on this book in *NTS* (1974), pp. 216–18, has shown that the meaning of the noun and adjective overlap the meaning of the verb and that justification does not depend on righteousness in Christ. 'Paul consistently represents justification as initiating the relationship in which righteousness is possible.' Ziesler seems to miss the point of Käsemann's argument that righteousness is both subjective and objective. He comments, p. 11, 'E. Käsemann also of course represents the subjective genitive view and for him it is God's own saving power', and refers to pp. 100f. On p. 100, Käsemann says, 'It is beyond dispute that the general tenor of the Pauline utterances on the subject, like that of the Reformation tradition, which determines our attitude, tells in favour of the objective genitive': 'Gottesgerechtigkeit bei Paulus', *EVB*, 2 181ff., *NTQT*, pp. 168ff. Ziesler quotes from an earlier translation in *Journal for Theology and Church*, vol. 1.

and "make righteous", gift and service, freedom and obedience, forensic, sacramental and ethical approaches.[5] The solution to the problem is Paul's account of the righteousness of God as a power, as the redemptive activity of God, as a gift which is never separated from its giver, as the power by which the Lord enters and remains on the scene.

The relationship of the righteousness of God to ethics springs from its central place in the theology of Paul, replacing (Rom. 14:17) the theme of the kingdom of God in the teaching of Jesus.[6] It sums up Paul's theology and has a wide range of implications. Righteousness points to the final goal of all things for 'the whole Pauline eschatology is therefore nothing else than the acting out of the righteousness of God, the saving and sovereign manifestation of the God who keeps his pledge to his creation and maintains justice within it.'[7]

With eschatology goes christology, for it is through Christ that God fulfils his justice and it is Christ who shows the nature of that fulfilment. 'The central proposition of Pauline Christology would therefore be, that God establishes justice through Christ and that he carries out this justice in and with Christ.'[8] To eschatology and christology we finally add ethics. The effect of the righteousness of God is to create new life and to reconcile men with God. From this new life and reconciliation flow the meaning and possibility of obedience and righteous life. Those who were slaves of sin now give themselves to the service of righteousness and the fulfilment of a holy life.[9] Beginning outside ethics, righteousness finishes as the source of a good life. Paul takes ethics seriously. 'What matters is that God's saving righteousness does two things for men and does them inseparably: it restores their relationship with God and makes them new (ethical righteous) beings.'[10]

Ethics will never cut loose from this origin. There is an inseparable connection between power and gift,[11] so that the Lord who calls man to serve enables him to perform the service. He must always be on the move, accepting each day the call of his Lord, remaining thereby in

[5] See E. Käsemann, 'Gottesgerechtigkeit bei Paulus', *EVB* 2, 184; *NTQT*, pp. 171f., and *An die Römer* (Tübingen, 1973), pp. 18–29 and 85–94.

[6] See, E. Jüngel, *Paulus und Jesus* (Tübingen, 1964), p. 266, 'Die *dikaiosunē theou* als "Thema" der paulinischen Rechtfertigungslehre erkannten wir als ein die ganze paulinische Theologie bestimmendes eschatologisches Phänomen. Die *basileia theou* als "Thema" der Gleichnisse Jesus erkannten wir als ein die ganze Verkündigung Jesu bestimmendes eschatologisches Phänomen.'

[7] P. Stuhlmacher, *Gerechtigkeit Gottes bei Paulus* (2 Aufl., Göttingen, 1966), p. 205.

[8] P. Stuhlmacher, *op. cit.*, p. 209.

[9] Rom. 6:15–19.

[10] Ziesler, *The Meaning of Righteousness in Paul*, p. 189.

[11] See E. Käsemann, 'Gottesgerechtikeit bei Paulus'. *EVB* 2, 187; *NTQT*, p. 174.

the gift which he has received and finding that gift renewed and effective.[12] The way of salvation is always through the justifying of the
ungodly and there is never a point when man stands over against God
as an independent ethical performer, unless he has been abandoned in
the sense of Romans 1:24. God's righteousness and his faithfulness, his
loyal love for his people, cannot be divided and it is in this dependence
on a righteous and faithful God that all Christian behaviour must be
placed.[13] The dynamic never disappears; one instance of this may be
seen in the precepts of holy law which point to an awareness that life
is now lived in the presence of a righteous God. Antithetical sentences
like 1 Cor. 3:17, 'Anyone who destroys God's temple will himself be
destroyed by God', show that Christians knew that they were already
under the judgement of their returning Lord. Other passages, such as
1 Cor. 14:38, 16:22; 2 Cor. 9:6; Mark 8:38, indicate the presence of a
righteous God among his people, of a Christ who reveals, guides, judges
and thereby realises the divine righteousness on earth among men.[14]
In all this righteousness never becomes a private matter. Man is justified by faith alone but never justified alone; for this act makes him
part of God's new creation. This is that saving work of God which
concerns the whole universe and not just the human race, let alone
man's subjective apprehension.[15]

Matthew is constantly concerned with a 'way of righteousness', for
at least three reasons: he sees the person of Christ as the fulfilment of
the Law,[16] he clarifies the Christian position in the face of Jewish
consolidation,[17] and he corrects antinomian enthusiasts.[18] John the
Baptist 'came in the way of righteousness',[19] fulfilling what God
required of man; but he was rejected by God's people. Righteousness
is an all-inclusive term for goodness and obedience. This is what Jesus
preaches and presents; even before the public ministry of Jesus, Jesus
and John join in the same work of declaring righteousness. Matthew
has taken the structure of Mark, drawn a line from birth to death and

[12] *Ibid. EVB* 2, 188; *NTQT*, p. 175.

[13] *Ibid. EVB* 2, 191f.; *NTQT*, pp. 179f.

[14] For an examination of these and other passages and for the development
of the ideas of this paragraph, see E. Käsemann, 'Sätze des heiligen
Rechtes im NT', *EVB* 2, 69–82; *NTQT*, pp. 66–81.

[15] E. Käsemann, *EVB* 2, 192f.; *NTQT*, pp. 130ff.

[16] Bornkamm, Barth and Held, *Tradition and Interpretation in Matthew*
(ET London, 1963), pp. 125–59; C. F. D. Moule, 'Fulfilment-Words in
the New Testament', *NTS*, 14 (1968), 293–320.

[17] W. D. Davies, *The Setting of the Sermon on the Mount* (Cambridge,
1964), p. 315.

[18] E. Käsemann, 'The Beginnings of Christian Theology', *NTQT*, pp. 82–97;
EVB 2, 82–104.

[19] Matt. 21:32.

resurrection and given an account of the life of Jesus. He shows the fulfilment of scripture in particular events, and links the person of Jesus to actual situations, insisting that the time of Jesus is a time of climax in the history of God's saving work. The time of Jesus is important on ethical grounds. The preaching of Jesus is concerned with righteousness, the demands of God, with moral or ethical prescriptions and therefore Jesus comes into conflict with scribes and Pharisees. The Pharisees claim to interpret the Old Testament correctly, but Jesus shows a different way of righteousness. In his teaching, life is a response to the claim of the kingdom which is now. Jesus fulfils in himself both God's commandments and man's final salvation; he does this as the judge of all the world. The life of Jesus is a distinct period of time. The prophets were important because they pointed ahead to a just climax of saving history: Jesus reveals this justice and fulfils the promise of the one who is to come. When Jesus has been rejected by the Jews, saving history continues through the church which has his message; but because Jesus brought ultimate righteousness, the church now looks back to the life of Jesus and to the 'holy past'.[20]

In this way the life of Jesus gives empirical content to the notion of righteousness and links it with the sphere of the contingent. The rules and exhortations of the New Testament show an equal respect for the contingent. Many of the exhortations of the New Testament are to be found in the writings of contemporary Judaism[21] and the parallels are for all to see; but one of the most common forms of exhortation or paraenetic in the New Testament is the catalogue of virtues and vices which contrasts good with bad, light with darkness. Such catalogues may be descriptive in form, contrasting bad types and good types, threat and promise (1 Cor. 6:9ff.; Gal. 5:19–23; Rom. 1:18–32; Rev. 21:7ff. and 22:14ff.; Matt. 5:3–12, 25:31ff.); or they may be directly paraenetic, urging the abandoning of the old way and the acceptance of the new (2 Cor. 6:14–7:1; 1 Cor. 5:9–13; Rom. 13:12–14; and Col. 2:20–3:17). It is possible that different forms arise from the different routes by which they reach early Christian writing. The sharp antithesis between good and evil is first found in Persian cosmology. The descriptive form is taken directly from Persian cosmology by Jewish anthropology. The two ways of behaviour point to two

---

[20] See G. Strecker, *Der Weg der Gerechtigkeit* (Göttingen, 1966), p. 188 *et passim*.

[21] Cf. R. Bultmann, *Theology of the NT* (London, 1955), 2, 226: 'The schemata of moral teaching, particularly Haustafeln [schedules of household duties], such as Hellenistic Judaism had already taken over from the hortatory practice of Hellenism, are now impressed into Christian service.'

spirits of light and darkness, one of which man must choose to follow. The paraenetic form comes through hellenistic syncretism where it acquires an astrological turn. The soul comes from beyond the planets and as it descends to the earth it is encircled and clothed by their influence, landing on earth as a prisoner of the flesh.[22] Both these forms come to express the same exhortation to the right way and both are inspired by eschatological motives. The radical contrast of the two ways reflects the nearness of the End.[23]

The call to a greater righteousness than that of scribes and Pharisees implies continuity in regard for law, for law expresses the demand of a righteous God for radical obedience. Lesser righteousness uses precepts of law as a protection against radical obedience. The classic example is the rich young ruler who kept all the commandments, but was not ready to obey.[24] Greater righteousness goes beyond the letter of the law to the total obedience which God requires, and is appropriate to the last days. As Matt. 28:20 points out, the teaching and observation of his commandments continue to the end of the age in the constant presence of the risen Lord.

Righteousness can suffer distortion. It may harden into a system of law as it had for some Jews and some Christians. Any table of rules which is not dominated by the divine act and power is a legalist distortion of righteousness. The letter to the Galatians shows how easily this could happen, and the letter to the Romans shows its wider roots in the piety of the pious. Any response to God's grace which adopts the abstract principle of natural order is an abstract distortion of the same; there is little evidence for this in the New Testament.[25] In order to stand between the two, righteousness must be more than a virtue: it must be a manifestation of the gospel itself: the power of God for man's salvation.

The pictures that go with justice are those of the path or way in which the just man treads, not swerving to the right or to the left, the balance which gives to each his due, the vindication of the oppressed, the acquittal of the guilty, and the ideal man or archetype like Noah, Abraham, and finally Jesus the righteous one, who, like Plato's just man, is crucified.

---

[22] Cf. *Corp. Herm.* XIII.
[23] For an extended discussion see E. Kamlah, *Die Form der katalogischen Paränese im NT* (Tübingen, 1964), especially pp. 214f.
[24] R. Bultmann, *Theology of the NT*, 1, 16.
[25] The passages normally cited are Rom. 1:26 and 1 Cor. 11:14, but C. K. Barrett has seriously challenged their relation to natural law theory: *A Commentary on the First Epistle to the Corinthians* (London, 1968), p. 256.

DISCIPLESHIP

The second pattern of the New Testament is that of discipleship, or of
the simple words 'follow me'. Christians are the followers of Jesus
Christ. The strangeness of this command is central to the whole of the
gospel. The mystery of the son of man is that in his humiliation he
remains a compelling figure as his call to discipleship sounds out. Jesus
did not make constant claims concerning his divinity, but the conviction that he was more than man grew upon those who came to him,
in spite of the barriers which he placed in the way of this conclusion.
Discipleship is linked directly to the person of Jesus who calls his
followers and joins them to himself. His call marks a new beginning, a
new freedom and a dependence on divine grace. To be a disciple
means to be with Jesus, to serve him, to leave all and follow. To follow
means to take up the cross and to share the humiliation of Jesus in
promise of his glory.[1] The death of Jesus brought an end to the visible
following of Jesus on the roads of Palestine; but the disciple now saw
his Lord as the exalted Christ who went before his followers into all
the world. Discipleship became again a present reality. Matthew 8
shows Jesus as the Lord who speaks of the homelessness of the son of
man, of leaving all to follow; Jesus enters a boat and the disciples
follow. The disciples call for help from their 'Lord', who rebukes them
for their lack of faith. The story has become a challenge to discipleship
in the face of the storms of temptation and distress.[2] Discipleship points
to the central significance of the earthly Jesus in the gospels. The
gospels enable the believer to identify the earthly Jesus with the risen
Lord and to follow one, who, by his very inaccessibility, stands over
and commands the allegiance of those who would follow him. Discipleship points also to the continuing link between eschatology and ethics
in the New Testament. The disciples receive the powers of the new age
and spread the borders of its victory (Luke 10:17ff.). The twelve are a
symbol of Israel, of the eschatological people of God (Mark 3:14f;
Matt. 19:28). The faithful disciple knows that in the last day his Lord
will own him. The disciple who does not confess his Lord will not be
owned on that day.[3] The notion of discipleship is concerned with the
direction of Christian life. The idea did not undergo a basic change
after Easter. The same simplicity and mystery of commitment were

[1] E. Schweizer, *Lordship and Discipleship* (ET London, 1960), p. 20.
[2] G. Bornkamm, in Bornkamm, Barth and Held, *Tradition and Interpretation
in Matthew* (ET London, 1963), pp. 52ff.
[3] See G. Bornkamm, *Jesus of Nazareth* (ET London, 1960), pp. 149ff.

there. Side by side with a discontinuity in the concept there went a continuity of self-understanding in the believer.[4] The same call pointed away to the Lord who went before his disciples.

Discipleship displays a distinctive element of biblical ethics. For the Hebrew as for the Christian, ethics were concerned with the will of a personal God rather than with ideas and definitions. God gave both commands and promises to his people and revealed himself with the call to imitate his holiness: 'You shall be holy as I am holy.' The new element Jesus brings is not a reduction of the law to the two great commandments, but the command to 'love *as I have* loved you'. Imitation of Christ involves dependence on him for strength to follow.[5] The disciples are the 'little ones' who receive the divine gift.[6]

Where did the command 'Follow me'[7] originate? It has been traced to both prophetic and rabbinic sources; but neither account is convincing. Slender antecedents may be seen, but the words themselves came from the originality of Jesus who used them as his distinctive call. The command could not be the construction of the early church for whom the exalted son of man could not be 'followed' in direct visible dependence. It is rather an authentic saying which has to be related to what comes after it.[8] Its originality springs from the position of Jesus as Messiah and the nearness of the kingdom. His divine audacity has no parallel other than God's calling of his prophets in the Old Testament.

[4] H. D. Betz, *Nachfolge und Nachahmung Jesu Christi im NT* (Tübingen, 1967), pp. 188f.

[5] T. W. Manson, *Ethics and the Gospel* (London, 1960), p. 68: 'The living Christ still has two hands, one to point the way, the other held out to help us along.'

[6] G. Barth in *Tradition and Interpretation in Matthew*, pp. 121ff. Barth lists among other qualities of discipleship: understanding, faith and conversion.

[7] Kittel, *TWNT*, I, 210–15. Epictetus and Marcus Aurelius spoke of 'following' God or nature, using the New Testament *akolouthein*. Generally *hepesthai* was preferred, as when Plato spoke of following God. The Hebrews had less place for the idea, since their God was a consuming fire. Here Philo followed Greek rather than Hebrew usage. The New Testament does not talk about following God but talks a great deal about following Jesus. The word *akolouthein* is restricted to the followers or disciples of Jesus and the command 'Follow me' gains messianic overtones. Discipleship is seen as a gift through which one shares in the salvation which Messiah brings as well as the cross which he must carry. It is an activity or event, not an idea.

[8] 'Das "Charisma" Jesu durchbricht die Möglichkeiten einer religionsphänomenologischen Einordnung. Gerade auch die einzigartige Weise, in der Jesus einzelne zum "Nachfolgen" berief, ist Ausdruck dieser unableitbaren "messianischen" Vollmacht': M. Hengel, *Nachfolge und Charisma* (Berlin, 1968), pp. 97f.

In the presence of the kingdom he called men to a break from all other ties and to unconditional solidarity with himself. And when, according to Mark and Q, the disciples were sent out, they had the same authority of the kingdom as their master had shown. In the community after Easter, discipleship became equivalent to faith as every believer was seen in the immediate service of the son of man. When the missionary outreach of the early communities was read back into the gospels and linked with Jesus, there were historical grounds for the move. The call to discipleship is a key element in early Christian missions and the tradition concerning Jesus.[9]

How does discipleship become ethical? Does it imply imitation? The evidence is not as strong as might be expected. Believers are called to follow the example of God in love to enemies (Matt. 5:43ff.), in forgiveness of others (Matt. 18:23ff.; Eph. 4:32f.), in love for brothers (1 John 4:7–11) and in holiness of life (1 Pet. 1:14–16). Christ's example is to be followed in self-sacrifice and service (Mark 10:45 and Luke 22:26–7). In the fourth gospel the action of footwashing is given as an example and the disciples are to love as Christ has loved (13:15 and 34). While for Paul the divine humility (Phil. 2:1–8) and self-giving (2 Cor. 8:9) are accompanied by his own example (2 Cor. 5:12–15), Christ's example of patient suffering (1 Pet. 2:21–5a), of obedience (Heb. 12:1–3), and holiness (1 John 2:6 and 4:17b), is to be followed. The Christian is to order his life by the example of God in Christ, in love (Rom. 5:5 and 8), patience (2 Thess. 3:5) and holiness (1 Cor. 6:11; 1 Thess. 4:3–8).

Such a selection is itself an indication of the marginal position of 'imitation' in New Testament thought. There is never any ground for the reduction of discipleship to external imitation. Whenever imitation of God or Christ is commended, it depends entirely on the work of salvation present in the believer.[10] The terminology of 'following' has no connection with that of 'imitating'. With one exception (1 Pet. 2:21) *akolouthein* has a religious meaning while *mimeisthai* moves in the ethical sphere. The two ideas are joined in Mark 8:34, perhaps through rabbinic (ultimately hellenistic) adaptation of the Old Testament phrase 'to go after'.[11] Imitation merges into discipleship because, coming from

---

[9] M. Hengel, *op. cit.*, p. 99.

[10] A. Schulz, *Nachfolge und Nachahmung* (München, 1962), pp. 305f., 'Jede neutestamentliche Imitatio nimmt ihren Ausgang im Empfang des christlichen Heilstandes, der als solcher die seinsmässige Befähigung dazu bietet.'

[11] A. Schulz, *op. cit.*, p. 335. Imitation has evoked considerable interest. Stanley argues against Michaelis' account of 'following' as primarily obedience. He does not produce evidence beyond that cited above and found wanting. Further, the kind of imitation for which he argues seems to be precarious in the face of historical criticism of the gospels. Ignatius of

a very different background, it expresses an intimate communion or participation.[12]

Later, discipleship involves obedience to those words of the Lord which have been handed down, for they possess an ultimate authority.[13] But discipleship does not simply provide emotional colour for legalism. It involves an endeavour to express in a new and changing setting both the spirit or attitude of Jesus and the ethical teaching which he was believed to have given. To be *ennomos Christou* means just this. It is a deep intention to carry out the will of Christ as it has been ordained and commanded.[14] The formal development of the office of apostle, which is part of the early catholicism[15] incipient in Acts and the Pastorals, cannot be examined fully. It appears that the notion of office, as a guarantee of continuing validity, receives a sharp rebuff in the Johannine literature. For the writer of the fourth gospel there is no explicit doctrine of church office and the constant theme is the immediacy of Christ and the equality and unity of his followers. He who has seen Christ has seen the father. In him his own abide as branches in a vine. They are his friends and his brothers in the family of God.[16]

Antioch has been the subject of debate. Th.Preiss ('La mystique de l'imitation du Christ et de l'unité chez Ignace d'Antioche', *RHPR* [1938], pp. 237–41) has argued that his mysticism has little relation to the incarnation and is largely non-biblical and gnostic. E. J. Tinsley (The *imitatio Christi* in St. Ignatius of Antioch', *Studia Patristica* II [Berlin, 1957]) maintains that it is incarnational and centred on the historical life of Jesus. Ignatius is difficult to classify, highly mystical and concerned with the total event of incarnation rather than with its historical detail.

On the imitation of Paul and Christ, see V. Furnish, *Theology and Ethics in Paul* (Nashville, 1962), for a balanced presentation of the evidence and recent assessments. Commenting on 1 Cor. 11:1; 1 Thess. 1:6f. and 2.14; Phil. 3:17; and 1 Cor. 4:16–17, Furnish identifies two themes of *imitatio*: the need for selfless service and the need for obedience in suffering: 'To imitate Paul and Christ means to be conformed to Christ's suffering and death in the giving of one's self over to the service of others' (p. 223).

[12] See H. D. Betz, *Nachfolge und Nachahmung Jesu Christi im NT, passim.*
[13] W. Schrage, *Die konkreten Einzelgebote in der paulinischen Paränese* (Gütersloh, 1961), p. 238.
[14] C. H. Dodd,'*Ennomos Christou*' in *Studia Paulina* (Haarlem, 1953), p. 109.
[15] The term 'Frühkatholizismus' has been frequently misunderstood. It is linked with a fading of apocalyptic hope, and the emergence of 'a theoretical principle of tradition and legitimate succession'. See E. Käsemann, *EVB* 1, 128–34; *ENT*, p. 87; *EVB* 2, 239–52 and 262–7, *NTQT*, pp. 236–59. Note the qualifications of C. K. Barrett, *Luke the Historian in Recent Writing* (London, 1961), pp. 7of.
[16] E. Käsemann, *Jesu letzter Wille nach Johannes 17* (Tübingen, 1966), pp. 53–100, ET *The Testament of Jesus* (London, 1968), chapter 3,

Paul speaks of being 'in Christ' where there is a new creation. In Christ he has a high calling. Conversely, Christ lives in him. The phrase could often be replaced by the words 'determined by the fact that Jesus Christ died and rose'.[17] It points to the present realm over which the Lord rules, in which salvation occurs and the powers of the coming age are present. There is a continuing personal reference.[18] Christians must conform to the pattern of Christ's behaviour.[19]

Eschatology is the chief clue to the meaning of discipleship after Easter and its expression in the phrase 'in Christ'. The resurrection of Jesus was never seen as an isolated or finished event. It marked the beginning of the general resurrection and was the first step of the triumphant son of man on his way to his throne of total sovereignty. Those who believed in him shared now in his risen life and were incorporated in him. By his Spirit they were made part of his body. Through the Spirit, through the baptised members of his body, Christ the Cosmocrator takes the world to be his own. To be 'in Christ' is to be a part of this event.[20]

The union of indicative with imperative is again the point of ethical interest. While *en Christōi* is generally used with an indicative verb, *en kuriōi* is normally found with the imperative. While it has been suggested that the indicative is concerned with what has been achieved in Christ and the imperative with what remains for the Lord to fulfil, one must hesitate to divide precisely. In particular, the designation of the church as *en Christōi* and the world as *en kuriōi* suggests a separation which would make nonsense of the dynamic outward thrust of the members of the body which is the church.[21] For the life in Christ is not a 'religious' life in the sense of withdrawal and inwardness; it moves

pp. 27–55. E. Käsemann, 'Einheit und Vielheit in der neutestamentlichen Lehre von der Kirche', *EVB* 2, 264; *NTQT* p. 255. 'Once again the fourth gospel makes a notable counter offensive against this development; it contains no explicit idea of the Church, no doctrine of ministerial office, no developed sacramental theology.'

[17] F. Neugebauer, 'Das paulinische "in Christo"', *NTS* 4 (1957/8), 131. Cited W. Kramer, *Christ, Lord, Son of God* (London, 1966), p. 143.

[18] C. F. D. Moule, *Idiom Book of NT Greek* (Cambridge, 1953), p. 80.

[19] *Konformitäts-Schema* is the term used by N. Dahl, *Formgeschichtliche Beobachtungen* 6. See Kramer, *Christ, Lord, Son of God*, p. 118.

[20] E. Käsemann, 'The Beginnings of Christian Theology', *NTQT*, p. 107; *EVB* 2, p. 104; 'The Pauline Doctrine of the Lord's Supper', *ENT*, pp. 114ff., *EVB* 1, 17ff.

[21] Such a separation seems to be found in Neugebauer's account: 'Sie wird Ereignis in der Ekklesia *en Christōi* ... Dieses Tun aber muss sich notwendig in dem durch die Geschöpflichkeit des Menschen gesetzten Rahmen abspielen, ihn ausfüllen und zugleich erfüllen. Das geschieht *en kuriōi*', *In Christus* (Göttingen, 1961), p. 148.

outwards towards others in sharing and daily obedience,[22] taking its shape from the changing circumstances which it meets.[23] It is an objective sharing[24] by every believer in the life of the risen Lord.

One example of the ethical application of *en Christōi* must suffice. Phil. 2 has long been a source of disagreement and difficulty. It seems to be an exhortation to follow the example of Christ who did not reckon equality with God in terms of snatching but took the way of costly sacrifice. We have here 'a deeply Christian comment – a revolutionary comment on the world's values and its quantitative notions'.[25]

How far does discipleship involve ascetic discipline? The evidence is conflicting. On the one hand, Jesus and his disciples are commonly criticised for their positive attitude to the world; Jesus explains why his disciples do not fast (Mark 2:18ff.; Matt. 9:14ff.; Luke 5:33ff.) and disapproves of the public fasting of hypocrites (Matt. 6:16–18). He is attacked as the friend of publicans and sinners and as a glutton and wine-bibber (Matt. 11:19). On the other hand, discipleship means renunciation of family and possessions. The way of Jesus is the way of poverty (Luke 6:20; 9:58). One cannot serve God and mammon. John the Baptist, whose mode of life is typically ascetic, is commended as supreme among men. The early community, described in Acts, involves the renunciation of personal possessions and a sharing of material goods; this pattern did not spread widely or last for long. Paul's attitude to marriage in 1 Cor. 7 requires careful analysis. Marriage must not limit the total obedience of the Christian to his Lord. Yet the attitude here is hardly ascetic.[26] In verses 36–8 he is talking about engaged couples and the special circumstances of the time.[27] Elsewhere he seems to assume an ascetic position in order to show the deficiencies of that position.[28] The same rhetorical move is made by Paul on the subject of tongues (1 Cor. 14). Glossolalia must not be silenced but it is better to speak five intelligible words than a thousand in a tongue. The best known parallel is Mark Antony's speech after the murder of Caesar in Shakespeare's *Julius Caesar*.[29] He condemns the 'honourable

22 M. Bouttier, *Christianity according to St. Paul* (London, 1966), pp. 24 and 90.

23 *Ibid.* p. 118.

24 'Die objektive ontische Gemeinschaft', A. Schulz, *Nachfolge und Nachahmung*, p. 180.

25 C. F. D. Moule, 'Further Reflections on Philippians 2. 5–11', *Apostolic History and the Gospel, Biblical and Historical Essays presented to F. F. Bruce* (ed. W. W. Gasque and R. P. Martin, Exeter, 1970), p. 274.

26 C. K. Barrett, *The First Epistle to the Corinthians* (London, 1968), p. 155.

27 *Ibid.* p. 184.

28 H. Chadwick, 'All Things to All Men', *NTS*, 1 (1955), 261–75.

29 Act 3, Scene 2.

men' by powerful innuendo, never by direct attack. Dualism is rejected as a ground for abstinence; what God has made is good (1 Tim. 4:3–5). Dying with Christ is something more fundamental than ascetic practices. It is the practice of death rather than the practice of suffering. Paul sees the signs of his apostleship as the marks of the cross; hardships are not self-imposed but are to be patiently endured as they confront him.

Elsewhere in the New Testament dualism is rejected as a ground for askēsis; what God has made is good. Jewish tradition was generally strong in world affirmation; but ascetic practices were general in New Testament times.[30] The same contrast may be seen in the New Testament; asceticism was to develop and never entirely disappear.[31] Ascetic practices may be necessary from time to time in the total service of Christ. They are neither right nor wrong in themselves; when taken as necessary and important they must be condemned. Nothing from outside can defile a man (Mark 7:15) and nothing in the world is unclean in itself (Rom. 14:14). That is why 'the New Testament can give no such answer to the question whether asceticism is right or wrong in itself', for 'there is nothing holy or sanctifying for man outside perfect obedience in the following of the obedient and merciful Christ'.[32]

The following of Christ is a picture as well as a pattern. Related images are those of the obedient soldier, the athlete straining towards the goal and the flock following the shepherd. He who follows must take up the cross which is the visible symbol par excellence. From fellowship in the sufferings of Christ comes discipline in service; as the athlete knocks his body into shape (1 Cor. 9:24–7), so the Christian endures hardship in mission.

Here again there may be distortion. Legalist distortion can occur in two ways. Discipleship may become a sign of ecclesiastical office and authority. Paul writes of the 'superlative apostles' who were a source of pride through their historical or pseudo-historical position (2 Cor. 11:5; 12:11).[33] This formal hardening removes the dynamic element in discipleship. Mark tells of two followers who wish to change their dis-

[30] See H. Strathmann, Geschichte der frühchristlichen Askese (Leipzig, 1914), pp. 16–100.

[31] A useful popular account of the general issue may be found in J. A. Ziesler, Christian Asceticism (London, 1973). For a valuable concise account of attitudes to wealth, see E. Bammel, art. ptōchos, TWNT, 6, 888–915.

[32] H. von Campenhausen, Tradition and Life in the Church (London, 1968), p. 122.

[33] See C. K. Barrett, The Signs of an Apostle (London, 1970), pp. 36ff. Also see E. Käsemann, Die Legitimität des Apostels (Darmstadt, 1956), p. 21.

cipleship for seats of authority on the right and left of the Messiah. The
only privilege of discipleship is the cross which is the cup and baptism
of the Lord and his followers (Mark 10:35–9). The risen Christ,
according to Johannine tradition, firmly reminds Peter that the only
job of the disciple is to follow and not to meddle with the position of
others: 'What is it to you? Follow me' (John 21:22).

A second legalist distortion may be found in undirected asceticism.
The Sermon on the Mount attacks hypocrites whose fasting gains
instant recognition and reward. Paul rejects the loveless martyr who
gives his body to be burnt (1 Cor. 13:3). The excesses of ascetics have
sometimes been viewed as extremes or extravagances. This is not the
case. Undirected asceticism stops short and holds back from full discipleship; it treats suffering as an end rather than a means. For the
taking of the cross should always be a way of following Christ. When
removed from this obedience it is without control and may run off into
strange abuses. These distort discipleship because they isolate the
element of mortification and deny the dynamic relation between
disciple and Lord. Some of this distortion may be seen in the Colossian
heresy with its dualism of spirit and matter. On the other side a trium-
phalist distortion of discipleship may be seen in the Corinthian enthusiasts who are wise, strong and honourable in Christ (1 Cor. 4:10). The
enthusiasts believe that they are 'reigning in Christ'. Paul argues from
eschatology to show that all disciples of Christ are followers, not full
possessors, for the great day of resurrection has not yet arrived.

FAITH AND FREEDOM

The lack of respect for faith in classical Greek thought provided a
problem for early Christian apologists. The Old Testament saw better,
with its obedient trust in a faithful God, and this was taken up in the
New Testament, where faith was expanded to cover the whole relation
of man to God. There is a close link with patience and hope. Above all,
faith is acceptance of Christ as Lord, dependence on the word of God
and life under grace. Faith is the path to salvation, a turning from the
world, a way of knowing and a life of love.[1]

The freedom of the Christian is described by Paul in Romans 8. In
contrast to the law which enslaves, the law of Christ is a law which
makes man free. There is no condemnation to those who are in Christ
Jesus. Here and now they anticipate the freedom of sonship to God and
may cry, 'Abba Father'. The freedom of faith is not a relaxation of
claims, but a recognition of one ultimate claim and of one point of

[1] Kittel, *TWNT*, 6, 182–230.

dependence. Freedom has to be held firmly. The Galatians are to stand fast, to hold on to the liberty in which Christ has made them free (Gal. 5:1). The only way in which they can stand fast in this liberty is by faith, dependence on Christ as saviour (Gal. 2:20 and 3:22, 23).

Freedom and faith both point to contingency, to the dependence of the believer on Christ in present frustration and suffering. There were those who imagined that, because they had received the Spirit of God, they were free from all obligations or any limitation upon their inclinations. The Corinthian enthusiasts believed that they had already within themselves all the righteousness of God, the blessings of the last day, as the Spirit filled them and enabled them to speak the words of God. Theirs was a freedom, a richness which, they believed, completely fulfilled the gospel. Paul replied to the Corinthians from the ground of eschatology, and in Romans 8 he used a similar argument. Christian faith is the faith of a pilgrim, the faith of one who looks in hope and who has not yet arrived. It is important for him to realise that he has not yet received the object of his hope; because it is only as he shares in the contingency and the frustration of the world that he has the right to the freedom which calls God 'Father'. The whole creation is waiting for the revealing of the sons of God and, until that day, Christians live within a world where freedom can only survive through faith. They are killed all day long. They are subjected to physical suffering and to every form of trial; but they are sure that nothing can separate them from the love of God which is in Christ Jesus and in this faith they are free. 'The power of Christ's resurrection becomes a reality, here and now, in the form of Christian freedom and only in that. Christ differs from the other lords in that he effects freedom...It is enough that we reach out, with the world, for his freedom and let it consecrate us.'[2] The freedom of Jesus shows itself in his attitude to outcasts and his sense of co-humanity with them. Mark's gospel is full of the first wave of enthusiasm for the deliverance and freedom which Christ had brought. There is never Christian freedom without enthusiasm. The Corinthian error was not an excess of freedom but a misunderstanding which tried to separate the cross from Christian freedom; but freedom depends on the cross and on the faith which fulfils the first commandment and hangs on God alone. The way of faith is shown in the total obedience of Christ on the cross, the one place, said Luther, where the

---

[2] E. Käsemann, *Der Ruf der Freiheit* (Tübingen, 1967), ET of 3 ed., *Jesus Means Freedom* (London, 1969), pp. 154–6. The paragraph is derived from this perceptive work. See also E. Käsemann, 'Der gottesdienstliche Schrei nach der Freiheit', *Paulinische Perspektiven*, pp. 211–36; ET, *Perspectives on Paul* (London, 1971), pp. 122–37; and *An die Römer* (Tübingen, 1973), pp. 202–41.

first commandment has been obeyed. Freedom can only come from this faith. All things belong to those who are Christ's in the way he is God's. Like a cliff climber suspended from one point, the Christian is free to move where he will as he is freed by faith in Christ alone.

The remarkable thing about this faith is the element of steadfastness.[3] Paul points to a faith which is held against difficulties at every stage. The difficulties or temptations which come to faith are a necessity for its existence. It is only, Paul would seem to say, when one is conscious of the overwhelming threat to faith that one can believe and be free. Freedom is neither a removal from difficulty nor a shutting of eyes to the problems of the world; but freedom and faith are what the Christian lives by in a world where, for the present, he will not see the fulfilment of his hope nor the object of his faith. The endurance of faith is underlined by the picture drawn from popular moral philosophy, of the athlete striving towards his goal. For Paul the *agōn* of faith requires renunciation, perseverance to one goal, always being on the way and never in this life reaching the end. Similarly the *agōn* for the faith is Paul's striving to spread the gospel and requires renunciation, earnestness, total exertion, wrestling against opposition and physical suffering. In the key passages of 1 Cor. 9:24–7 and Phil. 3:12ff., Paul's own *agōn* is meant as an encouragement and a pattern to all believers.[4]

Why have Christians always found it hard to hold on to their freedom? Paul tells the Galatians that Christ has called them to freedom and they are free from the enemy which has held them captive. Their freedom is threatened on two sides, by law and by flesh. Legalism and lawlessness come from the same root of selfishness and the cure for them both is to love one another. The freedom of faith is active in loving service (Gal. 5:13). Because freedom means abandoning oneself it must always be a precarious and threatened thing. Freedom means to die with Christ, to crucify oneself to the world and the world to oneself (Gal. 6:14). The threat of antinomianism would turn the Lord of the new life into the servant of the old man and cover up the manoeuvre with proud and pious phrases. Only love, says Paul, can preserve the freedom in which Christ has called us.[5]

If this pattern should seem subjective and individualistic, it is worth remembering that the forces which enslave men are cosmic forces and cultural entities. 'Paul sees the life of the church and of the believer,

---

[3] cf. G. Ebeling, *The Nature of Faith* (ET London, 1961), pp. 162ff.
[4] See V. C. Pfitzner, *Paul and the Agon Motif* (Leiden, 1967), for a clear and comprehensive account.
[5] See G. Bornkamm, *Das Ende des Gesetzes* (München, 1958), pp. 133ff.; *Die christliche Freiheit*, note especially p. 138.

and the role of the Holy Spirit, in terms of this dynamic and victorious struggle with social-metaphysical, that is, cultural giants.'[6] Solidarity with the world is essential to Christian freedom. Paul is not concerned with Stoic detachment. The cosmic powers of which he spoke were the apparently insuperable forces of evil in the world of the day. 'We conclude, then, that the New Testament in general and Paul in particular, offer at the very centre of their message a theological basis for social-cultural action. The primitive church was undoubtedly engaged in such action, in the transformation of pagan civilisation and culture, and was conscious of this action as inherent in the Gospel.'[7]

Faith is a response to God's grace and to daily life in the world. Paul praises the wisdom and mercies of God, then calls his readers to the worship of God in the world, to the sacrifice of their bodies, as well as to inward transformation and the renewal of their minds (Rom. 12:1, 2). Under this heading he gives a compendium of Christian ethics. Such worship of God must be rational and not the irrational enthusiasm of those who feel themselves entirely possessed by the powers of the age to come. It must take place in the world and its variety is shaped by the needs of the world. Such faith is marked by humility (Rom. 13). It involves the recognition that the sovereignty of God does not depend on man, that to stand in the presence of God is to be humble, not with a humility that looks to a time when it will cease to be humble, but with a lowliness which to all eternity will gaze in wonder at the loving mercy of God. All of which is said best by Bach in the Christmas Oratorio: '*Fallt mit Danken, fallt mit Loben, vor des Höchsten Gottesthron.*' So to live by faith, to have the *facultas standi extra se coram deo*, is to know the freedom and the joy of the children of God. Faith stands in the world under the grace of God. It takes the way of the cross. 'God's mercy comes from the cross of Christ to us, and it cannot remain what it is unless *tapeinophrosunē*, the suffering and dying with Christ, remains the mark of its recipients.'[8] It serves the Lord of all the world. 'The reason for "one must be subject" is, for the apostle, the need to verify Christian existence and one's stand before the Lord, who claims the world as his own, in that he confronts it continuously through his servants with the eschatological sign of his lordship, namely *tapeinophrosunē*.'[9] Humility comes from faith which depends on grace

---

[6] A. N. Wilder, 'Kerygma, Eschatology and Social Ethics', in *The Background to the NT and its Eschatology, C. H. Dodd Festschrift* (Cambridge, 1956), p. 532.

[7] *Ibid.* p. 534.

[8] E. Käsemann, 'Grundsätzliches zur Interpretation von Römer 13', *EVB* 2, 206; cf. ET, *NTQT* (London, 1969), p. 198.

[9] *Ibid.* p. 219; cf *NTQT*, p. 213.

(Eph. 2:8–10). It is the dominant aspect of the mind of Christ (Phil. 2:1–8) and is integral to the gospel. Two points are worth noting: the strangeness of this virtue to ancient ears and its difficulty of attainment. There was some place for humility in Hebrew thought, in Plato and in the Greek distaste for hybris; but the dominant morality of the day associated it with meanness and grovelling. It is linked with adjectives like ignoble, abject, servile, slavish, downcast and low. Epictetus names it first in a list of moral faults.[10] Faith as response to grace underlines the shape of Pauline ethics as dependent on the power of God, directed to a future which belongs to God and derived from Christ's death and resurrection as the decisive event of grace.[11] But, as with righteousness and discipleship, it is essential to grasp the corporate nature of these things. Grace never comes homogenised into human life, but as charisma it makes each man what he is, giving him something which only he can do within the body of Christ. The one Spirit produced many gifts. Distinctive as each is, it only finds existence and fulfilment as part of the body by which the Lord is taking his kingdom to himself. Obedience in daily life is offered within the family of charismata which spread the power of Christ in the world and look to the final enthronement of their Lord. 'Grace presses home its attack to the very heart of the world; it liberates it from the demons. Grace alone can do this. The whole of life, including death, stands under the promise of the gift of charisma, in so far as it is Christians who are living this life and dying this death. There is no passive membership in the body Christ.'[12] Within this fellowship of charismata there are three principles.

(1) 'To each his own', for a man's charisma is his only ethical option, Rom. 12:3; 1 Cor. 3:5; 12:7; Eph. 4:7; cf. 1 Cor. 7:7, 'Each has his own charisma from God'.

(2) 'For one another', since grace frees a man from himself for the service of others, 1 Cor. 12:3.

---

[10] For a comprehensive treatment see the excellent article, 'Demut', in *RAC* 3, 735–78, by A. Dihle. For a brief summary of evidence see M. J. Enslin, *The Ethics of Paul* (New York, 1930), p. 259. Enslin claims humility as part of the inheritance from Judaism. There is an important difference. The Jew looks to the final triumph when he will not need to be lowly. Christian humility, as has been noted, is something which deepens through eternity as grace is left without competitors. Augustine thought that pagans had a better chance of reaching humility than did Jews (*Sermon* 203.2).

[11] See V. Furnish, *Theology and Ethics in Paul* (Nashville, 1962), pp. 162–80 and 212–34.

[12] E. Käsemann, 'Ministry and Community in the NT', *ENT*, pp. 72f.; *EVB* 1, 117.

(3) 'Submit yourselves to each other in the fear of Christ', Eph. 5:21, cf. Rom. 12:10; Phil. 2:3; 1 Pet. 5:5, since humility must always be shown to the presence of Christ as encountered in the charisma of a brother.[13]

A legalist distortion of faith is found in the substitution of creed for living faith. When the object of faith ceases to be a person and becomes a series of propositions, faith is no longer Christian faith. In this sense the devils believe (James 2:19). The transition to this distortion is made easy because of the need to identify the person who is the object of faith. An enthusiastic distortion of faith is found in the libertarianism which argues that all things are lawful (1 Cor. 6:12 and 10:23).

LOVE

The meaning of the New Testament word for love (*agapaō*/*agapē*) may be seen against its general and particular use. In common usage *agapaō* takes the place of *phileō* before the first century B.C. The two verbs remain synonymous (as may be seen from John 21). The decline of *phileō* may be observed from the beginning of the fourth century B.C. The use of the noun *agapē* is stimulated by the greater use of its verb. The noun has a further advantage in that it has a wider meaning than *philia* which means friendship not love.[1] It is important to see the kind of linguistic innovation that has taken place. It is not the simple philological change from *phileō* to *agapaō*. That was independent and already achieved. It was the linking of *agapē* to the life, death and teaching of Jesus that made it a new thing. What happens in the New Testament is not the introduction of a new word but the giving of a distinctive content to an existing word. This is the word-event which is central to the New Testament.

Agapē and *agapaō* take pride of place through Jesus' summary of the law. Love to God demands all, yet strangely impels love in two other directions. Love for neighbour is joined by love for enemies. The newness of this love springs from the new situation which Jesus brings;

---

[13] *Ibid. ENT*, pp. 76ff., *EVB* I, 119ff.
[1] See R. Joly, *Le vocabulaire chrétien de l'amour, est-il original?* (Brussels, 1968), p. 48, 'On a parfois pensé que le christianisme précédé par les Septante avait accompli une révolution en la matière, imposant *agapaō* et condamnant *phileō* à la disparition. Il n'en est rien: *phileō* est mort, si l'on peut dire, de sa belle morte païenne. Ce qu'on a pris pour une cause n'était en réalité qu'une conséquence: le vocabulaire chrétien (et juif) est tel parceque tel était déjà auparavant le vocabulaire païen.'

only God gives this mysterious love. Those who are forgiven much will be able to love much. A merciful father has merciful children. For Paul, love directs God's saving will and shows itself in the love of man for God and his neighbour.[2] The command to love is always concrete and takes many different forms in the New Testament. In Mark it contrasts moral obedience with cultic performance, while in Matthew it is the key to the interpretation of the whole law. In Luke there is strong practical concern, and the story of the Good Samaritan drives the point home. Both Matthew and Luke use the tradition concerning love of enemies. Mark does not give the command a central place; his main concern is with following Jesus. In Matthew the command runs through from the Sermon on the Mount to the final judgement, when all nations are claimed for God's obedience and love. Luke's concern for the need and for the peace of the world is the content of his use of the love-command. Paul stresses the priority of the divine love to men. God gives man what love he has (Rom. 5:6–8). Freedom is not limited but made possible by love. The man in Christ, claimed for service in the realm of grace, is for the first time really free to love (see 1 Cor. 8; Rom. 14 and 15). In the fourth gospel the love-command points in a new way to Christology and eschatology. Jesus, as the bearer of the new age, commands his followers to love one another so that they will fulfil the mission which they take up from him in the world. Their distinguishing mark will be a love which brings the world to faith. Finally, in the first Epistle of John we have a striking emphasis on the two-fold command. Here the love of brother is the love of neighbour. God is love (4:16). Love is of God and all who love are born of him (4:7). Their mutual love is proof of their salvation (3:14).[3]

Paul claims that nothing of value exists without love. He describes love in a way which seems to be derivative from accounts of the earthly Jesus. Love is a part of the new age which is already here and which will always remain. Knowledge is imperfect and will be superseded. Tongues are temporary things and the time will come when talking does not have any place, but faith and hope and love will last on, and the greatest of them all is love (1 Cor. 13). Love is the summing up of the law. Just as Jesus summed up everything that had gone before him so all that God had required of his people is summed up and contained in love (Rom. 13:9, 10; Gal. 5:14). The image of the body of Christ does not point in the first instance to the unity of the Christian community, but rather to its diversity (Rom. 12; 1 Cor. 12). Christians are different from one another; but, because their new life comes from one

[2] Kittel, *TWNT*, 1, 44–55.
[3] See V. Furnish, *The Love Command in the NT* (New York, 1972), for the main points of this paragraph.

source, they are joined in one body of different members, and show their common life in the service of their lord and head. Love is related to the charismata as Christ is related to the members of his body. It is an anticipation of the new age and a sign of the presence of Christ in his church. Love is the realm of God's grace which is prior to the faith of the believer and makes that faith possible.[4] Sacrificial love for others is the core of Christian behaviour and the final standard of Pauline exhortation or paraenetic.[5]

Paul in particular and the New Testament as a whole include many other ethical prescriptions beside the command to love. *Pleonexia* is not just the contradiction of *agapē* (1 Thess. 4:6, cf. 2 Cor. 7:2); it is forbidden as greed and lust for gain (1 Cor. 5:11; 6:10). Sins are not defined by Paul as different negations of *agapē* and Rom. 7:7 sums up the law as 'You shall not covet', *ouk epithumēseis*. 'Love stands not only above but also under the commandments.' Love goes beyond the prescriptions of the law but not away from them.[6] In the New Testament the command to love is never a simple alternative to rules but goes beyond rules.

In the development from Pauline thought in Ephesians, the place of love is reasserted. The church as the body of Christ is now a cosmic entity, growing from earth to heaven. Love builds the church up (Eph. 4:16). For Paul, love was already the power of the new creation, by which the world is reconciled to God and all things are made new (2 Cor. 5:17). Now the power of cosmic love is seen as the fullness of God, which may be grasped in its infinite breadth, length, height and depth, by those who find their root and foundation in this same life-giving power (Eph. 3:18, 19).

A different development is seen in the fourth gospel where again love finds a dominating place. The turning point of the gospel comes when Jesus knows that he must leave the world and go to the Father. 'He had always loved his own who were in the world and now he was to show the full extent of his love' (John 13:1). He washes his disciples' feet and says, 'Then if I, your lord and master, have washed your feet, you ought also to wash one another's feet. I have set you an example: you are to do as I have done for you.' Jesus goes on in the same discourse to put this concrete act into a more general prescription. He

[4] G. Bornkamm, 'Der köstlichere Weg', in *Das Ende des Gesetzes* (München, 1958), p. 110.

[5] W. Schrage, *Die konkreten Einzelgebote in der paulinischen Paränese*, p. 253.

[6] W. Schrage, *op. cit.*, pp. 270–1. This is said against H. Preisker, *Das Ethos des Urchristentums* (Gütersloh, 1949), for whom the command to love is the whole or nearly the whole of Christian ethics.

gives a new commandment[7] which is to constitute a new people of God, a new Israel, who have passed through waters of baptism as their fathers of old passed through the Red Sea. They receive a new law that they should love as their Lord has loved them. Love has this backward reference to Jesus as the pattern and the cause of love. 'I give you a new commandment: love one another; as I have loved you, so you are to love one another. If there is this love among you, then all will know that you are my disciples.' 'Love as I have loved you' implies 'Love because I have loved you'. God has always been beforehand in loving, and because of the cross, Christians are able to love one another.

In chapter 15 love is linked with the keeping of commandments and Jesus shows his love by communicating his father's word. In chapter 17 the disciples are sent into the world as Jesus had been sent into the world, to declare the word and love of God. So they stand under the same sign of divine love. 'John binds love inseparably to the event of the word, that is to the speaking of the word on one hand and its acceptance and preservation on the other.'[8] This is true of the relation of the Son to his church. It is true that in some places love is seen as the sacrifice of life but as soon as the writer of the gospel begins to clarify the meaning of love, it is linked with the word. 'Just as faith means acceptance of the word for one's self, so love means giving one's self to the word in service.'[9] The word is active in the world where it shines in the darkness and the love which unites the church is always linked with encounter with the word. Brotherly love is the command of the Johannine Christ. Such love is unity and solidarity with God, an earthly extension of heavenly reality. 'Therefore it can exist only within that realm which can reflect the heavenly reality, namely the realm of the divine Word.'[10] As the Word participates in the communion of Father and Son, it reproduces the divine unity on earth. The same Word is proclaimed in Christian mission so that the outsider may become a brother and be brought within the divine love.[11] The prayer of Jesus for a universal brotherhood is 'that they may all be one'. Love is the substance of the divine unity 'that the love with which you have loved me may be in them and I in them' (John 17:26).

The legalism of love is found in the concentration on any charitable act without the domination of love. To give all to feed the poor or even to die a martyr's death, without love, has nothing to commend it (1 Cor.

---

[7] See R. Bultmann, *Das Evangelium des Johannes* (15 Aufl. Göttingen, 1957), pp. 351–71, 'Die Konstituierung der Gemeinde und ihr Gesetz: 13, 1–20.'

[8] E. Käsemann, *Jesu letzter Wille nach Johannes 17* (Tübingen, 1966), p. 109; ET *The Testament of Jesus* (1968), p. 61.

[9] *Ibid.* p. 111; ET p. 62.

[10] *Ibid.* p. 123; ET p. 69.   [11] *Ibid.* p. 125; ET p. 70.

13). Paul's shocking statement drives home the point. On the other hand the enthusiastic distortion of love which is puffed up and self-centred meets final condemnation from the Lord who was present in the homeless, hungry and naked (Matt. 25). Inasmuch as it is done to the least, it is done to the Lord, and the cup of cold water will not lose its reward. Love exhibits most clearly the respect for the contingent and the challenge of perfection.

NEGATIVE ETHICS[1]

Each of the four patterns can go wrong in two ways. Legalism and enthusiasm threaten the dynamic quality of each pattern. Righteousness, discipleship, faith and love are powers which find expression in a process. They are not to be hardened into fixed assets or softened into emotional evasion. Nor can the matter be left here. For the rejection of legalism and enthusiasm includes the rejection of much of the content of ethics. The New Testament presents serious problems to anyone who would take ethics seriously. It rejects moralities which would have been known and respected by its readers or hearers. Mark gives a picture of Jesus standing against the conventions of his time, perpetually in conflict with the moral authorities of his community. A popular story of a Dutch flood illustrates this point. When the congregation were told by their pastor that God wanted them to break the Sabbath and repair the flood walls on Sunday morning, they would not move. Jesus may have broken the Sabbath in the interests of human need, but, said an Elder of the congregation, 'I have always had the feeling that Jesus was a bit of a Liberal.'[2] In Matthew the great antitheses ring out, 'You have heard that it was said to them of old, but I say to you'. The pattern of the law is broken and Jesus stands as a threat to moral order. Paul had already said these things before the gospels were written. No man was just in the sight of God. None of his works, his fulfilment of moral codes or duties or laws, none of these counted in the sight of God. For Paul, as we learnt in Romans 1:24, man is never an independent ethical performer, except when he has been totally rejected by God. Then alone he stands on his own feet and does his own ethics. And the fourth gospel shows us the conventional criteria of morality rejected as external by Jesus who stands over against religious and

[1] The best account of negative ethics is given by T. E. Jessop, *Law and Love* (London, 1940); see p. 11, 'He exposed the badness not merely of good men but of goodness itself', and chapter III, 'The Badness of Goodness'.
[2] E. Käsemann, *Der Ruf der Freiheit*, p. 28; ET *Jesus Means Freedom*, p. 16.

moral authorities and who claims that he is light and that they are darkness.

When we turn from the negative polemic of the gospels against morality to the account of the moral process as the New Testament sees it, we find further evidence for negative ethics. Just as Christianity begins with a negative theology insisting that God is not as other gods, so it begins with a negative ethics, giving an account of the moral process which leaves little place for man's moral activity. Righteousness is the power by which God forgives, vindicates and saves mankind. It is something by which man is brought to be righteous, for it creates new life and reconciles man with God. From this new life and reconciliation flow the meaning and possibility of obedience and righteous life. Those who were slaves of sin now give themselves to the service of righteousness and the journey of a holy life. The second pattern, of discipleship or following, is again negative in ethical content. The disciple does not imitate his lord as an equal. He does not say: 'Jesus was humble, therefore today I shall be humble; Jesus went around helping people, today I shall go around helping people.' He is continually confronted with the negation of what he is by taking up the cross. The rich young ruler had used the commandments to protect himself against the radical demand of Jesus. These were a hindrance to discipleship. He was to leave all and follow.

Faith is acceptance of Christ as Lord, dependence on the word of God and life under grace. Each of these points negates the action of the believer and places the positive side of the relation on the God who is believed. The word of God is depended on and life is lived by grace. Faith comes to God with empty hands. It is having a sentence of death upon oneself. Lastly, love is so defined as to distinguish it from what is usually called by that name. Disciples are to love their enemies. They are also to love one another as Christ loved them. Love is marked with the sign of the cross, self-abandonment to the word in service. The divine love is present in those who receive from Father and Son the quality of life which is distinctive of the godhead.

The same problem has been approached in another way. The tension of indicative and imperative is at the centre of New Testament ethics. 'If we live by the Spirit, let our behaviour come from the Spirit too.'[3] Because man is justified he is to serve, because the kingdom is here man is to follow, because he has been loved he should love. Christ is our righteousness.

The outcome of the negative ethics of the New Testament is that

---

[3] Gal. 5:25. See R. Bultmann, 'Das Problem der Ethik bei Paulus', *ZNW* (1924), p. 140, and V. Furnish, *Theology and Ethics in Paul* (Nashville, 1962), p. 225.

there is a sovereign good, namely, God.[4] There is none good but God. This God, by his radical gift and demand, becomes for men the source of goodness. There is only one to whom the word 'good' may properly be applied. Everything else is to be derived from this sovereign good. The righteous God is powerful to justify men. The Lord chooses, calls and enables his disciples to follow. The faithful God is the giver of the faith which saves. And the strange love of Christ enables his own to love one another as he has loved them. Everything ethical in the New Testament is *extra nos*. It begins outside man, and man's only hope of finding goodness is through a turning from his own ethical business to God who alone is good and justifies men.

One major consequence of a sovereign good, or sovereign grace, was grasped clearly in early centuries. Time and again Jesus appeals to the ethical judgement of people who do not believe in him.[5] Paul refers to a law in the heart of the Gentile who does right. This divine prevenience was for Jesus and Paul just as much a matter of grace as that given in the fuller response of faith. When the fathers came to speak of God's dealing with man they saw the seed of the divine Word in every man. This implanted seed or divine image was given by God. Instead of saying, 'Whatever we say as Christians is good', Justin and those who came after him said, 'Whatever then has been well said among all men belongs to us Christians.'[6] This has been seen as the distinctive theme of Christian ethics until Augustine. All is of grace. The sovereign Good does not wait on the faith of man.

Yet with the insistence on the sole goodness of God and his transcendence of ethical standards, there is a striking sense of the ethical newness of the Christian way.[7] The result of negative ethics is not that there is no goodness, but that there is a new kind of goodness which can only be found after the rejection of old kinds. This is parallel to Christian theology where the effect of negative theology is not that there is no longer a God, but that there is a God who is so different from all other gods that he has to be seen in a new way. God is a God who justifies the ungodly, who raises the dead and who creates out of nothing. The newness of the law of Jesus is shown in the antitheses of the Sermon on the Mount and in the contrast between this law of life

---

[4] Mark 10:18. The great importance of this verse for the second century is shown by Justin when he quotes it with an anti-Marcionite development, I *Apol.* 16.7 and *Dial.* 101.2. Clement of Alexandria cites or hints at the verse twelve times.

[5] See A. N. Wilder, 'Equivalents of Natural Law in the Teaching of Jesus', *JR* (1946), p. 132.

[6] Justin. 2 *Apol.* 13.4.

[7] See K. Prümm, *Christentum als Neuheitserlebnis* (Freiburg im Breisgau, 1939), *passim*.

and the law of sin and death. Following points to the future which is always the direction of discipleship and there is no better way of indicating something which is entirely new. The impact of Jesus upon his hearers was the impact of an innovator. No one had ever spoken like this man. The newness of faith is the basis of a new covenant between God and man. It follows from repentance which implies a profound change. Faith shows the way to a new righteousness, and faith is a new kind of activity which takes over the whole of man's relation to God. The love of the Christian is also new. The love of tax gatherers and harlots is directed solely to those who love them. The Christian lives with a love which is new and which goes beyond the love of others. Justin's citations of these verses from the Sermon on the Mount substitute the word 'new' for the word 'extra'.[8] 'What new thing do you do?' Christian love goes the second mile and thereby transforms the concept of friendship. Men can understand the kind of love which is directed towards a good and worthy object. One might even die for the sake of a good man. But the love of God is commended because it is directed to sinners and not to the righteous. The strange love of the followers of Jesus is a divine transplant which changes those who receive it.

Reasons for negative ethics may be found in the polarities already noted in the positive account. In the first place, there is a constant challenge to perfection. Commenting on Matt. 5:48, 'Be ye perfect', A. Boyce Gibson wrote, 'It is the most impossible requirement imaginable. We are to become as good as men as God is as God and that is more than we can possibly be. There is no way round by under-translating the Greek word *teleios* as "fulfilled" or "self-realised": that is bad scholarship as well as a miserable concession to the 1920s.'[9] Since we are concerned in the Sermon on the Mount with an offer rather than a demand, the challenge to perfection cannot be dismissed. Christ becomes to us wisdom, sanctification and righteousness. The difficulties of this challenge were noticed by external critics of Christianity in its earliest days. Trypho objects, in Justin's *Dialogue*,[10] that the commands of the gospel are too difficult. The rejection of ethics in the New Testament is accompanied by a challenge to perfection of righteousness, obedience, faith and love. In the gospels there is only one person on earth who meets this challenge, and he is Jesus, who goes to the cross

[8] Justin, 1 *Apol.* 15.9.
[9] A. Boyce Gibson, *The Challenge of Perfection* (Melbourne, 1968), p. 6. Cf. 'an unattainable and even inconceivable perfection', C. H. Dodd, *Gospel and Law* (New York, 1951), p. 76, and A. D. Lindsay, *The Moral Teaching of Jesus* (London, 1937), chapter one, 'The Gospel of Perfection'. Also cf. J. Knox, *The Ethic of Jesus* (London, 1962), p. 22.
[10] *Dial.* 10.2.

in striking solitude. For Paul in Philippians 3, there is a total concentration upon a goal which has not yet been reached, the goal of sharing the sufferings and resurrection of Christ and becoming like his death.

The other side of this polarity in the New Testament is the insistence upon the importance of the contingent and particular. The challenge to perfection condemns legalism which would limit and make practical the demand of God. The importance of the contingent is a rejection of enthusiasm. The synoptic gospels begin from enthusiasm, and the Jesus of freedom whom we see in Mark is one who strides across the world and calls men to follow along his new and total way.[11] Yet in the synoptics there is always a reminder that the disciples are known by their fruits. Matthew writes against antinomian enthusiasts.[12] The Sermon on the Mount is a new law, and concludes with the parable of the man who built on the rock and the man who built on the sand. Not everyone who called 'Lord, Lord', would enter the kingdom of heaven, but only those who had done the father's will. Professions of enthusiastic devotion are of little account. The man who hears the words of Jesus and does not do them is like a man who builds, not on rock but on sand. Again, Matthew points to the final judgement of the righteous God, where those who have professed Christ will come to him only to receive condemnation because they have not given to the least of his brethren a practical and contingent service. In the fourth gospel, enthusiasm is checked by the constant link of love to the word or command of Christ. The word connects the perfect and the contingent. In chapter 15, love is linked with the keeping of commandments, and Jesus shows his love by handing on his father's word. In chapter 17, the disciples are sent into the world to declare the word and the love of God. The problem of enthusiasm in Paul is clearer than elsewhere in the New Testament, and the classic writings of this controversy are the letters to the Corinthians. The Corinthians, who believe that they have arrived at perfection, are pointed to the way of the cross and of obedience to the word in details of personal behaviour.

Contingency is important in another way. Man's particular acts cannot answer the challenge of perfection.[13] Side by side with the recognition of the perfection which God is and to which God calls, there is always an awareness of man's imperfection and temporal limitation. All flesh is as grass. And while man is better in God's sight than the flowers of the field and the birds of the air, he can do nothing about his tomorrow, but has to leave that to God. He knows not the

---

[11] E. Käsemann, *Der Ruf der Freiheit*, chapter 2.
[12] E. Käsemann, 'The Beginnings of Christian Theology', *NTQT*, pp. 82–107; *EVB* 2, 82–104.
[13] A. Boyce Gibson, *The Challenge of Perfection*, p. 22.

day nor the hour of his reckoning. He knows that whatever he does for
his master, he will still be an unprofitable servant. The sense of his own
contingency brought Paul to an awareness of the perfection of God (2
Cor. 1–4). The answer of death which he found in himself provoked
him not to trust in himself but in the God who raised the dead. Whatever derives from the flesh, that is, from man, is a mixture of 'yes' and
'no'. The son of God is yes, amen and the glory of God. Man is
never sufficient to himself; his only sufficiency comes from God. Even
as he gazes on the glory of the Lord and is transformed from glory to
glory, the light is always the light of God which reveals the darkness of
man. The treasure is always in earthen vessels so that the great power
may be God's and never his. Contingency presses on the believer from
every side. He is perplexed but not in despair, persecuted but not
abandoned, he is struck down but not destroyed. And his bearing about
in the body the dying of Jesus is a means to showing in the same body
the life of Jesus. The things which are seen are temporal, the things
which are unseen are eternal.

The early Christian communities were clearly conscious of this tension between perfection and contingency. There was an early attempt
(Act 4:32) to live by absolutes in 'messianic licence'; but casuistry
became necessary to apply the absolutes to life. 'The absolutes constitute the peculiarity, though not the totality of the teaching of
Jesus.'[14] The words of Jesus are used to determine particular forms of
conduct. This is not a relapse into legalism but an awareness of the
identity of the exalted Lord with Jesus the teacher. The radical ethic
is understood only within the mystery of the person of Jesus himself.[15]
The Sermon on the Mount brings together sayings of Jesus, spanning
the gap between grace and law and joining 'demands such as those of
"the right strawy epistle" of James with the Pauline profundities'.[16]

Respect for the contingent is shown in two ways which point beyond
Christian sources. Matthew shows how radical words became regu-
latory through the development of Christian Gemara, explanatory
additions or comments.[17] This is common rabbinic practice. Again the

---

[14] W. D. Davies, 'The Moral Teaching of the Early Church', in *The Use of
the Old Testament in the New, and Other Essays* (ed. J. M. Efird, Duke
U.P., 1972), p. 322.
[15] W. D. Davies, *The Setting of the Sermon on the Mount* (Cambridge, 1964),
p. 433.
[16] *Ibid.* p. 440. Davies concludes, 'Thus it is that our effort to set the SM
historically in its place finally sets us in our place. And the place in which
it sets us is the Last Judgment, before the infinite succour and the infinite
demand of Christ.'
[17] *Ibid.* pp. 387–401, and F. W. Beare, 'Concerning Jesus of Nazareth', *JBL*
(1968), p. 134f.

use of Jewish and Gentile *Haustafeln* represented the application of the absolute demands of the gospel to specific areas. The use of these prescriptive forms again showed continuity with Jewish ethical thought. It is important not to treat detailed prescription as totally irreconcilable with the absolutes; for it is through detailed prescription that the final allegiance can be shown.[18] Negative ethics illuminate the problems of legalism, fulfilment and forgiveness. Legalism is 'the intention to claim God's favour by establishing one's own rightness',[19] using the law as a means to this end. It stands in contrast to an attitude of reverence for the law as a revelation of God's will. Paul challenges the Galatians to keep the whole law (Gal. 5:3) instead of trying to make it serve their self-centred ambition. The penitent publican is justified rather than the proud Pharisee. Justification by faith brings obligation and penitence at deeper levels than those reached by legalism.[20] But legalism and pietism will never be convinced that this is so. It is a sign of authenticity that Paul's account of justification still continues to disturb pietism and legalism. For Paul is not concerned to attack a Jewish phenomenon; the letter to the Romans demolishes the piety of the pious, whether they be Jews or Christians. This gives value to the criticism that 'Paul went too far'[21] and had an antinomian tendency;[22] for the critic in question shows more clearly than others the 'deeply pietistic heritage' of the last two hundred years.[23] Legalism will always treasure Paul's continuing respect for the Law and minimise the distance which Paul moved from his earlier attitudes. However violent the change in any person's life he has to acknowledge his past and gradually come to terms with it. Paul's conversion would still leave

[18] 'Diesem Herrn aber, so betonen die Haustafeln, gehört der Gehorsam nicht in einer ghettohaft von der Welt abgregrenzten Sphäre, in die man sich weltflüchtig-asketisch zurückzieht, nicht in reiner Innerlichkeit oder allein in einem kirchlichen Binnenbereich, sondern auch in den gesellschaftlich-sozialen Bereichen. Das ist der tiefste Grund, warum im Kol. überhaupt erstmalig im NT eine Haustafel auftritt.' p. 22, W. Schrage, 'Zur Ethik der Neutamentlichen Haustafeln', *NTS*, 21, 1974.

[19] C. F. D. Moule, Obligation in the Ethic of Paul, in *Christian History and Interpretation, For John Knox* (ed. Farmer, Moule and Niebuhr, Cambridge, 1967), p. 393.

[20] *Ibid.* p. 399. Such penitence is 'a voluntary entering with God into the pain and distress which one's own sin has caused, and which, in God's hands can be turned into the creative means of healing and repair'.

[21] J. Knox, *The Ethic of Jesus in the Teaching of the Church* (London, 1962), p. 110.

[22] *Ibid.* pp. 86f.

[23] P. Schubert, 'Paul and the NT Ethic in John Knox', in *Christian History and Interpretation* (ed. Farmer, Moule and Niebuhr, Cambridge, 1967), pp. 370f.

some relation to that Law which was part of his world. It is hard to realise the violence of his rejection of legalism. There is more historical ground for Bultmann than for the innuendos of his critics.[24]

Negative ethics illuminate another problem, that of fulfilment. In what sense did Jesus fulfil the Law (Matt. 5:17)? It could mean that in the story of Jesus a great number of predictions were literally fulfilled, but it is more likely that it refers to covenant and promise. Jesus showed in his relationship to his Father a unique finality or fullness of all that a covenant could mean.[25] The new covenant which he inaugurated brought together all the imagery and hope of Jewish expectation. There was a 'rebirth of images' as the totality of their consummation in the Son, Jesus, was grasped.[26] So Jesus can 'bring to its final conclusion all that the Law stood for',[27] by completely realising the perfect will of God.[28] The fulfilment of the Law supersedes all legal prescription. So Jesus is able to abrogate and fulfil simultaneously. The concept of

[24] W. R. Schoedel, 'Pauline Thought: Some Basic Issues', in *Transitions in Biblical Scholarship* (ed. J. C. Rylaarsdam, Chicago, 1968). This article is remarkable for its sustained illogicality and a deep distrust of Paul's negative statements about law. There is no awareness of the hermeneutic principle that simply to reproduce the words of Paul cannot convey his meaning. (See G. Ebeling, *Word and Faith* [London, 1963], p. 18.) No distinction is made between logical possibility and historical probability. The cumulative innuendo of the article does not provide any argument: p. 267, 'It is possible, I believe, to cast doubt', p. 272, 'Is it too much to claim'; p. 273, 'The emphasis, to be sure, is probably on the work of the Spirit by which God's will is realised – nevertheless, since the term "law" also occurs in this connection, it does not seem artificial to ask what elements in Moses may have been regarded by Paul as expressing the essence of the law's requirement.' The mixture of logical terms and qualifiers creates the false impression that something has been said: p. 274, 'Paul, I should guess – But this does not exclude the possibility that – '; p. 275, 'I think it is clear'; p. 276, 'angels remain in some sense the executors of God's will'; p. 277, 'this may suggest that something is wrong'; p. 279, 'we see the possibility – Seen within the framework we have uncovered(!), we can perhaps understand what this may mean'. The conclusion consists of two negative entailments of negative conclusions.

[25] C. F. D. Moule, 'Fulfilment-Words in the New Testament', *NTS* 14 (1968), 298.

[26] *Ibid.* p. 300: 'Already an Israel-figure and perhaps a messianic title, the term "son" is given a completely new depth in Christian tradition by Christ's own interpretation of sonship in terms of his own life of self-dedication even to death. It is summed up in Christ's new use of Abba.'

[27] *Ibid.* p. 314.

[28] S. Schulz, *Die Stunde der Botschaft* (Hamburg, 1967), p. 182, cited, Moule, 'Fulfilment-Words' p. 316. ' "Erfüllung" kann hier also nur "verwirklichen" bedeuten. Der irdische Jesus verwirklicht eschatologisch das ganze Gesetz, das will heissen: den grundsätzlichen und allein wesentlichen Gotteswillen.'

negative ethics makes sense of the non-legal way in which the Law is fulfilled.

Finally, the place of forgiveness is illuminated by negative ethics. There is none good but God; no man can come before God except as a repentant sinner. The impossible ethical ideal of Christ shows the place of repentance and hope, as it displays the weakness and corruption of man. Man knows his finitude as he meets the infinite in the cross of Christ.[29] 'A good conscience is an invention of the devil'.[30] The precepts of Christ lead through judgement and exposure of human need to the infinite mercy of God and his forgiveness.[31] In forgiveness one may learn the quality and direction of Christian living. The quality is that of patient and unselfish respect for others and the direction that of overcoming evil with good.[32] Here again negative ethics have positive effect in concrete situations. Take, for example, Jesus' demand for total renunciation of wealth and his insistence that joint service to God and mammon is impossible. No one can ever claim to have kept these commands and all are therefore in need of forgiveness; 'and yet, if you take them seriously at all, they will make themselves felt in every single thing you do that is concerned with the disposal of your money.'[33]

In summary, we may say then that there is a case for both positive and negative ethics. To acknowledge the evidence on both sides is to begin to understand the ethics of the New Testament. Today, a rejection of negative ethics may spring from a distrust of Bultmann (e.g. Schoedel) or a concern for moral order (e.g. Knox). The rejection of positive ethics may spring from distrust of convention (e.g. Situation Ethics) or a concern for moral freedom (e.g. 'new morality'). In each case some of the New Testament evidence is put on one side. The more sensitive writers on Christian ethics have argued for both sides.[34] Negative ethics are not antinomian, but point to the inadequacy of man's efforts after goodness and to the sovereignty of good. Negative theology is not atheistic but points to the inadequacy of human accounts of God and the divine transcendence. Negative ethics point to recurrent polarities which are found in the New Testament – perfection and contingency, indicative and the imperative, mercy and demand, grace and law, enthusiasm and legalism, absolute and contin-

[29] R. Niebuhr, *An Interpretation of Christian Ethics* (London, 1936), pp. 131–45.

[30] A. Schweitzer, cited by C. H. Dodd, *Gospel and Law* (New York, 1951), p. 77.

[31] *Ibid*. C. H. Dodd, p. 62.   [32] *Ibid*. p. 81.   [33] *Ibid*. p. 76.

[34] E.g., A. Boyce Gibson, in *Christian Ethics and Contemporary Philosophy* (ed. I. T. Ramsey, London, 1966), p. 115, and *The Challenge of Perfection* (Melbourne, 1968).

gent, new and old. The sensitivity of Christian ethics to both sides of each antithesis prevents it from becoming just another account of the good life. Yet it does make for a precarious balance and gives ground for the earlier accusation of 'incurable unintelligibility' in Christian thought. As negative ethics point to these polarities so they also have their own polarity with positive ethics. For Christianity is still concerned with moral excellence. The fruit by which the believer is known is his good life. He is ruled more firmly by the pardon than he ever was by the law.[35] It is no accident that the New Testament and early Christian literature are full of concrete ethical prescription. Justification by faith, or life under grace, while it lies beyond morals 'becomes the one hope of a truly moral life'.[36]

The history of Christianity subsequent to New Testament days confirms the analysis we have made. The negative ethics, transcendent goodness and challenge to perfection of the New Testament are found in an uncompromising form in Gnostic and Marcionite heresies. For the Gnostics there was a radical dualism between spirit and matter, between God and the world, between the perfect and the contingent. The life of God was entirely distinct from the life of the world. There were two ways of living, one was the way of knowledge and perfection, the other was the way of frustration, ignorance and contingency. The God of the gospel was, said Marcion, a strange God, foreign to all the ways of men, with a goodness utterly beyond man's ideas of justice. Marcion could not combine perfection with contingency or the new with the old, because he grasped the wonder of the perfection and the catastrophic novelty of the new.[37] The experience of newness was the distinctive experience of the second-century Christian as he found himself increasingly unable to bridge the gap between himself and his own past.[38] He saw the danger of compromise and he did not see how he could bring perfection and contingency together without limiting them both. So he kept perfection and rejected contingency. The followers of Carpocrates and Epiphanes, says Clement, think that wives should be common property. 'Through them the worst slander has become current against the Christian names.' Epiphanes gave the following account of *dikaiosunē* –

[35] R. T. Brooks, cited by C. F. D. Moule, 'Obligation in the Ethic of Paul', *Christian History and Interpretation*, p. 404.
[36] C. K. Barrett, *A Commentary on the Epistle to the Romans* (London, 1957), p. 129.
[37] The Antitheses began, 'O Wonder beyond Wonder, what a rapture, power and surprise it is that man can neither say anything about the gospel nor think of it, nor compare it with anything!' See A. von Harnack, *Marcion, Das Evangelium des fremden Gottes* (Leipzig, 1921), pp. 81 and 137.
[38] See K. Prümm, *Christentum als Neuheitserlebnis*.

The righteousness of God is a kind of universal fairness and equality. There is an equality in the heavens which is stretched out in all directions and contains the entire earth in its circle. The night reveals all stars equally. The light of the sun which is the cause of the daytime and the father of light, God pours out from above upon the earth in equal measure upon all who have power to see. For all see alike.

The universality of God's fairness is clear. 'It is regulated by no law, but is harmoniously available to all through the gift of him who gives it and makes it grow... But the laws, by presupposing the existence of private property, cut up and destroyed the universal equality decreed by the divine law.'[39] When man began to think in terms of mine and thine, he introduced laws to prevent the common use of earthly goods. God meant all things to be held in common, with a universal fairness and equality. Man's laws do not merit respect. God's decree ensures the permanence of the human race, for there is in the male a strong burning desire which neither law nor custom nor any other restraint can destroy. The followers of this sect celebrated their higher righteousness in sexual orgies which re-established the righteousness of God. Here the antithesis between God's righteousness and laws is extended and the path of perfection knows nothing of particular obligations or of contingent limits. The disposition of heaven belongs to man upon earth, and the earthly laws which have been contrived must be totally rejected by those who are now and always citizens of heaven.

The same kind of instant perfection was available to Christian discipleship. *Koinōnia*, which replaces the notion of following, has no limitations or frustrations. The followers of Nicolaus believe that 'All things were one; but as it seemed good to its unity not to be alone, an idea came forth from it, and it had intercourse with it and made the beloved. In consequence of this there came forth from him an idea, with which he had intercourse and made powers which cannot be seen or heard.'[40] The origin of all things is a communion which implies sexual intercourse. The words of scripture are perverted to justify promiscuity, and Clement writes, 'It is to the brothels that this "communion" leads.' There is no scope for following, no scope for obedience. The Gnostic followers of Prodicus insist that they are by nature the sons of the first God, 'But they misuse their noble birth and freedom and life as they desire. And their desire is for pleasure, thinking that no one is superior to them as they are lords of the Sabbath and are

---

[39] Clement, *Stromateis*, 3.2.5f. Translations of *Stromateis* 3 follow H.
Chadwick, *Alexandrian Christianity* (London, 1954), with modification.
[40] *Strom*, 3.4.29.2.

royal sons above all the rest of mankind. To a king, they say, there is no law prescribed.'[41]

The Gnostic rejection of faith requires no precise documentation since it was this move which gave the tendency its name. The dichotomy between faith and knowledge assigned faith to the area of the contingent, both believer and the object of belief being contingent, while knowledge belonged to the perfect, both knower and known suffering no defect in their perfection. The newness of the way of Christ could not be joined to any other way.

Marcion did not separate faith from knowledge, but concentrated his sense of newness upon the God who was believed. For Marcion it was the newness of Christian love which overwhelmed him. He could not believe that the good and loving God of the gospel could be the just God of the Old Testament. Perfection of love could not be associated with the world of sin and death.

Each of the moral patterns of the New Testament has been distorted through a perfectionism which has rejected the contingent. Here is an enthusiasm which grasps the newness of the gospel, but cannot link it with the way of the cross or with the cup of cold water given in Christ's name. It is interesting to note how Clement replies to this serious challenge.[42] Echoing Plato, he writes,

> We must follow where the word leads;[43] and if we depart from it we must fall into 'endless evil'. And by following the divine scripture, the path by which believers travel, we are to be made like unto the Lord as far as possible.[44] We must not live as if there were no difference between right and wrong,[45] but to the best of our power we must purify ourselves from indulgence and lust and take care for our soul[46] which must continually be devoted to the deity alone. For when it is pure and set free from all evil, the mind is somehow capable of receiving the power of God and the divine image is set up in it. 'And everyone who has this hope in the Lord purifies himself' says the Scripture 'even as he is pure'.[47]

Knowledge of God cannot come to those who are under the control of their passions. 'Nor can the view that pleasure is the supreme good be reconciled with the view that only the beautiful is good or that only the Lord is beautiful and God alone is good and is alone to be loved.'[48] In their grasp after perfection the heretics have denied the transcendent and unique perfection of God. In trying to reject contingency

---

[41] *Ibid.* 28.1 and 30.1.
[43] Plato, *Republic* 394D.
[45] *Ibid.* 176–7.
[47] 1 John 3:3.
[42] *Strom.* 3.5.42.4–6.
[44] Plato, *Theaetetus* 176B.
[46] Plato, *Phaedo* 107C.
[48] *Strom.* 3.5.43.2.

they have made a contingent thing, pleasure, their goal or perfection. But neither perfection nor contingency may be compromised.

> It is the manner of life which shows up those who know the commandments; for as a man's word is, so is his life. The tree is known by its fruit, not by its blossom and leaves. Knowledge, then, comes from the fruit and from behaviour, not from talk and from blossom. We say that knowledge is not mere talk, but a certain divine knowledge, that light which is kindled in the soul as a result of obedience to the commandments, – which enables man to know himself and teaches him to become possessed of God.[49]

The problems of the New Testament have led us into the second century and to Clement who saw where heretics went wrong. We move now to Clement and his account of the four patterns, his preservation of both perfection and contingency and his restatement of the positive and negative aspects of Christian ethics.

[49] *Ibid.* 44. 1–3.

2

CLEMENT OF ALEXANDRIA[1]

Clement had already wandered far, when he came to Alexandria, looking for knowledge. He found the teacher he wanted in Pantaenus, a converted Stoic. After nearly thirty years in Alexandria, he left during the persecution of 202; this is probably the reason why his successor, Origen, who had strong ideas on martyrdom, never mentions him. We hear of him again in two letters written in 212 and 215. The first letter confirms his survival until 212. The second letter establishes his death prior to 215 for it speaks of him as one of 'those blessed fathers who have gone before us'.[2] His three main writings *Protrepticus* (*Exhortation*), *Paedagogus* (*Instructor*) and *Stromateis* (*Miscellanies*) form a progressive account of Christian knowledge. The *Exhortation* calls men to faith and salvation. The *Instructor* guides the believer to a Christian life. The *Miscellanies* present 'gnostic notes concerning the true philosophy', and have been the subject of much controversy. It seems likely that they represent the highest stage of Christian knowledge for their disordered contents are rich in thought and insight. They show the Christian philosopher or teacher as the ideal which determines Clement's own approach to life and morals. Clement discredits the gnostic heresy by putting forward a true form of gnosis.[3]

Christianity did not come to terms with classical thought gradually. As with Judaism the decisive steps were taken quickly. During the second century the problems of converted intellectuals, of pagan ridicule and philosophic attack combined to make Christians insecure. The Apologists had to think quickly and argue strenuously. The church universal was just as acutely and rapidly Hellenised as were Gnostic sects. The process is most rapid in Clement. We are concerned solely with his moral theory but the claim holds for all parts of his

---

[1] The following abbreviations will be used in this chapter: *Ex.=Exhortation or Protrepticus; P.=Instructor or Paedagogus; S.=Miscellanies or Stromateis: Q.D.S.=The rich man's salvation or Quis dives salvetur?*

[2] Eusebius, *H.E.* 6.11.6. and 6.14.9.

[3] For a brief account of the issues, see E. F. Osborn, *The Philosophy of Clement of Alexandria* (Cambridge, 1957), pp. 5–7 and 13f.

thought. After him Christian theology developed along deeper and critical lines. Doctrines were clarified and truths were better stated. Yet during the first five centuries Christian theology never became more Greek, never merged more fully with classical philosophy than it did in Clement.[4] For this reason we shall look at the debts to Hellas in his ethical thought. Those who came after him have little to add in this connection.[5]

As for philosophy in general, so for ethics in particular, Clement is crucial. Whatever has been said against his philosophical theology, and, after all, his obscure method deserves to be misunderstood, no one denies his importance for the history of Christian morals. Philosophy for him includes the good life. Moral issues move him most deeply and occupy most pages of his writing. The *Exhortation* dwells on the wickedness of the heathen and their need to change. The *Instructor* gives detailed moral prescriptions of fascinating variety. The *Miscellanies* include a closely argued section which orders all Christian morals around one great principle, as well as an extended account of what grace might do for those who go on towards perfection. It is small wonder that book after book has been written on Clement's ethical thought.[6]

Second-century Christians were upset by the moral rebuke of pagans, and by false brethren who gave point to the rebuke. Historians may discount the moral slur which, from earliest times, was part of the case against heretics. It is always easy to believe that those who disagree are bad; but there is much to suggest that at this time their moral misdemeanours were a major reason why heretics were noticed. One

---

[4] 'Avec Clément, cette hellénisation devient pleinement consciente et volontaire', O. Prunet, *La morale de Clément d'Alexandrie* (Paris, 1966), p. 243.

[5] Pseudo-Dionysius adds an extreme application of Neoplatonic philosophy in the sixth century.

[6] The works of Prunet and Völker are especially rewarding. For details, see bibliography. Prunet shows great sensitivity to the complexity of Clement's thought: 'Mais une réponse pleinement satisfaisante ne sera pas donnée de sitôt aux questions qu'il pose. Le domaine est trop étendu, trop complexe... La personnalité de Clément, tiraillée entre les tendances du Christianisme moderne, échappe en réalité à nos étiquettes et nous transporte dans un autre monde, bien loin de nôtre, mais déjà aussi bien loin du Christianisme apostolique' (p. 247). Völker's work is thorough and comprehensive. Marrou's comments are always concise and to the point; for example, his article in *Studia Patristica* (Berlin, 1957), concludes (p. 546), 'Où est passée l'Alexandrie du second siècle, ce milieu si caracterisé dans son extériorité par rapport à nous ? Au coeur de cette situation relative, nous avons retrouvé l'élan central qui animait le moraliste chrétien et avec lui nous nous sentons en pleine communion.'

might be a fool for Christ's sake but not a knave. Clement talks about
the Carpocratians and their connubial communism. The ascetic
extremes of Marcionites and others were more subtly dangerous, for
they lifted the good life out of the world in which men had to live.
Clement sees man in the world as his central concern.[7] We shall look
at the four patterns which were seen in the New Testament, noting
in each case some Stoic, Platonic or Aristotelian terms that are used.
A few of these terms were already in the New Testament; but their
use was far more restricted.

RIGHTEOUSNESS

(i) *The only really shameful thing is vice*

There is only one thing of which one should be ashamed and that is
badness and all it produces.[1] The *Protrepticus* condemns pagan morals
and commends the Christian way,[2] the true word leads men back to
piety. Even pagans have seen the sinfulness of sin. The king of the
Scythians shot an arrow into a subject who had been sexually depraved
by mystery worship; he did not want moral infection among his people.
Moses sensed the same danger when he excluded certain people from
the congregation.[3] Yet few recognise moral danger when they see it,
for example, in the gods of the heathen who are wicked demons bent
on slaughter. Sacrifice is merely murder in a sacred setting.[4] Art comes
from idols and demons on whose behalf it deceives the unwary; erotic
pictures lure men to sin with their eyes. Those who do not know God,
who worship the creature rather than the creator, are guilty of impiety;
they, not Christians, should be punished on this charge.

The scripture provides universal instruction, for there are ten thousand passages whose fulfilment is certain. The Lord, the Holy Spirit,
who has spoken them all, does not speak as teacher, master, or even as
God, but as a father who gently guides his children.[5] The *Paedagogus*
gives precepts for the upright in heart. Practical rather than theoretical
he creates right disposition and good character, the practice of duty
in obedience to commandments.[6] As Lord God, he forgives our sins
and, as man, he trains us not to sin. He, the Word of God, became flesh
and revealed to us a virtue which is both practical and contemplative.
What he says is law and his commands give the short, straight path to
immortality. His precepts are coloured by persuasion and not by fear.[7]

[7] For an outline of the Encratite position and its development, see H.
Chadwick, 'Enkrateia', *RAC* **5,** 343–65.

[1] *P.* 2.6.52.2.   [2] *Ex.* 1.2.3.   [3] *Ex.* 2.25.1.   [4] *Ex.* 3.42.9.
[5] *Ex.* 9.82.2.   [6] *P.* 1.1.2.1.   [7] *P.* 1.3.9.4.

He uses a tactful and gentle approach to the moral change which conversion requires.

Instruction covers all parts of life. Food should be used not for self-indulgence but for building the body with plain nourishment. Excess is to be always avoided and food and drink are to be taken in a dignified way. Right reason permits the use of wine in winter as protection against cold, at other times as medicine, or as a cup of friendship in enjoyment and sobriety.[8] Laughter should always be kept within limits of propriety.[9] Women who pretend to be graceful have found a disgusting way of drinking from narrow vessels; they toss their heads back and bare their necks, gulping down all they can and displaying more than modesty permits. Too much wine loosens the tongue, relaxes the lips, and makes the eyes roll widely. The power of vision has to swim through the excessive moisture. Those who are drunk think everything is going around them, and they cannot observe single things from a distance. 'Indeed it seems I can see two suns', said the old man of Thebes in his drunkenness. The sight is distorted by the heat of the wine. Clement writes of banquets, where those who 'in their gluttony are more like pigs or dogs than men, try to stuff themselves so quickly that both cheeks bulge at once and the veins on their faces stand out; not to mention the perspiration that pours out all over them as, tense with insatiable greed, they pant in their indulgence.' The glutton buries his mind in his belly like a certain fish which, according to Aristotle, carries its heart in its stomach. The effect of wine on the young is especially vicious, 'For it is wrong to add fire to fire by pouring wine, the most fiery of all liquids, into the burning years of life.'[10]

(ii) Harmony, reason and nature

Sin is all that is contrary to right reason, while virtue is a harmonious rational state in the whole of life. Stoics call right what is appropriate and fitting, and the commandments which express these things point to man's end of eternal rest in God.[11] *There is an order or harmony which fills the universe and against this harmony all that is evil and pagan has worked.*[12] Clement attacks the account of cosmic harmony which Epiphanes put forward in his *Concerning Righteousness*. For Epiphanes the righteousness of God is a universal fairness and equality. There is a balance in earth and stars and the harmony of all things points to the divine equity. But righteousness for Epiphanes leads to a shameful form of communion, which is unrestrained sexual licence.[13]

[8] *P*. 2.2.29.2 and 32.1.   [9] *P*. 2.5.46.1,2 and 47.3.
[10] *P*. 2.1 and 2.   [11] *P*. 1.13.102.2.
[12] *Ex*. 1.5.1.   [13] *S*. 3.6.54.1.

'Luxury has moved everything out of its place; fastidious extravagance has brought shame to man. It seeks everything, tries everything,
does violence to everything, and throws nature into confusion.'[14] Order
and stability bring consistency in behaviour.[15] Music must be scrutin-
ised, because of its strong influence on behaviour. It should express
gravity and modesty without fancy harmonies or florid figures.[16]
Moderation should always be our aim; over-exertion and weariness
cause illness. Avoiding both licentious pleasure and puritanical self-
denial, we should hold a middle course. It is proper to attend to our
own needs and look after ourselves instead of having others to wait
upon us; unless of course, we return the service received and promote
a reciprocal justice. Moderate drinking and eating produce a body
which is in accordance with nature.[17] Rational beings will not call
servants by whistling with their lips or through their fingers, nor will
they be always spitting, clearing throats or blowing noses in public.
Especially at the table, we behave like human beings and not like
oxen or asses who don't know the difference between a manger and a
dung heap. If you have to sneeze, don't explode! Don't belch with
open mouth and violent wind; but control the discomfort and conceal
the inward upset.[18]

A just man is a noble hymn of praise to God. Only in the soul of a
wise man can God write truth, love, reverence and humility. Man has
reason and with this he may come to know God;[19] but this knowledge
is not innate. The final invitation of the *Exhortation* calls on men to
come to Jesus and to be placed in an ordered arrangement under God
and the Word of God. Man has been given reason and is offered the
further gift of immortality. By receiving this gift he receives God himself. The Word of God is present in him and brings him into unity with
the will of the Father. So man is faced with a choice between judgement and grace, beween life and destruction.[20] Man does not become
good simply by nature. He has to learn about goodness and be trained
just as a doctor or a pilot needs to be trained. Perfection in virtue comes
not to those who have perfect natures but to those who persevere in
training towards a virtuous life. It is true that God has made us to live
together in righteousness, but justice or righteousness does not spring
unaided from within. The commandment stirs up the good which the
creator has placed in us and the soul is then trained to choose what is
best.[21] Nature is the work of the Logos and God himself directs it.[22]

[14] *P.* 3.3.21.3.   [15] *P.* 3.12.85.4.   [16] *P.* 2.4.44.5.
[17] *P.* 3.10.51.2 and 11.64.2.   [18] *P.* 2.7.60.2–3.
[19] *Ex.* 10.107.1ff.   [20] *Ex.* 12.120ff.   [21] *S.* 1.6.35.1.
[22] See F. Quatember, *Die christliche Lebenshaltung des Kl. von Alexandreia*
(Wien, 1946), pp. 114ff.

Luxury is irrational for it mistakes the purpose and end of man.[23]
Man has been made by God who cares for him and knows how and
for what he is formed. It is wrong to pluck out hairs because God has
counted their number and thinks them important. Luxury throws all
things out of order. It does not observe the course of nature or the
proper order of things.[24] Pleasures and luxury bring men to shipwreck
and go against all that is true.[25] The irrational effects of luxury are
shown by the neglect of orphan children, and the pampering of pets
by those who 'prefer irrational to rational creatures'.[26] Wearing a
festive crown in revelry is wrong, because the *logos* is in the brain and
should not be encircled with something that has been dedicated to
idols.[27] Wisdom is not bought with earthly coins, nor is it on sale in
any market. It can be bought in heaven, where it is sold for 'the true
coinage, the immortal word, the royal gold'. Drinking all night cannot fail to foster drunkenness, lust, and shameful behaviour. Disorderly
music, frenzied beating on cymbals and drums, turn a banquet into a
display of drunkenness.[28]

What belongs to the nature of man should not be taken from him,
but controlled and defined; it is natural for man to laugh, but he should
not always be laughing, any more than a horse should always be neighing. As a reasonable creature, he moderates and relaxes harmoniously
the tension and austerity of his serious endeavour.[29] Women will wear
white shoes except when travelling, when shoes may be greased. They
should wear shoes most of the time, because bare feet should not be
shown, and 'a woman is inclined to slip and is easily hurt'.[30] Gluttons
are not true men but are all jaw.

> Greedy and anxious, gluttons seem to sweep the world with a net to
> satisfy their extravagant tastes. With frying pans sizzling all around
> them, they wear all their life away with pestle and mortar, holding
> on to matter as does fire. Still worse, they even take the goodness
> out of plain food, like bread, by straining out the nourishing grain.
> The only necessary part of food is an embarrassment to luxury.
> There is no limit to men's greed for dainties. It has brought them to
> sweets, honey-cakes and dried fruits, to concocting countless desserts,
> and always looking for different kinds of dishes. This sort of man
> seems to be nothing but jaw.[31]

Man who follows virtue turns into light, and the same word is used for
'light' and for 'man'. They are in fact different words but Clement

[23] *Ex.* 10.92.4   [24] *P.* 3.3.19.4 and 21.3.   [25] *P.* 3.7.37.1
[26] *P.* 3.4.30.3.   [27] *P.* 2.8.72.2.   [28] *P.* 2.3.39.4 and 4.40.2.
[29] *P.* 2.5.46.2.   [30] *P.* 2.11.117.1.   [31] *P.* 2.1.3.2–4.1.

argues from their similar spelling.[32] In particular Abel was a righteous man and his blood cried from the earth. The Lord saves man with fear and grace. God puts before us life and death. We should choose life without delay. Yet men persecute the rational and loving man of God when he calls them to righteousness. A man who is firmly fixed in righteousness and who carries the words of truth on his heart will live for ever. God gives life; but man's evil deeds bring remorse and punishment after death.[33]

(iii) *Just and good*

The great theme of the righteousness of God takes a new form in Clement. Marcion has denied that justice could ever be good or be the means of man's salvation; he has tried to drive a wedge between justice and goodness. Clement comes back with an insistence on the unity of goodness and justice especially as they are found in God. Goodness and justice differ from other things. Justice is not good because it possesses virtue, but goodness and justice are virtue, and are good in themselves. They cannot be separated. The one God is both just and good. Of course the divine Word acts out the justice and goodness of God in many ways. He is concerned to save God's children and uses every form of reproof, correction and guidance in order to bring them to their right end. The Hebrews forgot the mercy of God and made him a master rather than a father. But God remains one God who is both just and good. He is all things and he is the only God. He showed his justice by sending his Word to us. So justice came to man both in written and bodily form, in the law and in the Word. In both ways it was good and brought man to a repentance which could lead to salvation. The great number of exhortations to goodness and warnings against evil fulfils the promise that there would be 'no peace for the wicked'.[34] Marcion's antithesis between goodness and justice is false. The commandment of Moses, when interpreted symbolically, gives a right way of life and a right understanding of God.[35] However unpleasant, law is able to lead the wicked back to a good life and such correction is the 'greatest, most perfect good'.[36]

(iv) *The right use of the world*

The morality of the *Paedagogus* is strongly ascetic but never runs into dualism. Clement values highly the Christian's place in the world. His description of Christian life in second-century Alexandria gives

[32] *P*. 1.6.28.2; *phōs*.   [33] *Ex*. 10.90.3.
[34] *P*. 1.8–10.   [35] *S*. 6.16.   [36] *S*. 1.27.

useful information concerning social and domestic relations in his day.[37] As God rejoiced over his work in creation, so man still wonders at it and thanks God for it. The cosmos is made holy by the creative work of God. Clement praises the right use of the world as had Plato and the Stoics before him.[38] Wealth and marriage are valued highly for they are both ways of receiving God's gifts. Yet some ambivalence remains; Clement has been described as both a defender of the world and a preacher of flight from the world.[39] God makes body and soul and unites them to form man; soul can only do right through body. The incarnation of the Word has delivered them both from the power of sin.[40] The exhortation to *apatheia* or passionlessness does not contradict their unity, for *apatheia* is merely freedom from passions.[41] The true gnostic shows his righteousness in his body, which bears the stamp of a righteous soul.[42]

The bath presents many problems. It is absurd to have gold and silver fittings in a bathroom. It is improper to strip in front of slaves and have them scrub one's body.[43] One should never take a bath just for pleasure, or to warm or cool the body. Too much bathing causes weakness and dizzy spells. One should certainly not have a bath when one is tired or when one has eaten too much. In the end, the only important thing is to wash the soul from pollution. It is moral cleanliness that counts.[44]

Money presents fewer problems. It is wrong to abandon the wealthy to their almost hopeless condition. A Christian should pray for the rich man and help him to find eternal life in spite of his possessions. Riches are not to be thrown away, but to be used for the benefit of our neighbours and ourselves. Wealth is an instrument which may be used for righteousness or for evil. One can get rid of worldly wealth, but still be rich in passions and miss salvation.[45] Clement puts forward a social, not a solitary, morality and gives a much more important place to woman,

---

[37] The accuracy of this picture has been challenged because Clement uses other sources, but examination suggests that the greater part of the work is a useful source of knowledge concerning Egypt in Clement's day. See discussion in H. Marrou, *Le Pédagogue I, SC*, pp. 86–91.

[38] Cf. W. Völker, *Der wahre Gnostiker nach Clemens Alexandrinus* (Berlin and Leipzig, 1952), p. 198.

[39] W. Wagner, *Der Christ und die Welt nach Clemens von Alexandrien* (Göttingen, 1903).

[40] F. Quatember, *Die christliche Lebenshaltung*, ch. 5.

[41] T. Rüther, *Die sittliche Forderung der Apatheia in den beiden ersten christlichen Jahrhunderten und bei Klemens von Alexandrien* (Freiburg, 1949).

[42] *S.* 6.12.103.5.

[43] *P.* 3.5.32.3.

[44] *P.* 3.9.48.2.

[45] *Q.D.S.* 14 and 16.

especially as mother of a family, than was usual in his day. A woman is of the same nature as a man, and equally capable of virtue.[46]

Kissing is a perilous procedure, and the kiss of charity needs to be watched. There are those who have no love in their hearts but yet make a great noise in church with their kisses. There is a holy kiss which is made with a pure and closed mouth by those who have tasted the kingdom. There is also an unholy kiss which is poisonous and fraudulent. Just as spiders, by touching the mouth, can cause pain, so kisses can inject poisonous lust. Those who like public display are fond of kissing; but this does not mean that they love those whom they kiss.[47] There are other social problems; men should not spend their time gossiping in barbers' shops and taverns, nor should they play dice, especially for money.[48]

In this account of righteousness, Clement has drawn from Plato the bond between virtue and knowledge. The only things that are bad are ignorance and action against right reason. Goodness does not come by chance or by innate aptitude, but by learning and practice. For Clement, as for Plato, education is important. Harmony, as a definition of goodness, had been used by Plato, Pythagoras and Heraclitus. Clement wrote of a divine harmony with which men must keep in tune, and insisted that as rational creatures we should tune ourselves temperately, 'harmoniously relaxing the sternness and high tension of our serious pursuits, not discordantly breaking them up'.[49] Clement quotes Plato on the importance of care of body for harmony of soul. Plato, says Clement, saw the dangers of opulence and indulgence in exotic foods. No one who had been brought up in luxury could become wise, for any natural ability would be destroyed. Plato learnt from the Hebrews to prefer sufficiency to luxury.[50] From Aristotle comes the doctrine of the mean, which is determined by reason and which guides human action; for Clement the mean should always be sought. The Stoics had spoken of living harmoniously or living harmoniously with nature; Clement uses the theme of harmony with nature to move to the notion of harmony with God, insisting that the latter is the original notion which the Stoics altered. As the Stoics insisted, all virtues are joined together, 'It is evident that if we examine these virtues in turn, we can make this observation concerning them all: whoever has one virtue gnostically, has them all, because they go together.'[51]

Clement uses certain passages from Musonius Rufus concerning clothing and luxury. His literary dependence is not extensive but it is

---

[46] *P.* 1.4.10.1; cf. also *S.* 4.8.   [47] *P.* 3.11.81.2.
[48] *P.* 3.11.75.1–2.   [49] *P.* 2.5.46.2.
[50] *P.* 2.1.18.1–2.   [51] *S.* 2.18.80.3.

quite clear.[52] Clement's frequent use of other philosophers and poets was never a problem to him: the Greeks had stolen from Moses. All truth comes from the Word. When Greeks drew their ethics from the law of Moses, they found the virtues of courage, self-control, wisdom, righteousness, endurance and patience, dignity and self-restraint as well as piety. While Clement's account of righteousness affirms reason and moderation, he has no place for mediocrity. There is a zeal for righteousness in all he writes. 'God, the true God, regards as holy only the character of the righteous man, and as unholy what is wrong and wicked.'[53] Again, while he is warmly human there is a liturgical quality to his humanism which sees the whole of life as a sacrament. For example, on the use of wine he follows Musonius in advocating a temperate limit of two cups; but he adds that every time we raise a cup of wine to our lips it should be regarded sacramentally. Our whole life should be a liturgy of praise to God; that is why *Paedagogus* ends with a prayer and a hymn.[54]

DISCIPLESHIP

(i) *Assimilation to God*

All Christian living has but one aim: to grow like God. Much has been written[1] on the meaning of assimilation to God, but, like all common formulae, it means what each writer wants it to mean. Here, as always, Clement's meaning is to be discovered from his usage.[2] There is no

---

[52] See A. C. van Geytenbeek, *Musonius Rufus* (Assen, 1963), pp. 116f. Also see H. Marrou, *Le Pédagogue I*, pp. 51ff.

[53] *S.* 7.4.26.2.

[54] *P.* 2.2.19.1. See H. I. Marrou, 'Humanisme et christianisme chez Clément d'Alexandrie d'après le Pédagogue', in *Entretiens sur l'antiquité classique, III, Recherches sur la tradition platonicienne* (Fondation Hardt, Geneva, 1955), 199, 'le caractère liturgique de cet humanisme, qui se réalise par le symbolisme et la vie sacramentelle', and 200, 'La vie du Chrétien toute entière est, doit être, une liturgie, une sacrifice de louanges, un hymne à la gloire du Père, du Fils qui nous a sauvés, de l'Esprit descendu jusqu'à nous.'

[1] See especially A. Mayer, *Das Bild Gottes im Menschen nach Clemens von Alexandreia* (Rome, 1942), and H. Merki, *Homoiōsis theōi* (Freiburg/Schw., 1952).

[2] The judgement of A. Méhat, *Étude sur les Stromates de Clément d'Alexandrie* (Paris, 1966), p. 374, is worth citing in full: 'Les doctrines de l'image de Dieu et de la ressemblance avec Dieu ont fait ces derniers temps l'objet d'un grand nombre de travaux desquels on ne peut malheureusement pas dire qu'il soit sorti une grande lumière. Il semble que ce soit une de ces formules où chacun mettait ce qu'il voulait...Il n'est pas sûr qu'au total elle ait exprimé plus que la vague religiosité syncrétiste de l'époque, le désir de prendre Dieu comme référence et comme "mesure" [Plato, *Laws*

question of acquiring either the divine form[3] or identity with divine virtue.[4] For Clement the process begins at baptism, moves through enlightenment and knowledge to end in continual prayer. Together with knowledge go purification, freedom from passion, freedom from need, good deeds, love, righteousness, piety and conformity or coherence of life.[5] When Clement exhorts the heathen as well as the faithful to follow God he is using a Platonic expression.[6] He makes no distinction between following God and assimilation to God, taking the latter from Plato's *Theaetetus*.[7] Philo had spoken in similar words of the need to grow like God, using the Platonic formula to describe a biblical doctrine. Following God, for Clement is obedience to God's command, and by obedience the Christian grows into the likeness of God;[8] but this can only be done because God takes the initiative and by his grace enables men to follow in Christ's way. God made us his children and set us in our true place within the universe. We should return the love which God has given, by avoiding bad examples and following the example of our master, so that we may fulfil what the scripture says about the image and likeness of God.[9] As we dress plainly in clothing suited to our age and nature, we remember the words of the divine apostle who tells us to put on Jesus Christ and make no provision for lusts. The highest beauty is spiritual, and the Holy Spirit inspires righteousness and wisdom, courage and self-control, love of good and modesty. To these should be added the beauty of a healthy and well-proportioned body.[10] Since even Pythagoreans hold the word of their master as a sufficient ground for belief, we should follow our teacher and saviour in the way of truth. Serving God through our saviour high priest, the Word of God, we live in a way which is appropriate to and like God.[11] Plato lays down the end as achieving likeness to God as far as possible and the Lord says to walk after the Lord our God and to keep his commandments. Assimilation and following, repeats Clement,

---

4, 716 D, cited *S.* 5.14.95.4]. La manière dont Clément multiplie les variations autour de ce thème dans toutes ses oeuvres, et surtout dans les *Stromates* ne signifie peut-être autre chose que son désir d'utiliser un mot à la mode. Il est difficile en tout cas de ramener ici à l'unité d'une pensée les *capitula* innombrables où l'on retrouve mention de la ressemblance avec Dieu. Ce n'est qu'un point de rencontre, non un véritable centre, mais qui se prêtait admirablement à cette manoeuvre de séduction par laquelle Clément cherche à attirer les philosophes.' This is a valuable warning against systematisation; but Clement uses the idea for other reasons besides the attraction of philosophers.

[3] *S.* 6.14.114.4.   [4] *S.* 7.14.88.5.   [5] *S.* 7.3.13f.
[6] *Laws* 4, 716A.   [7] *Theaetetus* 176.
[8] Cf. the conclusion of Michaelis concerning *mimeomai* that the central meaning is obedience, not imitation, *TWNT*, 4, especially 672f.
[9] *P.* 1.3.9.1.   [10] *P.* 3.11.64.1f.   [11] *S.* 2.9.45.7.

are the same thing.[12] Plato has declared that man's chief good is found in assimilation to God. This, claims Clement, is exactly what God had said in the scriptures where we are commanded to be followers or servants of God.[13] We look to the end of our life which is eternal rest in God and all that we do now serves that great end.[14] By contrast there are those who make a god of their belly and whose end is, in the words of the apostle, 'destruction'.[15] The gnostic is guided always by his love to God. He is a kingly friend of God and places here his first desire. He follows in the apostle's way which is in turn the way of God. This is clearly better than to follow in the dark way of the demons.[16]

The true following of the saviour is achieved 'when we seek after his sinlessness and perfection, adorning and regulating the soul before him as before a mirror and arranging it to be completely like him in all things'.[17] Christ calls us to follow him. He has given us new birth, set us free, healed and redeemed us. He promises eternal life and the vision of the face of God, the good Father. He calls us to abandon all earthly loyalties, to follow him to a rest and joy which are beyond all description. He is himself the life-giving bread by which we are nourished. He is our teacher. He is our champion who has wrestled with death on our behalf, and paid the penalty of death for our sakes. The call of Christ comes in the face of all the attractions of the earth.[18]

We are to follow God, stripped of pride and pretence, possessing what is our own and what is good – our faith in God, our confession to the Christ who suffered, our good works and good will to men.[19] Divine likeness is not achieved by gold and splendid clothing but by doing what is good and by needing as few things as possible. God himself needs nothing and we grow like him as we reject all ornament. The man, in whom the Word of God lives, does not try to alter his appearance. He does not worry about external adorning and beauty.[20] Man is joined to God and, as the Pythagoreans said, becomes one with God. Just as sailors pull an anchor and instead of moving the anchor, pull themselves towards it, so those who try to draw God towards them bring themselves to God. A life of reverence and contemplation, of worship, purification, holiness and constant self-control brings man as far as possible to assimilation to God. To know God is to know his Son, to be joined with him and made one in him.[21] In this way an original communion between man and heaven is restored.

The heretics have perverted the true doctrine of man's end. They shamefully identify communion with unrestricted sexual intercourse.

[12] S. 2.19.100.4.　　　　[13] S. 2.22.　　　　[14] P. 1.13.102.
[15] P. 2.1.18.3.　　　　[16] S. 7.11 and 12; S. 4.8.　　[17] Q.D.S. 21.
[18] Q.D.S. 23 and 24.　　　　[19] P. 2.3.36.
[20] P. 3.1.1.　　　　[21] S. 4.23 and 25.

This is not what the apostle teaches, for communion with God excludes all impurity and shame. Those who are still slaves of their passions cannot know God. There is no salvation for heretics, since they have no knowledge of God. The immoral communion of Carpocrates will be rejected by all who read the scriptures, for they know that true sharing is sharing with those in need, caring for the hungry, the thirsty and the lonely.[22]

The rich young man and Mary discovered that following Christ, or caring about Christ, was the way to eternal life. There is one thing that is necessary and the rich man is pointed to this one thing, while Mary is commended for having found it.[23] Eternal life so gained is heavenly treasure which comes to those who leave earthly treasure to follow Christ.[24] Our Lord, who showed to the Hebrews the pattern of true philosophy, did not wear elaborate shoes, but in all matters followed simplicity.[25] Foolish men abandon the sole pursuit of God to look for gold and jewels, yet God gave his own Word to all men. Because he made all things for all men, it is wrong for the wealthy to have more than is due to them.[26]

(ii) The third divine image

Man is made in God's image and may share further in God's grace.[27] Clement makes a distinction between image and likeness: the image is given to all at birth, the likeness has to be acquired.[28] By imitation of Christ man gains the likeness and becomes an image which is rational and like the Word of God, the true image.[29] What has been broken and defaced by sin is restored by the salvation of the Word.[30] We carry about in our nature an image of God which lives with us, is joined to us, is our guest and a constant bond of sympathy;[31] but if we look behind the elaborate decoration which people put on their body, we do not find a true image of God. Man finds beauty by adorning his mind, and by plucking out lusts rather than hair. The most beautiful part of man is his mind and this should be improved each day. Our Lord calls us to strip away the vanity and finery of luxury and seek

---

[22] S. 3.6.54.3.   [23] Q.D.S. 10.   [24] Q.D.S. 19.
[25] P. 2.11.117.4.   [26] P. 2.12.120.3.   [27] Ex. 1.5.4. and 1.6.3.
[28] S. 2.22.131.5. See my The Philosophy of Clement of Alexandria, p. 89, and Merki, Homoiōsis theōi, p. 45. Clement here differs from Irenaeus for whom man was made in the likeness of God and lost the likeness through sin.
[29] Ex. 12.122.4; S. 2.19.97.1; S. 3.9.69.4; S. 4.22.137.1; S. 6.7.60.3. See W. Völker, Der wahre Gnostiker nach Clemens Alexandrinus, pp. 113–15.
[30] Ex. 2.27.2f.; Ex. 12.120.4.
[31] Ex. 4.59.2.

salvation, carrying simply the tree of life.[32] Knowledge of self leads to knowledge of God, and this in turn leads to likeness to God.[33] The *Paedagogus* closes with a prayer for obedience to perfect the likeness of the image.[34]

Our Paedagogus leads and teaches us as children, who are able to enter the kingdom of heaven. Mankind becomes young in Christ. We are colts who are to be tamed by the divine colt-tamer. We are children who need training and guidance. In simplicity we follow Christ. As God's new people, we share in his new Word. Because we share in eternity, we live in a perpetual springtime. Inward truth does not wither when old age comes.[35] This childhood does not mean imperfection, for as soon as we are reborn we receive the perfection for which we long.

The true image of God is the Word himself. The human mind is an image of the image. Moses described this likeness when he spoke of walking after the Lord God and keeping his commandments. God's servants and followers display his likeness.[36] The soul of the just man is a divine image which enshrines men's leader and king. The eternal Word is 'one saviour individually to each and in common to all'. Being the exact image of God's glory, he impresses on the true gnostic the seal of this image, and makes a third divine image.[37] While all the faithful are noble and God-like, there are some who are more elect than others, and in their election are less conspicuous. They don't want to appear holy or noble; but they are the light of the world and the salt of the earth. 'This is the seed, God's image and likeness, and his true child and heir, sent here, as it were, on a kind of foreign service by the Father's great plan of salvation and appropriate choice.'[38]

No Christian needs a teacher from Athens to show him the way, for he has the Word himself and is able to draw on a superior source of instruction and knowledge.[39] A paedogogus took care of children on their way to school and assisted in their education. Paul spoke of the Law as a paedagogus (Gal. 3:24). Ariston of Chios and Maximus of Tyre had spoken of the paedagogus as one who gives moral instruction. Clement expands the idea to the full meaning of the gospel and of salvation through Christ. We are taught by God and our glory is the name of Christ. We feed on the milk of the Word who nourishes us in

[32] *P.* 3.2f.　　　　[33] *P.* 3.1.1.　　　　[34] *P.* 3.12.101.
[35] *P.* 1.5.20.4. The theme of infancy runs through *Paedagogus I* and is distinctively Christian. See Marrou, *Le Pédagogue I*, *SC* (Paris, 1960), pp. 23–9, for an excellent comment on 'L'esprit d'enfance', and on 'Jeunesse et nouveauté chrétiennes'. See also F. Quatember, *Die christliche Lebenshaltung*, pp. 95–108.
[36] *S.* 5.14.94.5f.　　　[37] *S.* 7.3.16.5f.　　　[38] *Q.D.S.* 36.　　　[39] *Ex.* 11.112.1.

his likeness.[40] It is not easy to tell what Clement means by 'logos' – human reason, the son of God or both. He plays persistently on the ambiguity to underline his idea of participation.[41]

(iii) *Askēsis*

As we become like God by sharing in his virtue, we train as athletes to maintain the excellence which has been given to us.[42] To achieve spiritual health and salvation, a rich man should find a man of God who will be his guide and trainer, giving criticism and direction. The director may be severe at times, but he will also spend nights at prayer on behalf of his pupil. He will be an ambassador with God, and will continually beg mercy for his charge. An example of concern for the soul of a young Christian is found in the story of St John and the robber.[43] The end of man is shown as he lifts his soul to God, turns from the lusts of the body and with fear and patience follows after God.[44] Every hindrance is left behind.[45] In strenuous endeavour we avoid pleasure and look for hardness, refusing a soft feather mattress and even sleep because the Word within us never sleeps. We get up at night to read or to work; by staying awake we live for a longer time.[46]

Self-control (*enkrateia*) is important for Clement.[47] He defends marriage against ascetic rigorists because it offers more daily trials than the celibate state.[48] The example of Christ may point to celibacy but that of the apostles points to marriage.[49] This does not mean that intercourse of husband and wife is ever a good thing. It may be practised in order to obtain children, but never to satisfy lust.[50] Christian marriage is a spiritual union[51] which anticipates the life of heaven.[52] Clement would see the superiority of his ascetic ideal in its extension beyond sexual matters which are the only concern of the heretics. The higher and true self-control extends to language, money, eating and drinking.[53] It must spring from love to the Lord and not from scorn

---

[40] *P.* 1.6.35.3.

[41] See Marrou, 'Humanisme et christianisme', in *Entretiens sur l'antiquité classique*, III, *Recherches sur la tradition platonicienne* (Geneva, 1955), p. 192, 'Tout le Pédagogue joue, page après page, sur l'ambiguité du mot grec LOGOS.'

[42] *P.* 1.12.99.2.

[43] *Q.D.S.* 42. John allowed himself to be captured by the robbers in order to win back their leaders who had deserted the faith.

[44] *S.* 4.3.9.5.   [45] *P.* 2.3.36.2.   [46] *P.* 2.9.81.4f.

[47] This paragraph is indebted to the article by H. Chadwick, '*Enkrateia*', *RAC*, **5**, 343–65, especially 358f.

[48] *S.* 7.12.70.7f.   [49] *S.* 3.6.49.1; *S.* 3.6.53.1.

[50] *S.* 6.12.100.3; *S.* 3.8.58.2.   [51] *S.* 3.8.58; *S.* 7.12.76.7f.

[52] *S.* 6.12.100.3; *S.* 6.13.105.1.   [53] *S.* 3.1.4.1ff.; *S.* 3.6.48; *S.* 3.6.59.1f.

for the world he has made. Continence is a gift from God but never a guarantee of salvation.[54]

Clement praises the martyr for his world rejection and self denial. The true Christian readily gives up his body and bears witness that he is faithful and loyal to God. He who chooses death suffers for love of God and finds salvation. We live by the suffering of Christ.[55] Martyrdom is seen as a struggle with demons who attack and tempt Christians. The army of the devil is drawn up against each Christian. Clement has less place for the positive value of suffering than for the victor's crown which it earns. The philosopher learns endurance so that he will conquer in the battle. Clement's idea of patience and endurance is both philosophical (qu'est le Sage grec, même épicurien, sinon un ascète?)[56] and biblical. The martyrs remain the peak of perfection. They show love for God in their gift of themselves. They are true imitators of Christ in the way of the cross. To die daily is the way to perfection.[57]

(iv) *Perfect Sonship*

The call of assimilation to God is a call to perfection, to be perfect as the Father is perfect, forgiving injuries and living free from passion. Perfection is the living of a blameless life in the obedience of the gospel. The paedogogus has received full perfection because he is one with God. He leads, teaches and guides.[58] Those who have grown so like Christ that they are true imitators have a first obligation to instruct others in the same imitation and discipleship. The aim of following and discipleship is restoration into perfect sonship through the son of God.

The continuous pursuit of passionlessness indicates the negative side of Clement's attitude to the world. The gnostic lives on earth as a foreigner. He is always prepared to leave the world and always regrets the restrictions which this life places upon him. He keeps himself away from the good things of the world, and even in a city he behaves as if he were alone. He doesn't go to the theatre or to games, does not involve himself deeply in earthly interests, but simply goes through the motions of being on earth.[59] The abandonment of the world is part of a process which finds fulfilment in martyrdom. Clement is always more concerned with the inside story. Freedom from passion is the important thing, not freedom from external goods. God is free from passion, and therefore becoming like God must involve freedom from all passions. God is above all the pulls and pushes of earth. Christ, the perfect

[54] *S.* 3.18.105.1.   [55] *S.* 4.4–7.
[56] H. I. Marrou, *Le Pédagogue I* (Paris, 1960), p. 60.
[57] *S.* 4.4.14f.   [58] *S.* 7.14.88.6 and *P.* 1.7.54.1.   [59] *S.* 7.12.

image, gained freedom from passion. Man is called to this way of likeness to God through becoming like Christ.[60]

Imitation and discipleship dominate the life of one who is baptised.
He should do everything for God. His soul should be turned constantly
to God, should lean on Christ's power and rest in the light of the
saviour as a ship rests in a harbour. Prayer should constantly allow him
to speak with God and he should avoid sleep because it keeps him from
his prayer. 'Show yourself always a partner of Christ who makes the
divine ray shine from heaven; let Christ be to you continual and
unceasing joy.' God who owns all things, treats the bodies of his
servants with care for they are his shrines and temples.[61] Illumination
gives the light of the knowledge of God and knowledge of him who is
perfect brings men to perfection. Baptism is perfection, for it makes us
sons of God, filled with his light and life.[62] He who is like God is truly
beautiful; he becomes divine because he wills what God wills.[63] Assimilation has as its final goal being made divine. The end of all piety is an
eternal rest in God.[64]

Deification of man has been a problem for many readers of Clement:
it means to receive the gift of immortality. The clue is in Clement's
comment that immortality is nearness to God.[65] Irenaeus had already
established the term in Christian writing when he spoke of sharing
in the divine glory,[66] of participation in God[67] and of seeing God
from within.[68] There are several reasons why the term should supplant earlier expressions. *Dikaiosunē* had been defined by Marcion
as inferior to goodness and by Epiphanes as a ground for immorality.
Koinōnia had been debased to mean sexual licence. *Homoiōsis* had
philosophical precedent and ethical overtones. Clement links it consistently with *apatheia*. Deification had smaller apologetic value.
Christians were minor images of God in a way that idols and stars were
not. Origen was to describe the insistence of the heavenly powers that
they should not be worshipped by Christians who shared the divine
nature.[69] The notion of deification was both variable and elastic.[70] Did
the term bring Clement dangerously near to the views against which he
was arguing? He is emphatic that man's virtue is not the same as

---

[60] *S.* 2.20.103.1; *S.* 4.22.138.1; *S.* 4.23.47.1; *S.* 7.3.13.3; *S.* 7.14.84.2;
    S. 7.14.86.5 On the link between *apatheia* and assimilation see S. Lilla,
    Clement of Alexandria (Oxford, 1971), p. 110.
[61] Clement, *To the newly baptised.*
[62] *P.* 1.6.26.1f.   [63] *P.* 3.1.1.5.   [64] *P.* 1.13.102.2.
[65] With reference to Wisdom 6:19, in *S.* 6.2.12.3. See Völker, *Der wahre
    Gnostiker,* p. 614.
[66] *Against Heresies,* 4.39.2.   [67] *Ibid.* 4.40.1.   [68] *Ibid.* 4.20.5.
[69] *Exhortation to Martyrdom,* 7; *Contra Celsum,* 5.11.
[70] As Harnack showed, *History of Dogma,* 1 (ET London, 1897), 119f.

God's. God's substance is as far from man as God's power is near.[71] Heretical gnostics claimed substantial identity with God. Yet Clement was concerned that his gnostic could not be surpassed by anyone. To become divine was the limit of excellence; Clement's picture is unclear and sometimes very close to perfectionism.[72] It is possible to show that he does not divide Christians into two classes and that his gnostic is not sinless on earth; but it is more important to notice his apparent lack of caution, for without some dangerous theology he could not have made his point.

The influence of Plato is strong in this part of Clement who quotes Plato to the effect that happiness is having one's daemon in good condition, and uses the *Laws* and *Theaetetus* to show the necessity of becoming like God. Pythagoras is said to have spoken the words 'follow God'. Plato developed the idea, and it also entered Stoicism. Posidonius has been credited with the exposition of the idea. Clement identifies the 'following' with assimilation to God, and quotes the key words of the *Theaetetus* more than twenty times.

Clement's extended treatment of this idea in *Stromateis* 2.22 is valuable for its theme and for its intricate content. It makes the familiar claim that Plato took from Moses his account of assimilation to God. Clement makes this come true by pushing Plato into a biblical mould. There are three elements in the totality of goodness – a starting point, an end and a good life which joins one to the other. These are for Plato: the daemon or rational part of the soul, the Good, eudaemonia or participation in the Good or assimilation to God. For Clement the three are: the divine image in man, God, assimilation to God or restoration to perfect sonship. These are further modified by stating that the end and the way of it cannot be separated, but are together a 'twofold end' or a 'twofold hope'. For Plato the Good which is participated in and the good life which participates are the twofold end. For the believer, what he has received and what he still expects make up his twofold hope. Paul speaks either of present freedom from sin and the end of eternal life, or of the hope which removes shame because of the present gift of the Holy Spirit. Ezekiel similarly speaks of the righteous who will live and the sinner who will die.[73] Clement's use of 'hope' instead of 'end' is a deliberate insistence on eschatology which was the hardest part of Christian belief for any Hellenist to accept. He pushes Plato and other Greeks into this mould. At the same time the Platonic sovereign Good preserves the priority of divine goodness or grace. Knowledge is always and only a gift of God.[74] Clement's account of image and likeness corrects a gnostic account which divided earthy

---

[71] *S.* 2.2.5.4.
[72] *S.* 3.8.62.2; *S.* 4.9.75.2.
[73] *S.* 2.22.135.
[74] *S.* 7.10.57.

men who had the image and animal men who had the likeness from a
spiritual elect who were identical with the divine.[75]

Among minor ethical ideas, Plato indicates the importance of self-
knowledge. The words of the Delphic oracle are relevant for Clement,
'Therefore it is, as it seems, the greatest lesson of all to know oneself,
for if one knows oneself one will know God, and knowing God one will
become like God.'[76] The value of knowing one's ignorance is reflected
by Clement and Plato. The ultimate vision of God fulfils Platonic
aspirations. Plato too had pointed to the soul as that part of man
which was supremely important, and his philosopher is concerned with
the practice of death. In similar terms Clement speaks of the suffering
and discipline which the Christian must undergo. Man made in the
image of God regains the likeness of that image by deliberate choice,
and not, as the Valentinians claimed, by some innate quality.

From Aristotle Clement draws the importance of end or purpose.
Like everything else, man has his function to fulfil. The Stoic virtue of
passionlessness is taken seriously but not consistently by Clement. His
ideal Christian withdraws from distress to the things which are his own,
and cannot be shaken in times of adversity. Clement does allow the
existence of good passions or feelings, and modifies the rigour of the
Stoic account. Passionlessness makes room for and never excludes
love.[77]

FAITH AND FREEDOM

(i) *One universal salvation*

Faith is the way man comes to God. Anointed with faith, he throws off
corruption and ascends to God.[1] The *Paedagogus* shows the necessity
of instruction before faith which is followed by baptism. Faith is the
one universal salvation of humanity, and is linked with freedom. The
law dominated by fear; but the Word is the master of free choice.
Faith supplants law and gives freedom in place of fear. Our Lord used
symbols to speak of his flesh and his blood; faith is the body and hope
is the soul of the church which is nourished by the flesh and blood of
Christ. Faith cannot live when hope goes.[2]

Clement gives an extended account of faith at the beginning of the
second book of the *Stromateis*. Here as later in *Stromateis* 5 and 7 he
is concerned to answer the objections brought against faith by intellectuals and false gnostics. Faith is the way which leads to truth. It is a

---

[75] *Excerpta ex Theodoto*, 54.1; cf. 50.1f.
[76] *P.* 3.1.
[77] See Chapter 6, pages 199f., for further comment on this point.
[1] *Ex.* 12.120. 5.   [2] *P.* 1.6.38.2.

barbarian philosophy. It lays hold on God who is hard to grasp but very near to us because he holds all things in his hands. Faith is a knowledge of those things which cannot otherwise be understood. Except you believe you will not understand. Greeks look down on faith but without faith there can be no knowledge of higher things. Faith becomes knowledge, a knowledge which is a habit and can stand up against reason and argument.[3] Learning depends on faith between teacher and pupil. It is no good throwing a ball unless someone is prepared to catch it. Faith travels by hearing and by the preaching of apostles. Repentance is one of its effects. Faith anticipates, faith is an act of will, faith understands in advance. Faith is something divine which shows up against good as well as bad things.[4] The true gnostic has stability through faith.[5] Faith looks both ways to the past in memory and to the future in hope. Faith believes that certain things have happened and that certain things will happen. A strange mixture of love and fear, faith brings power for salvation and strength for eternal life. It is a form of assent which, as the Platonists and the Stoics say, is necessary if knowledge and communication of any kind are to continue.[6] Faith has an immediate effect upon physical life; for self-control disregards the body through its confession of faith towards God. Faith establishes the one point of dependence so clearly on God that the body is ignored and brought to a state of self-control.[7]

Stromateis 5–7 begins with an emphasis on the intellectual aspect of faith.[8] Faith must not remain inactive but must always expand into investigation. We are to seek and find. As Paul, the divine apostle, saw, faith brings perfection to a man in Christ.[9] Faith is the beginning of Christian possession. To faith is given knowledge, to knowledge is given love, and to love the final inheritance. Faith simply hangs or depends on the Lord. It is possible to believe and still be very immature and mistaken; for example Christians who suffer for their own glory, or to escape from a punishment which is worse than martyrdom, are simply children in their faith.[10] Faith, freely chosen, is the only way to begin Christian life, and is the foundation of salvation; the Stoics spoke of the need for an initial voluntary assent. Faith may be directed towards the teaching which has been handed down, and as such, is the acceptance of the symbols of the truth. From this beginning faith moves on in stages. Clement turns the words of Paul 'from faith to faith' into an exposition of a two-fold faith: a common basic faith and a develop-

---

[3] *S.* 2.2.9.3–4. [4] *S.* 2.6.30.2. [5] *S.* 2.11.52.3f. [6] *S.* 2.12.54f.
[7] *S.* 3.1.4.1 For link between confession and faith see *S.* 4.9.71.1 and 73.3, *S.* 4.21.133. 1.
[8] Cf. T. Camelot, *Foi et Gnose* (Paris, 1945), p. 50.
[9] *S.* 5.1.11.1; *S.* 5.10.61.2f. [10] *S.* 7.10.56.1; *S.* 7.11.67.2.

ing faith which moves to perfection.[11] So faith is strength to salvation and power to eternal life.[12]

It is objected that faith is irrational and at best only an opinion. Clement therefore argues for the necessity of faith as a form of apprehension, an intellectual rather than a moral activity; for Clement the two are never quite separate since knowledge of God cannot be achieved by a purely intellectual process. With all his concern for growth and development, Clement does not want faith to be regarded as imperfect. Faith is perfect in itself, and does not lack anything. Knowledge and piety must always be built on faith. Clement has used many arguments to prove the necessity of faith, using all the philosophers as allies. After Plato and the Stoics, he turns to Aristotle and Epicurus. Aristotle shows that all proof depends on an unproveable first premiss. First principles have to be grasped directly and not deduced from other propositions. Aristotle used faith to describe the test of truth and falsity. 'Aristotle says that the act of judging whether a thing is true, the decision which follows knowledge is faith. Faith is then something superior to knowledge and its test of truth.' Even Epicurus argued for faith when he spoke of preconceptions.[13]

In what way is faith directed towards the historical Jesus? Origen and others will distinguish between faith which apprehends the Jesus of history and a higher knowledge which apprehends the divine mystery. But Clement insists that it is impossible to allot, as some do, faith to the Son and knowledge to the Father. 'They forget that one should believe truly in the Son, that is believe that there is truly a Son, that, and how and why he has come and has suffered; but that to know is to know who the Son of God is. Therefore there is no knowledge without faith, or faith without knowledge, any more than that there is a Father without a Son.'[14] Clement will not separate faith and knowledge nor will he separate the historical apprehension of Jesus from an apprehension of who he was and why and how he came.

---

[11] S. 5.1.1.

[12] S. 2.12.53.

[13] See my, *The Philosophy of Clement of Alexandria*, pp. 131–40, for these arguments for faith which are found in: S. 8.3.6f.; S. 2.4.13–16; S. 2.11.48; S. 2.11.54; S. 5.1.5.

[14] S. 5.1.1. It has been suggested that some of Clement's hierarchy of knowledge comes from the divided line of Plato's *Republic*, where (509f.) faith is placed with opinion as a way of apprehending sensible objects. After all Clement does say that it is better to know than to believe. (S. 6. 14.109). But, unlike Plato, Clement gives a higher place to faith than to *epistēmē* (S. 2.4.15). See Camelot, *Foi et Gnose*, pp. 64–8, for a discussion of this point.

(ii) *Free will and royal freedom*

Faith brings freedom and man must be free. Man can only be king and remain free when he does not submit to what is base and is not ashamed of the Lord, who offers freedom to those who run away into slavery.[15] The heretics claim that faith is innate in certain people; but Clement insists that it is the direct result of a free choice. We are not puppets pulled by strings.[16] We have chosen life and believe in God. By believing the Word we know what is true; if we disbelieve the Word we disbelieve God. In each case we have chosen.[17] God is not responsible for evil in the world. Sin is an activity of man and not an essence or a work of God. It is impossible for anyone to reach perfection without using his free will. We must be fixed upon the pursuit of the good and then receive the divine grace.[18] The image of God in man is closely related to the freedom of man to choose and to his ruling part or mind. Clement insists on the self determination (*autexousia*) of the human soul and attacks the blind determinism of heretical gnostics like Valentinus and Basilides. He plays down Paul's account of man's slavery under sin. Yet Paul was also concerned to insist that man had no one but himself to blame for his sin; and Clement saw no other way for captive man to attain to freedom except through the gift of his Lord. We have here the distinction between free choice and freedom which is to be important for Augustine.[19] Freedom is found when the free will of good men obeys the will of God. God made the world and gave what is in it for the use of good men. Even the thoughts of these men are the product of God's inspiration. Whole regiments of angels watch over nations, cities and individuals. Divine providence goes with human co-operation.[20] The Son is the Lord of all but he compels no one to receive salvation.[21] No one is saved against his will. His own free choice speeds him to salvation.

Clement sharpens the stress on free will, reward and punishment. Man's free choice is rewarding according to the rightness or wrongness of his action. Grace and free will work together and are not opposed.[22] In *Stromateis* 3 Clement attacks those who replace freedom with

[15] *Ex.* 9.83.1–2. [16] *S.* 2.3.11.1. [17] *S.* 2.4.12.1.

[18] *S.* 4.13.93.3; 'Sin is an activity, not a substance and it is therefore not a work of God.' See also *S.* 5.1.7.1–3.

[19] F. Buri, *Clemens Alexandrinus und der paulinische Freiheitsbegriff* (Zurich and Leipzig, 1939), shows how Clement overstates man's freedom in contrast with the account of Paul.

[20] *S.* 6.17.157.2–5. [21] *S.* 7.6.3.2; *S.* 7.7.42.4.

[22] With Clement as with later Greek fathers, teaching concerning grace is a form of synergism. See W. Telfer, 'AUTEXOUSIA', *JTS* (1957), p. 124.

licence. False gnostics assert that they are by nature the sons of the first God and may use their kingly status and freedom as they wish. Their desire is fixed on pleasure and as kings they are subject to no law. But there is no freedom or royalty in their licentious behaviour and their filthy conversation. They are frightened of being caught in their wrongdoing. The words of Paul that everyone who sins is a slave are amply true in their case.[23] Clement uses the attack of Paul in Romans 8 as a weapon against antinomians. The flesh and the spirit are different and Christians are no longer obliged to live according to the flesh. The spirit enables them to put to death the deeds of the body and by doing this they live. As God's spirit leads them they are God's sons and cry, 'Abba Father'. The spirit is given that we may know him to whom we pray and in this knowledge find freedom.[24] A man who has been freed in this way will not cease to honour God when he is threatened. Both men and women find it a noble thing to die for virtue and for freedom.[25]

(iii) Strong in face of hardships

The Christian attains to a self-sufficiency which is in contrast to the dependence of others. He is independent of passions and of external things. The freedom of the true gnostic is not the freedom of the philosopher who escapes to a higher form of knowledge or who submits to fate. It is a freely chosen obedience to the God to whom the future belongs. The way to the promised future is not easy, so the Christian athlete trains hard.[26]

The rich man cannot reach the salvation for which he longs unless he shows the same effort which athletes show when they compete for a perishable crown at the games.[27] Only by danger and toil is the heavenly kingdom achieved. God asks man to be his friend 'for neither faith nor love nor patience is the work of one day; but he who endures to the end, he shall be saved'.[28] The newly baptised are exhorted to endure hardship in their master's service. Their minds must always control their passions, and by looking towards God, bring quietness and steadiness to the whole of living. Let them live in gentleness, humility and peace, turn from care for the body and fix their hope on God;

> knowing this, make your souls strong even in face of hardships; be brave like a man in the arena who engages in his contests with dauntless courage and unshaken strength. Don't let your soul be

[23] S. 3.4.30.3.   [24] S. 3.11.77.2–78.4.   [25] S. 4.8.67.4.
[26] P. 1.12.99.2.   [27] Q.D.S. 3.   [28] Q.D.S. 2.

crushed down by grief, whether disease attack or another hardship oppress you; but nobly set your mind against these obstacles and in the midst of your troubles give thanks to God.[29]

The endurance of the Christian is built on his hope that the son of God will appear and restore good things to his own.

This pattern owes most to the opinions of philosophers where Clement specifically quotes them in support of the necessity for faith.[30] He adds to this Plato's insistence on man's responsibility. God cannot be blamed, the blame must fall on the one who chooses.[31] Lastly Stoic self-sufficiency and freedom is modified by Clement so that it is no longer acceptance of the inevitable but is creative discipleship. The stars have no hold on those who have been baptised.[32] Christian freedom looks to the future of God's kingdom and differs as sharply from Gnostic libertarianism as it does from Stoic indifference.[33]

LOVE

(i) *Entering into God*

Clement sums his *Exhortation* with the words, 'Let us hurry on to salvation, to new birth. Let us, who are many, hurry to be gathered into one flock in agreement with the oneness of the One Being. Similarly let us pursue unity by doing good, seeking the Good One.'[1] The goal of salvation is the union of many into one, the harmony of many sounds, the symphony under the one conductor. With these metaphors, Clement describes the goal of love as unity with God. The divine love comes to men when a spark of goodness is kindled by the Word of God within the soul.[2] The two great commandments require love. God has loved us and made us all that we are. Our only thanks is to love him in return. 'But the act of loving the Father with all our strength and power makes us free from all decay. *For the more a man loves God, the more closely he enters into God.*'[3] Paul shows the greatness of love as the way *par excellence*. His picture of love shows its perfection. 'But love comes with us into the divine fullness and will increase still more

---

[29] Clement, *To the newly baptised.*

[30] See above, section (i) of this chapter, and also, *The Philosophy of Clement of Alexandria*, pp. 131–40.

[31] *Republic* 617.

[32] *Excerpta ex Theodoto*, 78.

[33] Cf. J. Moltmann, 'Die Revolution der Freiheit', *Evangelische Theologie* (November 1967), pp. 595–616.

[1] *Ex.* 9.88.2.   [2] *Ex.* 11.117.2.   [3] *Q.D.S.* 27.

when perfection has been granted.[4] Love is quite consistent with passionlessness. Love is of God

> for love is no longer the desire of the lover but a loving union which has restored the gnostic to the unity of the faith, independent of time and place. He who has already gained his inheritance through love, and has anticipated hope through knowledge, does not desire anything, as he has exactly what he desires. He remains in the one unalterable disposition, knowing and loving. He will not try to be like beautiful things for he possesses beauty itself through love.[5]

(ii) *Service of love*

The *Paedagogus* declares love to be the heavenly food on which reason feeds. Love bears all things, never fails, and is the bread to be eaten in the kingdom of God.[6] Love also gives true beauty to men. Love rejects the unnecessary and artificial, resting in God and his Word.[7] Love, as Paul says, builds up, while knowledge puffs up.[8] Love is built on faith.[9] Love promotes fellowship, friendship and affection in accordance with right reason. It is linked with hospitality and shows itself in brotherly love. The virtues follow from one another and culminate in love. Love is a love of truth and leads to knowledge.[10] The Greeks did not understand love though some of them saw how false and dangerous Aphrodite was.[11] Marriage begins as pleasure and lust directed towards the proper procreation of children.[12] Yet marriage is helpful for the whole of life. Compared with friends and relations a wife cares and endures more, is more constant, sympathetic and patient. A long discussion of marriage in *Stromateis* 3 attacks heretics for rejecting it. Both marriage and celibacy are given by God. The apostles were married and, except for Paul, took their wives on their travels. The married man has less chance of being selfish in a solitary way; the need of others are always pressing on him.[13] Yet the true gnostic, like the apostles, lives with his wife as a sister.[14] The love of a Christian for his wife is entirely free of physical passion.[15] Their spiritual unity anticipates the heavenly life of angels.[16] Clement never quite reconciles his belief in marriage as the gift of a good creator with his conviction that sexual intercourse is a sign of imperfection.[17] He

---

[4] *Q.D.S.* 38. [5] *S.* 6.9.73.3. [6] *P.* 2.1.5.3.
[7] *P.* 3.1.3.1–2. [8] *S.* 1.11.54.4. [9] *S.* 2.6.30.3.
[10] *S.* 2.9.45.1–3. [11] *Ex.* 1 and 2. [12] *S.* 2.23.137.1.
[13] *S.* 7.12.70.6–8. [14] *S.* 6.12.100.3; *S.* 3.6.53.3. [15] *S.* 3.7.58.
[16] *S.* 7.12.76.7–77.6; *S.* 6.13.105.1.
[17] For an extended treatment of Clement's account of marriage, see J. P. Broudéhoux, *Mariage et famille chez Clément d'Alexandrie* (Paris, 1970).

says the first for Marcionites or other ascetic sects and the second for Carpocratians and any who doubted the supreme perfection of his gnostic.[18]

Neighbourly love is explained in the story of the Good Samaritan. 'For love bursts out in good works.'[19] Our nearest neighbour is always Christ himself, who heals the wounds of the souls of men and calls them to love him by keeping his commandments. Love of Christ leads to love of his brethren, respect for his flock and giving to the needy in a service of love. The rich as well as the poor have a claim on our love. Those who love the brethren cannot reject the rich as having no hope of salvation. In love Christians show their wealthy brethren the possibility and the path of salvation.[20]

(iii) Perfection in love

Christians must love their enemies if they want to be like God. The great enemy is not the body, as heretics have claimed, but the devil and those who are like him. Christians are attacked by the devil's minions but nothing can separate them from God's love. In this love they live and stand firm.[21] Love simply means to love God and neighbour; Clement of Rome has written of this love and commended the account of Paul. Clement proceeds in his *Stromateis* to say that sin is contrary to love but love responds with a song of confession when it has fallen into sin. Love offers the sacrifice of a broken spirit, works no evil against a neighbour and fulfils the law. So scripture shows Christ's love and discipline.[22]

In the seventh book of the *Stromateis* there is an extended account of Christian perfection. In the true gnosis faith goes to knowledge,

---

The licentious sects are the followers of Carpocrates, Nicolais, Prodicos, Severianus and the Antitactai. The encratites follow Marcion, Tatian or Julius Cassian (pp. 32–61). P. 60, 'Dans le domaine moral donc, les membres de la communauté chrétienne d'Alexandrie – l'auditoire de Clément – se trouvent confrontés à des courants contradictoires.' On the question of the relative merits of marriage and celibacy, Broudéhoux finds no clear response in Clement: 'Le problème n'offre d'ailleurs qu'un interêt assez secondaire: l'essentiel n'est-il pas qu'il ait parlé du mariage et de la virginité avec autorité et pénétration?' p. 201. The answer would seem to be, 'No!' See also the excellent study of F. Bolgiani, 'La Polemica di Clemente Alessandrino contro gli Gnostici Libertini nel III Libro degli "Stromati"', *Studi e materiali di storia delle religioni* (1967), **38**, 1 e 2, 86–136.

[18] This is the logic of apologetic, a logic of objection and rebuttal which answers each objection separately. See D. Allen, 'Motives, Rationales and Religious Beliefs', *American Philosophical Quarterly* (1966), pp. 111–27.

[19] *Q.D.S.* 28.   [20] *Q.D.S.* 3.   [21] *S.* 4.14.   [22] *S.* 4.18.113.4–5.

knowledge to love, and love reaches the final inheritance. One may appear to act rightly, but appearance means nothing unless the motive is love. The gnostic is a man in love with God.[23] Through love he knows God. As God is love he is known by those who love, as in his faithfulness he is known to those who are faithful. Plato insisted that only like could perceive like. Only those who love, argues Clement, can see and know the God who is love.[24]

The gnostic in his knowledge and love of God anticipates the blessedness of heaven. He will 'feast on that clearest and purest insatiable vision which is granted to greatly loving souls'. He already worships God in the whole of life. 'We are commanded to worship and adore the Word, in the conviction that he is our saviour and leader, and through him to worship the Father. We do this not on selected days, as certain others do, but continually through the whole of life and in every way.' He lives with God beside him. 'Celebrating a festival in all our life, and convinced that God is wholly present everywhere, we cultivate our fields with the voice of praise and sail the sea to the sound of hymns.'

Prayer is conversation with God and may be spoken or unspoken. God does not need tongues to tell him what is in our minds. 'It is possible therefore to send up a prayer without speaking, by concentrating the inner spirit alone on mental speech, in undivided attention to God.'[25] Clement gives the first extended Christian account of prayer, 'the whole life' of the true gnostic.[26]

No one surpasses the martyr who is 'faithful through love' and who confirms the truth of his preaching by his action. 'You will marvel at his love' and his gratitude in being united to what is akin to him. He leaves this life gladly 'through love to the Lord'. His saviour welcomes him with the words 'Dear brother' because of the likeness he has achieved. 'We don't hesitate to call martyrdom perfection, not just because a man has come to the end of his life as all men must, but because he displayed the perfect work of love.'[27] The spring of martyrdom is love and the reward of the martyr is assured and beyond price. The poet knows this when he declares that 'he who is not drenched with heart-eating sweat will not reach the peak of manhood.' Yet only love can make perfect. Of faith, hope and love, the greatest is always love.[28] The really blessed and true martyr is the one who ascends to love, who has testified to the commandments and to God. Out of love for Christ he gives himself wholly for God: 'giving up happily and lovingly his humanity when he is asked for it'.[29] Basilides who rejects

23 S. 7.11.67f.   24 S. 5.1.13.1.   25 S. 7.7.43.5.
26 S. 7.12.73.   27 S. 4.4.14. 3.
28 S. 4.7.54.1.   29 S. 4.9.75.4.

divine providence because of the fact of martyrdom, does not understand how important love is, when it is persecuted and endures for the truth.[30]

Here the influence of philosophy is clear, as we see a development from the second pattern, assimilation. The *perfect Christian may even now become divine* because God's love has come into his heart. The vision of the gnostic is reminiscent of Plato's ascent to the form of the good in the *Republic* and of ultimate beauty in the *Symposium*. The pursuit of goodness must be for its own sake. As Plato recognised this necessity in the *Republic,* so Clement insists that the perfect man does not act on grounds of expediency, but acts because he considers it right to do good. Aristotle developed the idea of virtue as the fulfilment of a function or excellence; Clement's account of perfection builds on the concept of completeness, 'the best and completest virtue in a complete life'. The various virtues need to be perfected in their own right. From the Stoics Clement draws his distinction between what is good and what is bad and what is intermediate or indifferent. For the Stoics good things are examples of virtue, bad things are examples of vice, and everything else is intermediate or indifferent. Clement can speak of simple salvation as the result of medium kinds of actions, and right salvation as the result of right action. There is no clear link between Clement and the Stoics on this point; but they share a general structure of three kinds of moral values instead of only two. Clement's ideal Christian follows virtue for its own sake, and like the sage of the Stoics is free, a king, a priest, noble and possessed of knowledge. His account of prayer and inner life has points of similarity with that of the Stoics, Epictetus and Marcus Aurelius, not to mention Platonists like Plutarch and later Plotinus.[31] Clement's picture has some striking differences. His joy is not detached but is linked with the world and with God. There are no parallels in Stoicism to his forgetfulness of wrong, sense of newness, love for others and loyalty to Christian community. Passionlessness for Clement does not exclude love and likeness to God nor even the final gift of martyrdom.[32]

The more one reads this section, the more one wonders how such an elaborate and optimistic account could be written. There is slender ground in the New Testament for a progression in Christian holiness.[33]

---

[30] *S.* 4.12.85.3.
[31] O. Dibelius, *Das Vaterunser* (Giessen, 1903), p. 32.
[32] See W. Völker, *Der wahre Gnostiker,* pp. 524–40 and 575.
[33] See W. A. Beardslee, *Human Achievement and Divine Vocation* (London, 1961), pp. 72ff., and the comment of V. Furnish, *Theology and Ethics in Paul,* p. 240, that the motifs of progress and growth have not been established in Paul.

The Stoic term *prokopē* is used once by Paul with ethical interest.[34] Certainly there is mature and immature Christian behaviour; but there is normally a negative twist as the immature are reproved for not having grown up. There are some pointers to the perfect Christian life. The beatitudes and 1 Cor. 13 indicate to legalists and enthusiasts what grace may do in human life. Clement builds on both beatitudes[35] and 1 Cor. 13.[36] There is clear affinity with the philosophical milieu of the time and Philo had blended Greek and Hebrew accounts of the higher life.[37] But this is not yet enough to justify the way in which the ideal figure dominates Clement's work. As always Clement makes sense only when he is seen as an apologist defending on at least four fronts. He wanted to show heretical gnostics that his model Christian was better than theirs. He wanted to convince imperial authorities that there was nothing morally dangerous in the new 'atheism'. Again both Greek and Hebrew traditions had taken perfection seriously and viewed Christianity with superior scorn. Socrates turned the direction of philosophy towards man and the good life. Plato followed with his concern for justice and Aristotle sees virtue expressed in a complete life. Stoic ethics were governed by the pattern of the wise man. Clement's gnostic answers the scorn which Christians had received from philosophers.[38] The Jews had a long tradition of perfection in religious and moral observance. They could not but regard Christianity as a decline from this.[39]

Each of the four objectors to Christianity has to be won over and to this end Clement's gnostic develops qualities which each group would admire. He finishes up as a more philosophic figure than the New Testament would provide: 'Our philosopher is concerned with these three things: first: contemplation, second: the fulfilment of the commandments, third: the making of virtuous men.'[40] This is the result of

[34] See the valuable article by G. Stählin, *TWNT*, **6**, 703–19.
[35] More than forty references to the beatitudes are found in Clement, e.g., *S*. 4.2.6.
[36] More than thirty references to this chapter are found in Clement, e.g., *Q.D.S.* 38.
[37] We are hampered by the lack of Middle Platonist ethical material. See Philo, *De prov.* 1; Apuleius, *De Platone*, 2; Plotinus, *Enn.* 1.44. See S. Lilla, *Clement of Alexandria*, p. 110. Note however Buonaiuti's comment, 'Ma Clemente non applica meccanimente al tipo ideale del cristiano gnostico i connotati dell saggio stoico o platonico', *Le origini dell'ascetismo cristiano* (Pinerolo, 1928), p. 126, cited Völker, p. 607.
[38] See *S*. 7.1.1; *Contra Celsum*, 1.27 *et passim*.
[39] See G. Delling, *TWNT*, **8**, 68–74. Trypho tells Justin he would have been better off if he had stayed with his philosophers instead of listening to worthless teachers and worshipping a mere man: Justin, *Dial.* 8.
[40] *S*. 2.10.46.

the background of argument. For philosophy provided the most effective answer to the instant perfection of the heretics.[41] The getting of wisdom was a long and painful process. Epictetus told beginners to expect the kind of pain that a visit to the surgery would bring. Plato wrote of the rare virtue of intellectual courage and of the practice of death. Clement insisted that 'neither faith, nor love nor patience is the work of one day'.[42]

It remains remarkable that he could set out such an extended picture. Granted the value of his sources and the apologetic pressures, there were further explanations. First, the lives of Christians were an argument for their faith which all men could read – Justin uses the evidence of changed lives in his *Apology*.[43] Secondly the Christ of the gospels prompted the thought – what would Christ be like if he lived in late second-century Alexandria?[44] This would correct gnostic distortion and enter the life and environment of the pagan contemporary.[45] Thirdly, all Christians needed to persevere because they might be called to face their final test at any time. A mediocre Christian could not be ready for martyrdom. Finally, for Clement the way to the end is part of the twofold end. So he brings together in one picture the whole range of moral values.[46] Only God is good, his goodness is inexpressible; but goodness may still be seen in the human parable of a life which shares in it.

To sum up, Clement is widely concerned with each pattern and is aware of both contingency and perfection. Does he show tendencies to legalism or enthusiasm? The many prescriptions of the *Paedagogus* suggest that each Christian must go through law before he finds the

---

[41] See above, p. 48, and also *S*. 6.9.78.

[42] *Q.D.S.* 32.

[43] Justin, 1 *Apol*. 16.4.

[44] See *S*. 1.24.159.5–6. Cf. Méhat, *Étude sur les Stromates de Clément d'Alexandrie*, p. 380.

[45] His success is remarkable. See p. 608, Völker, *Der wahre Gnostiker*. Ideas are torn from their setting and some unevenness remains. 'Aber aufs Ganze gesehen muss man doch urteilen, dass er erfolgreich und mit erstaunlicher Sicherheit und Kraft durchgeführt ist. Wurzelnd in Schrift und Tradition, unter weitgehender Benutzung der christlichen Literatur des 2. Jahrhunderts sowie geschickter Verwertung philosophischer Lehren schuf Clemens im Porträt des vollkommenen Christen, des Gnostikers, etwas Neues, was die Systeme der häretischen Gnosis ebenso wirksam bekämpfen wie als Grundlage für die Entwicklung christlicher Aszetik und Mystik in den kommenden Jahrhunderten dienen konnte. Darin liegt seine originelle Leistung beschlossen.'

[46] Prunet, *La morale de Clément d'Alexandrie*, p. 246. 'Vie intellectuelle, religieuse et morale ne progressent pas l'une sans l'autre...*askesis*, *mathesis* et *phusis* sont en relation réciproque.'

fullness of the gospel. There is no exposition of God's righteousness in the Pauline mode; but the argument for the goodness and justice of God hangs on a similar point. There is a firm insistence on the order of nature but no developed scheme of natural law. The account of discipleship has a strong ascetic tendency shown in the commendation of passionlessness and the perfection of martyrdom. There is a strong tendency to enthusiasm since man may become divine, willing what God wills; yet the true gnostic finds God in the contingency of his daily work. Faith does not harden to a creed; but it does become an intellectual adventure. There is neither libertarianism nor determinism; the account of freedom is carefully argued. He who enters into God through love will not be tripped up by pious works; but he may well be so caught up in ecstasy that he ceases to be moral. Yet even against this last threat there is a strong defence of marriage and the moral implications of love gain vehement exposition in face of the failure of Epiphanes.

Clement's opposite tendencies show sensitivity and balance. There are on every hand a respect for contingency and an awareness of perfection. Nothing could be more meticulous in its concern for the detail of life than the *Paedagogus* and no account of perfection could surpass the superlatives of *Stromateis* VII.

CLEMENT AND SEXTUS

The sayings of Sextus present a morality similar to that taught by Clement in a contrasting literary form. The aphorisms are used by Origen and, despite the many question-marks against them, seem to have been widely used during the third and fourth centuries. They are partially co-extensive with two other lists of maxims; one of these is designated as Pythagorean by Stobaeus in the fifth century while the other is found in a letter of the Neoplatonist Porphyry at the beginning of the fourth century. It seems that a Neopythagorean collection, which would inevitably be strongly Platonic in tone, has been revised by a Christian moralist about the beginning of the third century. We do not know who Sextus was. The work of Christian editing can be detected from unedited parallels: 'On the one hand, in content there is a Christianisation of pagan maxims; on the other hand, in form there is also a "paganisation" of Christian maxims.'[1]

Sextus diverges from Clement in two ways. First the gnomic form

[1] H. Chadwick, *The Sentences of Sextus* (Cambridge, 1959), p. 138. This work presents the text of Sextus with an extended discussion of authorship, origins and doctrine; to all of which the following account is indebted.

introduces ambiguity which Clement's extended context overcomes. Since ethical terms have an unusually wide range of meanings some statements can be transposed from Platonism to Christianity without verbal alteration. Other statements may require slight modification. However, context and application to particular cases give meaning to ethical propositions. With Clement this is maximal and with Sextus it is minimal. The second divergence is in the attitude to the world. Sextus has a much stronger ascetic strain than Clement. Both are ambivalent to the body and its uses; but Sextus requires every possible renunciation of the body which is the means by which temptation approaches. Conjugal affection gives place to competitive continence. Several reasons may have contributed to this intensification. A Pythagorean influence (*sōma sēma*) is present. Its presence may be due to editorial weariness or dullness. More probably it reflects the competitive element in self-mortification which Sextus clearly mentions. It would hardly be right to soften pagan stringency. Had not Justin proudly quoted the case of the young Christian who applied for castration? Any modification must be towards the death of the body and not away from it. Anything pagans can not-do, Christians can not-do better.

Righteousness

Sextus begins, as Clement does, from a rejection of every form of sin (11). His practical injunctions concerning food are similar to those of Clement. The wise man may eat meat, but would be wiser to abstain (109). Drinking is not forbidden; but it is madness to become drunk (268, 269). Appetites must be kept in check and food should never be taken for the sake of enjoyment, but only for the sake of nourishment (111).

The attitude to wealth is more strongly negative than that of Clement. The love of money is as much a trap as is the appetite for food. The wise man may not own any private property (79, 81). His only possession must be the goodness of his life (79). Private ownership of property is not consistent with the universal brotherhood under one father. Those who confess God as father should share all their worldly goods (228). It is a duty to give to the poor, and especially to give in such a way that the gift will be received without a sense of insult or inferiority (52, 339).

Discipleship

The theme of assimilation to God dominates Sextus as it does Clement; but ascetic rigour has been stepped up. The soul aims to become like

God (44–9). Believers are sons of God; but they must become his sons by acting like the children of the Father (58–60). Man's chief good is assimilation to God as far as it is possible (381, 45, 48). The soul must ever live in the presence of God (55). The soul strives towards sinless perfection (8, 234, 237). Leaving the world behind, it ascends to God by faith (402) through his word (420). God's light shines upon it, and it lives always in the presence of God, thinking of him more often than the body breathes (97, 288, 289). Time which is not given to thinking about God is time wasted (54). The wise man is God's noblest work (308), joined to God in mutual appreciation (421, 422), and exercising dominion as a son of God and through prayer (60, 375). He is revered as the living image of God (190). He is God among men (376a) and his soul is God in the body (82d). The move from a future to a present eschatology is complete. God is within. Yet man still offers to God the only sacrifice, which is to do good to men.

While the appetites of the body tie it to the earth, the soul gives to God the things which are his (78, 19, 20). As far as possible the body's needs are to be renounced for the sake of the soul. Sexual desires must be destroyed (232, 233). Castration is prescribed as a last resort for the man who cannot control himself (13, 273). Those who are already married are permitted to renounce their marriage for the sake of coming closer to God (230a). On the other hand, family life is compatible with the life of the wise man, provided he acts always from high motives and knows that he is living dangerously (230b). Because the body is a burden to the soul, death is welcomed (320). Yet the body bears the image of the soul, and because of this it should be kept pure (346).

Faith and freedom

The same foundation of faith is laid as in Clement and the link of faith and freedom is equally explicit. Faith is the basis of the good life, and all the teaching of Sextus is given to the believer (196, 400, 402). Sin has to be abandoned (234) and backsliders must never fall again (247). To the believer divine freedom has been given (36), and he under the rule of God rules over the world and his fellow men (43, 182). Wisdom and philosophy bring freedom (275, 306, 309, 392). What has to be done must be done willingly (388). God cares for the wise man by his great providence (423). Fate can neither produce (436a) nor control God's grace (436b).

Love

Love, for Sextus, is at once less human and less ecstatic than in Clement. Love is directed to those of like mind (106a), to God (106b) and truth (158). To love God is to do his will (442) and without love no one can come to God (444). To honour and to love another wise man is to honour and to love oneself (219, 226).

In conclusion, two points may be noted. Sextus lacks the respect for the contingent and the rich imagination of Clement's ethic. His literary form is, however, far more effective as instruction or propaganda. There is too much of Clement. The sentences of Sextus may well be the form in which Clement's ideas, after modification, are spread through a considerable part of the early Christian church.

3

BASIL THE GREAT[1]

Basil was born in Caesarea of Cappadocia about 330 of rich but honest parents. His father was a teacher of rhetoric, a lawyer and a wealthy land-owner. One of his grandfathers had died a martyr. The piety and devotion of Basil's mother was reflected in her children, three of whom became bishops, one a nun and another a monk. Three of these children were canonised. After careful training at home, he studied rhetoric and philosophy in Caesarea and Constantinople. In 351 he went to Athens where for five years he took advantage of its rich intellectual life. He returned to Caesarea as a professor of rhetoric for two years, and then turned from the bright prospects of his academic future, was baptised and entered a life of religious discipline. After visiting Egypt and Syria to observe the monks, he selected a quiet country retreat, and gathered a few others who wished to live a hermit's life. He wrote in moving terms of the rich beauty of his surroundings and of its silence. Seeing the dangers of solitary life, he organised monks into a community. He gave to his community a set of rules and a detailed pattern of life. Far more than Pachomius had done in Egypt, he put emphasis on the common life which members shared. Together with his learning, sanctity and perception, he had great powers of organisation. Monasticism in the East has retained the shape which he gave it. His programme of social relief produced hospitals and homes for the poor.[2] The Emperor Julian tried to bring him from his place of retreat to the splendour of the court, for they had been students together. This and other efforts to move him failed, but in 364 he was ordained and took an active part in the fight against Arianism. In 370

---

[1] The following abbreviations will be used in this chapter: *M.=Moralia; L.R.=Longer Rules; S.R.=Shorter Rules; Ep.=Letter; H.=Hexaemeron; S.=On the Spirit*. The first three works are quoted with some modifications from the translations of W. K. L. Clarke, *The Ascetic Works of Saint Basil* (London, 1925). See also the translation of B. Jackson (Oxford, 1845).

[2] 'For the first time, the hospital, the almshouse, and school become regular adjuncts of a monastic settlement.' K. E. Kirk, *The Vision of God* (London, 1932), p. 266. See for extended treatment, S. Giet, *Les idées sociales de S. Basile* (Paris, 1941).

he became Bishop of Caesarea, and held this office until his early
death in 379. From these years he is remembered as the defender of
the Nicene faith in the face of imperial Arianism. The Emperor
Valens came to Cappadocia, determined to stamp out opposition. The
rest of the province yielded; but Basil stood firm against all threats.
Confiscation of property meant nothing to him, since he only had an
old cloak and a few books. Exile was nothing to a stranger and pilgrim
in all the earth. Pain and death held no terrors. When a threatening
prefect expressed surprise at Basil's stand he was told that he had not
met a proper bishop before. The emperor talked with Basil on problems of faith with his household cook, one Demosthenes, in attendance.
When the latter entered the discussion, Basil suggested that a Demosthenes who could not speak Greek would be better making sauces in
the kitchen than improvising at theology. He once replied to a threat
of torture which included tearing out his liver with the comment that
he would be obliged for the treatment since his liver gave him a lot of
trouble where it was. He showed no consideration for himself or for his
few friends, once making Gregory of Nazianzus the bishop of a desolate
but strategic outpost.[3] His theological work was crucial but he saw
small reward for the struggles of his strenuous life. Jerome and others
accused him of pride. He was reserved, conscious of his abilities and
deeply concerned by the doctrinal dangers of his time. The body,
which he ill-treated, gave him great pain and he declared himself an
old man at forty-five. He died five years later, two years before the
second ecumenical council at Constantinople, to be remembered as
Basil the Great.[4]

His chief theological work concerned the Holy Spirit. The Spirit
must be 'counted with' and not 'counted below' the Father and Son.
'We glorify the Spirit with the Father and the Son because we believe
that he is not foreign to the divine nature.'[5] Basil did not write in the
abstract. His founding of monastic communities grew from a direct
awareness of the varied gifts of the Spirit. The 'enthusiasm' of the
earliest church had been exemplified in the behaviour of the Corinthians to whom Paul wrote. They wanted 'spirit without letter' and
believed that the fullness of the last days was already on them. The
second century rejected the Montanist movement which claimed even
greater heights of spiritual ecstasy. The third century faced the brief

[3] Sasima. See S. Giet, *Sasimes* (Paris, 1941).
[4] See Gregory Nazianzus, *Oration* 20; Gregory of Nyssa, *Funeral Oration*, *Life
of St Macrina*; Ephraem Syrus, *Encomium on Basil the Great*; Socrates,
H.E. 4.26; Sozomen, *H.E.* 6.15–17; Jerome, *De vir. illust.*, 116; *Dictionary
of Christian Biography*, *in loc.*
[5] *Ep.* 159.2.

problem of Cyprian's contemporaries who demanded martyrdom.
Monasticism saw the revival of enthusiasm on a wide scale. The spiritual gifts of the anchorites were not immediately disruptive because
they were exercised, in isolation, for the perfection of the individual.
They displayed all the intensity of those who would take the kingdom
by storm. In time the ideal of Antony led to excesses and the reforms
of Pachomius had moderating effects. It was left to Basil, however, to
establish the common life (cenobitism), through an appreciation of
spiritual gifts and their interdependence. Basil saw in the successors
to Antony a new hope for the church. God was pouring out his Spirit
and the day of Pentecost had come again. The community of monks,
indwelt and endowed by the Spirit, reproduced the earliest Christian
community. Their charismatic endowments were not for their own
elevation but for the enrichment of a common life. With sound theological judgement Basil turned to scripture for the direction and rule
of his community. He cites more than 1500 verses of New Testament.[6]
His exhaustive knowledge and continuous use of scripture point to
profound insight. Spirit without letter would be just as disastrous as
letter without spirit. The challenge and opportunity of his time caused
him to discover afresh the ethical patterns of the New Testament. His
rigour, enthusiasm and devotion cannot fail to move the twentieth-
century reader one way or another. Yet these are only half of Basil.
The other half is integration of these qualities in a fellowship of the
Spirit and an obedience to the Word. God has made us, like members
of one body, to need one another's help.[7] The need for community is
evident because Basil 'once saw a swarm of bees flying in military
formation according to the law of their nature and following their
king[!] in good order'.[8] Renunciation of the world is joined to an
affirmation of its order and beauty. The length of the elephant's trunk
is due to stiffness of legs which is due to weight of body.[9] Every season
brings its special fruits. Spring is the time for flowers, summer for
wheat harvest, autumn for apples and winter is the time for talking.[10]

   Basil is a strenuous Christian. The pictures of the soldier, the athlete
and the child come readily to his mind.[11] His monk is the Christian

---

[6] See J. Gribomont, 'Les règles morales de S. Basile et le NT', *Studia
Patristica* II (Berlin, 1957), 417ff.
[7] *L.R.* 7.
[8] *On the Judgement of God*, 214E. For 'king' bees compare Ambrose, *Hex.*
5.21.68, and Seneca, *De Clem.* 1.19.2. Dr A. Lenox-Conyngham has drawn
my attention to these parallel references.
[9] *H.* 9.5.   [10] *Ep.* 13.
[11] K. Holl comments, 'Eine merkwürdige Mischung kindlicher Einfalt und
heiligen Ernstes ist die Signatur des griechischen Christentums in seinen

soldier who takes the kingdom by force, the athlete who throws everything into the contest and the child who is saved with simplicity and
trust. Not that Basil ever loses his pride or activism; but they are tem-
pered by submission to the king, for whom he fights and in whose love
he finds his only rest.

RIGHTEOUSNESS

(i) *Rigorism*

The righteousness of the Christian is marked by excess. It abounds in
every way, goes beyond that of the scribes and Pharisees, and is
governed by the single standard of the Lord's teaching.[1] Frequent reference to the teaching of the Lord determines the quality of this
righteousness. The Lord sent his followers to teach *all* that he had
commanded and not, 'to observe some things and neglect others'. If all
commands had not been essential, all would not have been written
down. This righteousness is always superior to that of the law, and
goes beyond literal requirements. The Christian must neither speak
evil, do violence, fight or avenge himself. He never returns evil for
evil, but rejects anger, is patient and suffers, not in order to justify
himself, but rather to reform his brother. He must not slander his
brother secretly, nor may he joke, laugh or be idle. While he lives a
temperate life, he never thinks of himself as his own master. He does
not complain in time of need or weariness. Every action and word is
governed by one obedience. He is never glad when others go wrong
and always looks for reconciliation.[2]

With this extreme account of righteousness there is an insistence on
the gravity of all kinds of sin. There is no distinction between one fault
and another. Basil was troubled by the effects of sin and disobedience
in a divided church. From scripture he knew that all sin is a revolt
against God and must be punished. The New Testament makes no
distinction between large and small sins. He who commits sin is the
slave of sin, and the word will judge him: whoever does not obey the
Son will not see life, but the wrath of God dwells upon him. The only
possible distinction between sins is between those which dominate us
and those which do not. The large sin is one which is our master, the
small sin is one which we have mastered. So every thought should be

liebenswürdigsten Vertretern, ein naiver Sinn und eine abgeschlossene
Stimmung, die uns immer zugleich an die Jugendzeit des Christentums und
an das Sterbegefühl der alten Völker erinnern', p. 282, *Ueber das
griechische Mönchtum, Ges. Aufsätze* ii (Tübingen, 1928).

[1] *M.* 80.22.318C.   [2] *Ep.* 22.

obedient to God and every disobedient thought must be punished. God
does not condemn the number of our sins, nor their relative seriousness;
he condemns the plain contradiction of his will; so it is wrong to be
tolerant towards some sins and to condemn others. At this point Basil
is close to the Stoics who insisted that it was as easy to drown in one
foot of water as in ten feet; but the New Testament also told him what
happened to those who broke the least commandment, while the Old
Testament warned those who swerved to the right or the left. As all
sin is condemned, so all men are called to virtue. The will and commandments of God are found in scripture, which is interpreted according
to concrete situations. Distinctions may be introduced, but severity
and rigour remain. The letter of scripture is followed, for example,
when he who calls his neighbour a fool is condemned to hell, although
Basil explains, 'What is Raca? A vernacular word of mild insult, used
among friends and relations.'[3]

With God it must be all or nothing, obedience or disobedience. Sin
is the only source of evil. Like Clement and Origen, Basil strictly
separates evil from God and attributes it to man's free choice. Reason
in relation to conduct is called conscience. All men have an elementary
sense of good and evil. Man's pursuit of good should take the practical
route of conquering sin. Sin must be torn out. The words of the Lord
show the need for vigilance. He who defends a sinner is worse than he
who has made one to stumble and earned a millstone around his neck.
The unrepentant sinner is like the eye which should be plucked out
and cast away.[4] True repentance brings joy to the Lord. The sinner
who will not repent becomes as a Gentile and a tax-gatherer.[5] With
fear and tears the lost soul must turn from sin.[6] Repentance must be
obvious.[7] Great care must be taken before a sinner is trusted with any
office in the brotherhood.[8] Penitence is central in the life of every monk.
While love is the supreme virtue, the monk lives in continual penitence
through his desire to obtain remission of past sins. He prays for the
freedom of his soul. He practises mortification and good works which
help him to stamp out sin. He does not laugh because his Lord has
condemned laughter and because there are so many sinners to be
mourned. Sleep brings slackness in thoughts of God and, when over-
done, leads men to despise God's judgements.[9] Every idle word earns
judgement. It may be a good word; but, if it does not fulfil a purpose
in the Lord, if it does not edify faith, then it grieves the Holy Spirit.[10]

---

[3] S.R. 51. For the general point, see S. Giet, 'Le rigorisme de S. Basile'. RevSR
23, (1949), 333–42, and also D. Amand, L'ascèse monastique de S. Basile
(Maredsous, 1948), pp. 164–75.

[4] S.R. 7.   [5] S.R. 9.   [6] S.R. 10.   [7] S.R. 14.
[8] S.R. 18.   [9] S.R. 32.   [10] S.R. 23.

On the other hand if a sister does not sing psalms with fervour, 'Let her either correct herself or else be expelled.'[11]

In the church of God a minister must be upright. His life is examined before his admission to office.[12] Unworthy ministers should be dismissed and not replaced until worthy candidates are available. Yet the church has fallen upon sad days. Its laws are in confusion. There is no just judgement and no limit on vice.[13] The righteousness of God is the justice which all shall know when they receive the reward of their works. At present men enjoy the long-suffering of God, but in that terrible day, his justice will be made clear to all.[14] He is the one God of mercy and judgement,[15] who will duly reward those who have done well. Generosity, for example, earns his blessing. Whoever gives to the afflicted gives to the Lord and shall receive his reward from the Lord.[16] The soul looks to the great day when all creation shall stand before the judge to give an account of its deeds. That day and that hour must ever be remembered so that life may be lived in the fear of God.[17] The body is trained to work hard and the soul is accustomed to trials; but the end of everlasting blessedness with the saints is never forgotten.[18]

(ii) *Rule*

Basil's discourse on morals sets out in separate prescriptions what the New Testament tells Christians to do.

> Let us now try to fulfil in the name of our Lord Jesus Christ our promise concerning the *Morals*. As many things as we find in the New Testament in scattered passages forbidden or approved, these to the best of our ability we have tried to gather into summarised rules for the easy comprehension of whoever wants them.

The Rules fulfil the ministry of the word for the perfecting of souls. The life of the monk is governed in every aspect. His clothing, food, sleep, in fact, every part of his life is regulated. Many laws or canons cover particular sins and prescribe punishment in a wide variety of special cases.[19] Basil, an enemy of compromise, is always practical in his outlook. 'The saints that have gone before teach us that the use of the girdle is necessary...It is especially necessary that he who means to do work in person should be neatly dressed and able to move without hindrance.'[20]

[11] *S.R.* 281. [12] *Ep.* 54. [13] *Ep.* 92.2.
[14] *L.R.* Preface 328 and 329. [15] *L.R.* Preface 329 and 330.
[16] *Ep.* 150.3. [17] *Ep.* 174. [18] *Ep.* 42.4.
[19] *Ep.* 188, *Ep.* 199, *Ep.* 217. [20] *L.R.* 23.

Punishment is remedial and beneficial rather than retributive. A just judge requires that an evil doer should pay his debt with interest, 'if he is to be made better by punishment and render other men wiser by his example'. Such punishment is to be received willingly, 'as befits a son who is sick and at death's door'.[21] Correction and cure must be prescribed according to individual need. 'There is no fault that cannot be cured by care or overcome by the fear of God.' The privileged patrician needs a very distasteful job to help him to achieve the Lord's humility.[22] Special responsibility hangs heavily upon the superior, who shares the condemnation of a brother if he has not warned the brother concerning his sin and taught him a way of reformation. One of the greatest faults is to give wrong guidance and cause a brother to go astray.[23] A superior heals the weak brother, just as a doctor heals those who are sick in body. Surgery may be painful or drugs may be bitter, but they can achieve a cure. Godly sorrow is necessary.[24] The same principle is applied to heal diseases of body and of soul.

> We must take care so to use the art of medicine, if need arise as not to assign to it the whole cause of health or sickness, but to accept the use of its remedies as designed for the glory of God and a type of the care of souls. . . For as with the flesh both the putting away of foreign elements and the addition of what is lacking are necessary; so also with our souls, it is fitting that what is foreign be removed and what is according to our nature be received. Because 'God made man upright' and created us for good works that we should walk in them.[25]

The corporate aspects of sin are clear within the brotherhood. If one allows another to sin, one is guilty of that sin. As our Lord said to Pilate, 'He that delivered me to you has the greater sin.' We must not be silent when others sin. The Old Testament tells us to rebuke our neighbours and the gospel tells us to show our brother his faults.[26] Within the community any offence requires direct and drastic action. A man may provide such offence by transgressing the law, leading another to transgress it, preventing someone from doing God's will, or encouraging a weak man to do something which is wrong. There is intricate variety in the apportioning of blame.[27] Various community problems are considered. Laziness is linked with sin because one should be zealous and endure to the end.[28] Spiritual sickness may show itself in eating delicacies or in eating too much.[29] When a good man falls into

[21] *S.R.* 158.   [22] *L.R.* 10.   [23] *L.R.* 25.
[24] *L.R.* 52.   [25] *L.R.* 55.   [26] *S.R.* 46-7.
[27] *S.R.* 64.   [28] *S.R.* 69.   [29] *S.R.* 71.

sin, his condition is different from that of an indifferent man who has committed the same sin. The latter is corrupt in his whole nature and requires more drastic action.[30] Obedience is the answer to sin. When monks dispute among themselves and reject the commands of their Lord, the king is no longer among them.[31] Disobedience must be punished and if punishment does not cure the ill, then the diseased member must be cut off from the community. 'Insubordination and defiance are the proofs of a multitude of sins, of tainted faith, of doubtful hope, of proud and overweening conduct.'[32]

Moderation, quiet and self-control should rule the lives of those who receive what God gives from the wealth of his universe. The providence of God rules justly over all things and must never be questioned.[33] The true good of man is his soul, uniquely his soul and man should know himself, or as scripture says, take heed to himself. Health, beauty, youth, long life, riches, glory and power, must be regarded with moderation. Reason helps moderation. Basil answers reasonably the unreasonable question, 'if a brother having nothing of his own be asked by another for the actual thing he is wearing, what ought he to do, especially if he who asks is naked?' The matter of giving and receiving is a question of stewardship and there is happily a Pauline principle, 'Let each man abide in that wherein he was called.' Another problem shows moderation of appetite, 'How can a man avoid taking pleasure in eating?' The answer is that one must hold to the criterion of what is fitting and useful and regard pleasure as irrelevant.[34]

(iii) Order and natural law

The beauty of nature inspires quietness in the soul.[35] Basil marvels at the ordered beauty of the creation, and uses philosophy to explain the links between the ordered universe, the providence of God, and human responsibility. He rejects any argument which would threaten man's responsibility and freedom. The design of the creator is seen on every side. Appropriate herbs are provided to heal the various sicknesses of the body. Man must use God's world in a right way. The rich man must care for those in need. Divine judgement falls on the selfish. Money should not be lent or borrowed at interest, and if it is, both lender and borrower are selfishly at fault.[36] Basil's sermons on the six days of creation show how the order of nature is important to moral life. Nature teaches us by her example to show vigour in producing

---

[30] S.R. 81.   [31] On the Judgement of God, 214.   [32] L.R. 28.
[33] Ep. 2.6 and Ep. 6.2.   [34] S.R. 91 and 126.   [35] Ep. 14.
[36] On usury, see Hom. on Psalm 14 and Hom. on avarice.

good works.[37] The serpent symbolises the fickleness and shiftiness of sin. Justice and honesty must go together.[38] Fishes which move by regular laws of migration indicate obedience to the law of God. They have no reason in them but the inward law of nature tells them what to do.[39] The ox and the ass know their master and can even follow a known track when a man has lost his way. Man is not always able to show his superiority over dumb creatures.[40] Storks show qualities of kindness and care which shame many men. When the old lose their feathers others surround them to keep them warm. Man can learn also from the industry of the swallow who builds a nest by perseverance and before whose example no man can plead his poverty.[41] Nature is a good teacher. Man by standing upright on his two feet looks to his heavenly country, while cattle with their four feet bend towards the earth. 'Raise your soul above the earth. Draw from its natural shape the rule of your conduct; fix your way of life in heaven.'[42] The care which irrational creatures take of their lives warns us to watch over the salvation of our souls. The bear, the fox and the tortoise all know how to heal their wounds.[43] Basil does not hesitate to read off from nature recommendations concerning human conduct. Porphyry writes in similar vein of the lessons to be drawn from nature. Ants, bees and other gregarious animals preserve a communal and reciprocal justice. Doves are very strong on chastity and storks on kindness to parents.[44] Both these writers have a strong dualistic tendency which does not diminish their allegiance to natural order. Basil draws one violent conclusion from nature. The body is like a charging beast that must be whipped by reason to calm it down.[45]

DISCIPLESHIP

(i) *Seized by a vehement desire to follow Christ*

Throughout Basil's account of Christian discipleship, there sounds a ruthless call to self denial. Asceticism is required of all. He who is attached to this life or tolerates 'anything which even to a small degree draws him away from the commandment of God'[1] cannot be a disciple of the Lord. The glory of God is declared by doing his will.[2] Confession of the Lord and possession of spiritual gifts cannot save the disobedient from condemnation.[3] It is no help to live with others who please God and to preserve an outward appearance of virtue when one

---

[37] *H.* 5.7.   [38] *H.* 7.3.   [39] *H.* 7.4.
[40] *H.* 8.1.   [41] *H.* 8.5.   [42] *H.* 9.2.
[43] *H.* 9.3.   [44] *On Abstinence*, 3.11.   [45] *To the young*, 9(7).
[1] *M.* 2.   [2] *M.* 4.   [3] *M.* 7.

has no real virtue within. God must be obeyed in God's way.[4] Every
offensive thing must be cut away however necessary and dear it may
seem.[5] The Law condemns bad deeds but the gospel goes further and
condemns the inner passions of the soul. There is an initial act of
renunciation which cannot be avoided. The soldier must enlist. 'For if a
man has not first succeeded in denying himself and taking up his cross,
he finds, as he goes, many hindrances to following, arising from himself.'[6] One must renounce the devil, fleshly lusts, physical relationships,
human friendships, all behaviour contrary to the gospel, worldly
affections, parents, relations and possessions.[7] 'Accordingly perfect renunciation consists in a man's attaining complete passionlessness as
regards actual living and having "the sentence of death" so as to put
no confidence in himself.' The first disciples show the way. John and
James left their father 'and even the boat, their sole source of liveli-
hood'. Matthew left all and followed, not only leaving the profits
behind, 'but also despising the dangers that were likely to come upon
himself and his family at the hands of the authorities for leaving the
accounts of the custom-house in disorder'. All of this shows that anyone 'who is seized by the vehement desire of following Christ can no
longer care for anything to do with this life'.[8] Yet all is gain, for the
things which are given up are no better than dung, and what is gained
is the pearl of great price. Renunciation looses the chains which bind
us to all present, material and transitory things, and releases us from
human obligation 'making us more ready to start on the way to God'.[9]
So Basil's message is good news, because man is able to fulfil all the
commandments of God. God forgives all sins when we produce fruits
of repentance, and are washed in the blood of Christ. An inner spark
of divine love enables us to keep the commandments of God. For if we
love him we will keep his commandments, and the two commandments
to love God and our neighbour are all the law and the prophets. Yet
the promise does not remove the need for constant vigilance. None of
the saints of old won their crowns by living in luxury. They all passed
through the fire of affliction. The Christian follows the commandment
of his Lord and the example of the holy men of old who showed in
adversity their greatness of soul.[10] The athlete of Christ fights for
victory over sin, by straining every muscle. Christians struggle and
suffer together. They fight in the arena for the common heritage 'for
the treasure of the sound faith, derived from our fathers'.[11] Those who
are being attacked by Arians are congratulated on their good fortune.
They have won the blessings of persecution in a period of peace.[12] A

[4] *M. 16* and *M.* 18.   [5] *M.* 41.   [6] *S.R.* 237.
[7] *L.R.* 8.348f.   [8] *L.R.* 8.349.   [9] *L.R.* 8.350.
[10] *Ep.* 206.   [11] *Ep.* 243.4.   [12] *Ep.* 257.1.

soldier does not worry about rations or lodging, but faces dangers and
death for the reward of nearness to his king, the friendship and favour
of his king. 'Come, then, soldier of Christ, take to heart these small
lessons from human affairs and consider eternal blessings.'[13] Ascetic
life is a peaceful substitute for martyrdom, the peak of perfection. As
with Clement, each Christian should order his life as a preparation for
martyrdom. So Basil kept a direct link between the life of the monk
and the perseverance which gave to martyrs their perfection.[14]

(ii) *His glory as object and desire*

The ascetic life is not an end in itself. It is a means to the end of the
glory of God. 'Ever to be pressing the soul on beyond its strength to do
the will of God, having his glory as its object and desire.'[15] Prayer
should be unceasing but special times of the day have been chosen as
appropriate for the remembering of the blessings of God. These times
are the dawn, the third, sixth and ninth hour with a final service at
midnight.[16] All must be done to the glory of God.[17] Prayer is governed
by a sense of God's presence. When one talks with a ruler or a superior,
one fixes one's eyes upon him. Much more, when one prays, one fixes
one's mind upon God.[18]

Man and woman are equal before God[19] and possess two chief
faculties, reason and free choice. The beginning of the moral life comes
with the Delphic injunction, 'Know thyself', or the theme of Deutero-
nomy, 'Take heed to yourself.'[20] Self-knowledge is a condition of the
good life. One must consciously choose between animal life and
higher spiritual life. Quietness of mind and freedom from distraction
enable a soul to fix its gaze on God. The wax tablet must be smoothed
out before it can be written on.[21] Prayer should leave imprinted a clear
idea of God. In this way God dwells in the soul which becomes his
temple.[22] The inner man consists of contemplation and since the king-

---

[13] *Preliminary sketch of the ascetic life*, 200A.
[14] *Ep.* 252: 'the bond, as it were, of blood which binds the life of strict
discipline to those perfected through endurance'.
[15] *S.R.* 211.   [16] *L.R.* 37.383f.   [17] *L.R.* 55.401.   [18] *S.R.* 201.
[19] *Hom. on Psalm* 1.3 See S. Giet, *Les idées sociales de S. Basile* (Paris,
1941), pp. 71–5.
[20] When all has been said of hospitals and school, the monk's chief work was
to 'take heed to himself'. 'Von der Erkenntnis aus, dass die sittliche
Aufgabe in der Vollendung der eigenen Persönlichkeit besteht, ist das
Mönchtum zu einer intensiven Selbstbeobachtung geführt worden': K. Holl,
Ueber das griechische Mönchtum, Ges. Aufsätze, II (Tübingen, 1928), p.
277.
[21] *Ep.* 2.2.   [22] *Ep.* 2.4.

dom of heaven is within, this kingdom must be contemplation.[23] Basil praises the quietness and beauty of his new home in the country. 'However, the best thing to be said about the place is that being suitable for growing fruits of every kind, it nurtures what to me is the sweetest fruit of all, quietness.'[24] The life of a religious community enjoys tranquillity of soul through solitude. It is here, and here alone, that one may live the spiritual life, away from the noise and distractions of the world.

The *Longer Rules* begin with the exhortation to apply ourselves to the care of our souls for the love of Jesus Christ,[25] who calls us back from death to life and who has shared our weakness and disease that we might be healed. Only through him may we regain the image and likeness of God which man possessed in paradise before his fall.[26] The fear of God is important for all who begin to practise piety.[27] To follow God we must loosen all chains of attachment to this life. We must remove from our previous environment and forget all former habits. No distraction must threaten the achievement of our aim. If our minds wander we cannot hope to succeed in loving God and our neighbour. This art is to be learnt by concentration.[28] Solitude is a great help to a soul which wishes to avoid distraction.[29] To follow the Lord Jesus Christ means taking up the cross after him.[30] We must suffer and endure for Christ's sake,[31] continue in prayer and in vigils to the end that we may be disciples of Christ and conform to his pattern. As sheep we follow him who is our shepherd, as branches we bear fruit in him, as members of his body we are equipped with the gifts of the Spirit. We are the bride of Christ, temples of God, a sacrifice to him and 'children of God, formed after the likeness of God according to the measure granted to men'. It is a mark of the Christian that he sees his Lord always before him.[32]

We are called to be made like God.[33] We cannot become like God unless we know what he is like. Theological inquiry is necessary to find the truth which rules the goal of human life.[34] Perfection of life can only be found in the outward and inward imitation of Christ, the following of his example in life and death. Paul spoke of being made

---

[23] *Ep.* 8.12.

[24] *Ep.* 14. H. von Campenhausen comments, 'Anyone who is able to enjoy solitude to that extent cannot expect it to last forever', *The Fathers of the Greek Church* (London, 1963), p. 89.

[25] *L.R.* Preface 327.   [26] *L.R.* 2.339.   [27] *L.R.* 4.341.   [28] *L.R.* 5.341.

[29] *L.R.* 6.344.   [30] *L.R.* 8.348f.   [31] *M.* 55.   [32] *M.* 80.

[33] For the closely-woven Platonism of Basil's thought, there is no better summary than the account of his ethical outlook in the *Homilies on the Psalms*, given by A. Benito y Duran, 'Filosofía de san Basilio Magno', *Studia Patristica*, v, *TU* 80 (Berlin, 1962).   [34] *S.* 1.2.

like the death of Christ.[35] As every man is made in the image of God,
the blasphemy of the Arians, who deny that the Son is like God, is all
the more outrageous.[36]

Perfection calls man to continence, to the renunciation of every
worldly relationship, to fasting, to the study of scripture and to watch-
ing. There has been disagreement on the shape of Basil's thought. Some
have maintained that he describes a progress in gradual stages towards
the direct love of God, moving through an *ordo amoris* like that of
Augustine. A stronger case can be made for seeing his initial drive of
life and thought towards God alone. Duty to the world, neighbour and
church,[37] develop from this point. The perfect Christian is considered
on the Stoic pattern of the wise man. Moses too is described as a sage.[38]
Man must advance by degrees until he is completely like God. He
always has to fight against temptations and his life is a continual
struggle. Perfection is not secure or stationary. Life must be lived either
for or against God. There is no neutrality. The Christian life is always
a battle against demons and evil passions. Spiritual perfection can build
on the basis of the fear of God, whose terrible judgements are always
before us, and whose damnation will consign sinners to hell. The discipline of the monk is simply a continuation of the discipline which is
imposed on every baptised Christian. There is one morality of the
gospel, and it is this gospel which the discipline of Basil is concerned
to realise, a gospel of perfection. Passionlessness, a goal of Christian
living, is constancy, perseverance under suffering, and freedom from
passion through self-rule.[39] All of these are universal features of Christian moral exhortation; but as Basil develops them they show his
Hellenic background and personal extremism.

(iii) *Ever pressing the soul on beyond its strength*

Basil understands soul and body in much the same way as did Plato
and the later Platonists. The true self is the soul which has been made
in the image of God. The body is simply a dependent possession of the
soul. Basil shows admiration for the beauty of physical things, and he
shares with Plato an admiration for the excellence of man's physical
form. But the soul, for Plato and Basil, is the essential part of man. It

---

[35] *S.* 15.35.   [36] *H.* 9.6.
[37] Basil remains sensitive to social relationships. A strong case has been made
out for his social concerns, by S. Giet, *Les idées sociales de S. Basile*; but a
concluding reference to Basil's 'inlassable et géniale activité' (p. 425)
overstates the case.
[38] T. Spidlik, *La sophiologie de S. Basile* (Rome, 1961), pp. 24f.
[39] A. Dirking, 'Die Bedeutung des Wortes Apathie beim heiligen Basilius
dem Grossen', *Theol. Quartalschrift*, 134 (1954), 211f.

is what belongs to man as man. The soul must be liberated from its
prison within the body. It must be purified from the passions. Here
Basil talks like Plato, the Pythagoreans and the Stoics; Marcus Aurelius
spoke of man as a soul carrying a corpse. Yet Basil's account of temperance is based on Paul, and he quotes Galatians 5:16–18 and Romans
7:14ff. The Christian soldier fights against the flesh and against the
devil. Body and soul are irreconcilable. The soul can only be strong
through the body becoming weak. The victory of the soul is the defeat
of the body. An emaciated body is a sign of piety.[40] We must be grateful when woken for prayer because the soul perceives nothing in sleep
but meets God in prayer.[41] If anyone is annoyed when woken, he
deserves 'temporary separation and deprivation of food'.[42] There is
a tricky problem concerning the possession of a night shirt, if that shirt
is a hair shirt. More than one garment is forbidden; but hair cloth is
special. 'For its use is not on account of bodily necessity but for afflict-
ing and humiliating the soul.'[43]

Continence or self-rule, listed by Paul among the gifts of the Spirit,
is that self-mastery which comes through restraint, the suffering of
hardship and the buffeting of the body. Incontinence was the cause of
man's first disobedience while all the saints have practised continence.[44]
Laughter can be incontinent if it lacks moderation and control and
should not be confused with spiritual joy or hilarity.[45] Continence
mortifies the body, introduces eternal blessings and takes the sting out
of pleasure.[46] The demons know and fear the power of continence as
the Lord said that 'this kind does not go out except by prayer and
fasting'.[47] The monk must therefore chastise and mortify his body, for
the athlete of Christ trains his body in self-control.[48] The fear of God
purifies soul and body. It penetrates the soul so that the soul no longer
tolerates sin, and refuses to do anything contrary to the divine commands.

The monastic virtues are poverty whereby the monk treats nothing
as his own and cares for the property of his community, and obedience
by which the monk is subject to the authority of his superior. His
obedience must be perfect, enthusiastic and exact. Like the little
hungry child when it hears its nurse calling it to eat, he obeys commands with enthusiasm, for his life springs from their fulfilment.[49] The
monk lives in isolation from worldly pursuits, in detachment from the

---

[40] M. Viller and K. Rahner, *Aszese und Mystik in der Väterzeit* (Freiburg, 1939), p. 127.   [41] *S.R.* 43.
[42] *S.R.* 44.   [43] *S.R.* 90.   [44] *L.R.* 16.358.
[45] *L.R.* 17.   [46] *L.R.* 17.360.   [47] *L.R.* 18.362.
[48] *L.R.* 17.361. Amand, *L'ascèse monastique de S. Basile*, p. 201f.
[49] Amand, *op. cit.*, pp.318–35.

world, and from himself. His renunciation is shown in purity of conscience, poverty, humility and obedience. He mortifies himself both
physically and spiritually. His love and his renunciation must bear
fruit in prayer throughout the day, in work which all monks must do,
and in charitable service to those in need. He must dress in a way
appropriate to the temperate life, showing humility and avoiding
softness. The purpose of clothing is to hide nakedness and to protect
from the heat and the cold. The monk from his poverty will have only
one tunic. He is temperate in eating and eats whatever is put before
him. He eats what is necessary in order to live and observes a mean
between indulgence and self-torture. Fasting can get out of hand if it
depends upon the will of the individual, and it should be done under
the direction of a superior. All forms of luxury are to be avoided.[50]

The members of the brotherhood are not to be distracted. Their
parents and relations are no longer their private concern.[51] Under no
circumstances may the monk leave his community for the sake of his
family. He must no longer think in terms of what is his, but in terms
of what belongs to the community. Visits from his parents may awaken
memories of his past life, and it is generally forbidden for monks to
speak with their parents or with strangers. There may be some exception to this rule if spiritual advancement can be seen as a result. When
a monk talks with a nun he must do so under the direction of their
superiors who will choose persons, time and place for the conversation.
There should be two or three monks and two or three nuns of a serious
disposition. A monk must never meet a nun by herself. Basil writes
also of the danger of homosexual behaviour to the common life of the
monastery. The monk abhors such tendencies.[52]

It has been common to look for philosophical interest in Basil's
asceticism and tendency to dualism. While Basil's account of the Spirit[53]

---

[50] *Ibid.* pp. 212–42.   [51] *L.R.* 32.375.
[52] Amand, *L'ascèse monastique de S. Basile*, p. 242ff.
[53] H. Dehnard, *Das Problem der Abhängigkeit des Basilius von Plotin*
(Berlin, 1964), examines common expressions in Basil and Plotinus. The
similarities between Plotinus, Origen and Gregory are due to a common
philosophical tradition (p. 31). In *De Spiritu*, Basil has drawn on Plotinus'
metaphysical formulae to complete Gregory's account of the Spirit and
uses Plotinus' account of the world soul to describe the activity of the
Spirit; there is no evidence of any real influence of Plotinus. Basil uses
the common terms because they are the best he can find (p. 87). Dehnard
can find no trace of any dependence of Basil on Porphyry (p. 88)! D.
Amand, *op. cit.*, pp. 351–64, shows that Basil has taken over the
metaphysical dualism of later Platonism. The extent of Basil's debt to later
classical thought has been the subject of discussion. Courtonne shows
that his debt to classical literature is not great; Y. Courtonne, *S. Basile
et l'hellénisme* (Paris, 1934).

shows some awareness of Plotinus, his pessimistic view of the world is closer to Porphyry. Not that God made a bad world; he is not the source of evil.[54] Evil is separation from God and has no being.[55] But man remains a wanderer or fugitive in the world. Only through the incarnation of the Son and the gift of the Spirit can his release be secured.[56]

A world-denying strain of Platonism may be distinguished from a world-affirming strain in the tradition from Plato to Philo and the Hermetic literature.[57] The two strains continue in later Platonism. Plato commended the study of astronomy provided it left the stars alone.[58] Plotinus, for all his optimism, still pleaded for the flight of the alone to the alone.[59] The stronger pessimism of Porphyry is evident in his *On Abstinence from Animal Food*. The philosopher turns from the body and its passions to pure intellect and the supreme God.

Senses and passions work always on the irrational part of the soul, food and drink can poison the soul with passions. To stand against these things is a great struggle but there is no other way of purity.[60] As far as we can we should avoid contact with all that incites passions. That is why the Pythagoreans live away from the noises of the world. Plato chose an unhealthy part of Athens as the place for his Academy.[61] The philosopher meditating on death despises luxury and lives free from want on a slender diet. 'For he who in this way mortifies the body will obtain all possible good through self sufficiency and be made like the divine.'[62] The worship of the supreme God can employ neither material sacrifice nor verbal utterance – only silent contemplation is appropriate.[63]

This is the kind of Platonism which Basil knows and understands. In his *Discourse to the young*, he argues for the similarity of classical and Christian moralities. Socrates, when attacked, turned the other cheek. Alexander would not look at the daughters of Darius because after capturing men he did not want to be conquered by women; he was in effect fulfilling the precept against committing adultery in the heart.[64] But, to sum up, the body in every part should be despised by everyone who does not want to be buried in its pleasures as if in slime.' Both Plato and Paul warn us against the body. We should not

---

[54] Hom. *That God is not the author of evils, passim.*   [55] *Ibid.* 5.

[56] See L. Vischer, *Basilius der Grosse, Untersuchungen zu einem Kirchenvater des 4. Jahrhunderts* (Basel, 1953), pp. 29–38.

[57] See A. J. Festugière, *La révélation d'Hermès trismégiste*, II (Paris, 1949), x ff.

[58] *Republic* 530.   [59] Plotinus, *Enneads*, VI.9.9–11.

[60] *On Abstinence*, 1.33–5.   [61] *Ibid.* 1.36.

[62] *Ibid.* 1.54.   [63] *Ibid.* 2.33.   [64] *To the young*, 7(5).

pander to it but whip it with the lash of reason until it settles down. Pythagoras is quoted on the body as the prison of the soul.

> It was for this reason, in fact that Plato also, as we are told, providing against the harmful influence of the body, deliberately settled in the disease-infested part of Attica, the Academy, in order that he might prune away, as one prunes the vine of its excessive growth, the excessive well-being of his body. And I myself have heard physicians say that extreme good health is even dangerous.[65]

However wrong this estimate of Plato may be,[66] it is the one which Basil knows, a Platonism which is more dependent on Porphyry than on Plotinus. Like Clement he wishes to show that Christian sage can excel pagan philosopher. He admires the scorn of Diogenes for worldly things and his claim to superior wealth because he had fewer needs than the king.[67] Julian, of course, was critical of the moral influence of Christianity and the free forgiveness which it offered.[68] Basil could not afford to offer a morality less stringent than that of his imperial friend.

On the other hand Basil was no Manichee. He maintained a unity between the ascetic and the created world. The 'world' which he rejected was an attitude to life, a 'system of purely human values which takes no account of the judgement of God'.[69] The ascetic 'renounces also all the affections of this world which can hinder the aim of godliness'.[70] Yet the flesh can hamper us in the vision of God.[71] It is the heavy prison house of the soul.[72]

There is also a positive side to Basil's Platonism. With the sense of man's temporality and hostility between soul and body, there is that yearning for absolute beauty which only God can satisfy. God is beauty

---

[65] *Ibid.* 9(7).

[66] Nevertheless, it remains true that 'Neither Christians nor Platonists, if they are to be faithful to their deepest convictions, can simply be negative in their attitude to the body and the world, regarding them as wholly evil and alien. Their fundamental belief that the material world, with all that is in it, is good, and made by a good power simply because of his goodness, prevents them from becoming Gnostics or Manichees': A. H. Armstrong, *St. Augustine and Christian Platonism* (Villanova University Press, 1967), p. 10.

[67] *To the young*, 9(7).

[68] A. von Harnack, *Mission and Expansion* (ET, London, 2 ed. 1908) **2**, 215.

[69] J. Gribomont, 'Le renoncement au monde dans l'idéal ascétique de S. Basile', *Irénikon* (1958), pp. 282–307 and 460–75, esp. p. 298.

[70] *L.R.* 8.

[71] 'Because of the weakness of the flesh which enfolds us', *Hom. on Psalm 33*.11.

[72] *Hom. on Psalm 29*.6.

itself to whom all things look and from whom all things flow. He is
the ever-springing fount of pure grace, and a treasure which can never
be spent.[73] It is God's will that all should participate in his life.[74]

FAITH

(i) *Sound faith and godly doctrines*

Faith for Basil is the apostolic rule of faith. It must be guarded and
kept. Sound faith is the only basis for good living. 'For by these two
things the man of God is perfected.'[1] The exposition of the faith
requires care and discernment, for the devil is always trying to destroy
faith. Faith which works through love is a mark of the Christian. 'I
think it both fitting and necessary that I should now expound our
sound faith and godly doctrines concerning the Father, Son and Holy
Spirit, and then add the discourse on morals.'[2] Such faith is simple,
strong, quiet and full of light. Belief in the word of God is a living
faith which works by love and shows itself in good works. Faith is an
unhesitating assent to that which we learn from God. It is the full
conviction of the truth which is declared and taught to us by the grace
of God. Faith is firm and unshakeable, pure and exact, founded upon
scripture. Scripture is divinely inspired and is the source of all doctrine.[3]

If we are asked why we are Christians, we must answer that it is
through our faith.[4] Faith is linked with baptism as inseparable in
salvation. 'Faith is perfected through baptism, baptism is established
through faith.'[5] Faith is directed to the Father, Son and Holy Spirit,
and they who deny the trinity are acting against faith.[6]

Basil's faith is more static than Clement's. It does not go beyond
essentials. Christians should not puzzle over anything superfluous but
stand firm in the ancient faith. Let them confess one Name and one
God and avoid all kinds of novelty.[7] Yet there is continuity, for Basil
simply takes over all of Origen's negative theology.[8] God cannot be

---

[73] *Hom. on Psalm 1.3.*   [74] *Hom. on Psalm 29.4.*

[1] *De Fide* and Preface to *S.R.*

[2] *On the Judgement of God*, 223C.

[3] *Ep.* 2.3.   [4] *S.* 10.26.   [5] *S.* 12.28.

[6] *S.* 18. For additional comment on true faith, see Vischer, *Basilius der Grosse*,
pp. 66–72.

[7] *Ep.* 175.

[8] See also J. Gribomont, *L'Origénisme de S. Basile, L'homme devant Dieu*,
Mélanges offerts à H. de Lubac (Paris, 1963), 1,294, 'Des héritiers d'Origène
le plus discret est Basile.' Thanks to Basil's discretion, the influence of
Origen lived on, 'ramenée à l'essentiel et décantée'.

known in the way other things are known. Eunomius has shown in-
sufferable pride and presumption in his attempt to enter the being of
God;[9] 'to know God is to keep his commands'.[10] For Clement the
mystery of God is an invitation to pilgrimage from faith to knowledge,
for Basil it is a warning against intellectual impertinence.

The faith of the fathers stands as a fixed point of reference in times
of uncertainty. 'Now I charge you by the fathers, by the true faith, by
our blessed friend, lift up your souls.'[11] The struggle against heresy is
a constant fight in defence of the faith.[12] One should not waver concerning what the Lord has said but be convinced that every word of
God is true and possible. A man who doesn't trust the Lord in small
things will believe him far less in great things.[13] Human conditions can
never cancel out the commandments of God.[14] Faith must be steadfast
and immovable from the good things which are in the Lord.[15] The
mark of a believer is to hold fast to the faith which is 'unhesitating
conviction of the truth of the inspired Word.' What is not of faith, as
the apostle says, is sin.[16] The power of faith is recognised by animals,
for with it one may walk upon serpents and scorpions. The snake did
not hurt Paul because it found him full of faith. On the other hand, 'if
you have not faith, do not fear wild animals so much as your lack of
faith, through which you make yourself susceptible to all corruption.'[17]
When the waves of trouble seem to overwhelm Basil, he asks for
prayer that he might please God. He does not wish to be a wicked
servant who thanks his master only for what is good and refuses to
accept the chastisement of adversity. Rather, 'Let me gain benefit from
my very hardships, trusting most in God when I need him most.'[18]
Against the heretics the struggle must go on. Christians are called upon
to fight their way through temptations for the prize of the truth. They
must never cease to fight the good fight, nor throw away the achievement of past toil.[19] Anxiety is a good thing if it does not lead to dejec-
tion and despair. We must trust in the goodness of God, knowing that,
if we turn to him, he will not cast us off for ever, since he is with us
always.[20] The trial may be heavy, but no one who avoids the dust
and the blows of battle can win a victor's crown. The mockery of the
devil and the onslaughts of his minions are troublesome but despicable.
They combine wickedness with weakness. We should not cry too loud
when we are hurt. There is only one thing which is worth deep sorrow,

---

[9] *Against Eunomius*, 1.12.
[10] *Homily on the Martyr Mamas* 4. See Vischer, *Basilius der Grosse*, pp. 89f.,
for the contrast with Origen's unrelenting enquiry.
[11] *Ep.* 28.3.   [12] *Ep.* 125.   [13] *M.* 8.   [14] *M.* 12.
[15] *M.* 39.   [16] *M.* 80.   [17] *H.* 9.6.
[18] *Ep.* 123.   [19] *Ep.* 140.1.   [20] *Ep.* 174.

and that is 'the loss of one's own self', which comes from denying God and losing the eternal reward.[21] The endurance of the Christian philosopher is the endurance of the man of faith and is marked by the new virtue of humility.[22]

(ii) *Whose feet will you wash?*

Faith must always be linked to humility. We should not be proud of our good deeds,[23] nor should we choose any but the lowest seat at a meal.[24] Simple clothing shows humility.[25] Within the brotherhood the ideal of humility is shown by a superior as he performs acts of service to lower brethren. The brethren must readily receive such service and not resist. The dangers of pride and the need for humility are recognised in the ordering of communities.[26] Our Lord spoke of the dangers of exalting oneself and the apostle pointed the way of lowliness and humility.[27] The humility and endurance of the monk has many forms, and leads to patience and sweetness. Basil expounds humility with great persuasion, and shows how it should be practised. Humility is the virtue which places us in our right place in the order of being. It places us truly in the presence of God and springs from a sense of his glory. In a sermon on humility, Basil speaks of the moving example of the humility of the Word of God, who became flesh, descending from heavenly glory and abasing himself for our sake. He shows the child in the manger, the young boy in the carpenter's shop, always obedient and subject to his parents. He shows Jesus receiving baptism at the hands of his servant John and giving himself up as an innocent victim to his enemies, receiving injury, outrage, humiliation, and finally a shameful death. We are to imitate this humility of Christ, a humility which his apostles have also followed, and such humility will gain eternal glory. One may gain humility, not by the extravagance of ascetic extremes, but by quietness and moderation in daily life. Humility is bound to a recognition of the grace of God and to humble dependence upon him. It always sees the wonder of God's providence and trusts in that providence.[28] Humility cannot be practised except within a community. How can one follow our Lord's pattern of humility unless one has brethren who have feet to be washed? 'Whose

---

[21] *Ep.* 240.2.

[22] Morison points out that Basil does not describe his monk as a philosopher: *St. Basil and his Rule, A Study in Early Monasticism* (Oxford, 1912), p. 35; but the influence of the idea is clear.

[23] *M.* 57. [24] *L.R.* 21. [25] *L.R.* 22.

[26] *L.R.* 35. [27] *S.R.* 56.

[28] Amand, *L'ascèse monastique de S. Basile*, pp. 312–18.

feet will you wash? For whom will you care? If you live by yourself to whom will you come last?'[29] With humility goes silence.[30] 'For there are a tone of voice, a symmetry of language, an appropriateness of occasion and a special vocabulary which belong to godly men...These can only be learned by one who has unlearned his former habits. Now silence both induces forgetfulness of the past through lack of practice and affords leisure to learn good habits.'[31] Silence brings peace and unity, removing causes of tension. There can be a time for speaking, when the time for silence is past.[32] Yet even theological opinions do not normally provide a ground for breaking silence.[33]

(iii) Free will

Sin does not come from God, but from man's misuse of his free will. Sin is man's work. Basil's system, following Origen, is built upon the fact of free will which enables man to strive towards perfection. Sin may be seen negatively as the absence of good in the universe, positively as a revolt against God, a self-willed disobedience.[34] Greek thought, especially as mediated through Origen, moulds Basil's insistence on free will.[35] In the homily *That God is not the author of evil*, Basil declares, 'The origin and root of sin is what is in our own control and our free will.' In the sixth homily of the *Hexaemeron* he refutes astrology, using the anti-fatalist arguments of Carneades.[36] If man's affairs are governed by fate then there is no such thing as human responsibility; there can be no ground for the processes of law and no one can be blamed for moral faults. Fatalism is absurd. 'Under the reign of necessity and of fatality there is no place for merit, the first condition of all righteous judgement.'[37] Man is free to choose good or evil.

[29] *L.R.* 7.345–8.
[30] See Vischer, *Basilius der Grosse*, pp. 112–15, for a developed account of the following points.
[31] *L.R.* 13.
[32] *Ep.* 223.1.
[33] *Ep.* 9.3.
[34] Amand, *L'ascèse monastique de S. Basile*, pp. 146–51.
[35] Epictetus speaks similarly of self-determination: *Diss.* 2, 2, 3; 4, 1, 56; 4, 1, 62; 4, 1, 68; 4, 1, 100; see M. Spanneut, 'Epiktet', *RAC* **5**, 642–5.
[36] Cf. Sextus Empiricus, *adv. math.* v; Origen, *Philocalia*, 23, 17.
[37] *H.* 6, 7. D. Amand, *Fatalisme et liberté dans l'antiquité grecque* (Louvain, 1945), chapter 8, pp. 383ff.

LOVE

(i) *Wounded with love*

Basil begins the *Morals* with a reference to the first and great commandment to love God with all the heart, and the second to love one's
neighbour as oneself. Only by keeping God's commandments can love
for him be proved. The keeping of the commandments of Christ is
linked with the endurance of his suffering even to death.[1] 'Love to
God cannot be taught.' We were not taught to rejoice in life or to hold
on to life nor did anyone show us how to love our parents. There is
sown in the hearts of men the word which inclines to the love of God
and shows that there is nothing comparable with the beauty and
magnificence of God. The yearning of the soul for God as it cries, 'I
am wounded with love' points to the beauty which cannot be seen,
but is desired with an insatiable desire. The beauty of the morning
star and the brightness of the sun and moon cannot compare with the
glory of God.[2] To be separated from God is worse than all the punishment of hell. We cling to him who is our maker and whose goodness
is evident on every hand. Apart from the beauties of creation, we learn
the divine goodness in the humility and suffering of Christ. It is not
possible to say everything about the love of God but it is important
to remind the soul of it and to stir up a longing for God.[3] The love of
God is the first duty of the Christian life, the perfection of virtue, and
the supreme object of every baptised child of God. As the centre of
all religious and moral activity, it gives to the discipline of the monastery and to the whole life of perfection the one aim of union with God
in love. The soul is moved by love of God to prayer in which it is renewed and strengthened. Prayer gives to the soul a clear notion of
God. God dwells in the soul so that it may become his temple and be
conscious of him at all times, undistracted by worldly cares and
passions. Prayer, constant prayer, is union with God.[4] The love of
wisdom begins with the love of God whose wisdom made all things;
it is this love which grows to perfection.[5]

---

[1] *M.* 3. See, for example, Vischer, *Basilius der Grosse*, pp. 38f., on 'Die
Motive des asketischen Lebens'.
[2] *L.R.* 2.336–7. See Amand, *L'ascèse monastique*, pp. 295ff.
[3] *L.R.* 2.338–40.
[4] Amand, *L'ascèse monastique*, p. 91.
[5] T. Spidlik, *La sophiologie de S. Basile* (Rome, 1961) pp. 24f.

(ii) *The sure sign of Christ's disciples*

A Christian must be pure from hatred and must love his enemies. He must love his friends and be prepared to lay down his life for them. 'A sure sign of Christ's disciples is their mutual love in him.' One does not have the love of Christ towards a neighbour if one harms him in any way even though the harmful act may be permitted by scripture. The Christian is a man of peace and tries to pacify any man who may be vexed with him; but in love the Christian may grieve another for the other's good.[6] Hospitality should be practised among Christians in a quiet and frugal way.[7] One will not go to law even for the clothes on one's back, but one will strive to bring others to the peace which is in Christ.[8] Basil puts persistent stress on the need for neighbourly love. All begins with love of God. This is the first and greatest commandment, but a pure love of the glory of God is not yet fully Christian. The lover of God must also be a lover of his brother. This theme runs through all Basil's letters and is the reason why they were written.[9] He is delighted to know that Maximus the philosopher had discovered the highest good which is love to God and to one's neighbour.[10] The monk who treads the way to the mansions of the Lord has a love to the Lord God, which takes up all his heart, strength and mind;[11] and he must love when he is hated.[12] Friends know that to lose is to win, for love bears all things and never fails. 'He who subjects himself to his neighbour in love can never be humiliated.'[13]

The love of one's neighbour shows too in the requirements of social ethics. Marriage brings duties for husband and wife, for children and parents. Society brings obligations to all its members, especially to those who rule. The animals display a pattern of ordered community. The church is charged to follow the same way of peace. The clergy and the bishops have their obligation to one another. The care of poor and sick springs from personal interest; for there is a natural as well as a Christian law which requires this duty. It is wrong to give money only in old age or after death. Generosity should have personal discernment, and charity should have particular objects.[14] Man's response to God's

---

[6] *M*.5.   [7] *M*.38.   [8] *M*.49–50.

[9] 'God gave to those, who could not see one another in person, the great comfort of communication by letters', *Ep.* 220. See Vischer, *Basilius der Grosse*, p. 61, 'Ein grosser Teil der Korrespondenz des B. dient einzig dieser Absicht: Gemeinschaft herzustellen'.

[10] *Ep.* 9.1.   [11] *Ep.* 23.   [12] *Ep.* 43.   [13] *Ep.* 65.

[14] See J. Rivière, *S. Basile* (Paris, 1925), pp. 208–87. Also the comprehensive treatment of S. Giet, *Les idées sociales de S. Basile* (Paris, 1941), covers many aspects of the subject.

infinite love and mercy is in both commandments, for love of God and neighbour go together. What is done for the least of his brothers is done for the Lord.[15] Love for God and neighbour are both implanted in every human heart. At the moment of its creation the soul receives from God seeds of reason which prompt this love. Weakened by sin, love needs to be restored by grace which can lead it on to perfect communion with God.[16]

(iii) *One body having Christ as head*

The monks are members of Christ, and their community is his body. Souls are united and find concord and peace in him. The Holy Spirit distributes gifts in abundance and thereby maintains the life of the community. Every spiritual gift goes with a charge or an office which the gift should fulfil. The charge of the superior implies a special gift for commanding and ordering. Love of the brethren brings fulfilment of all the duties of the community. It is shown by good example, by prayer, by the work of our hands, by teaching or by hospitality. It cares for the sick, for travellers, for orphans. All this is a way of fulfilling the command to love the brethren. Common life is the core of Basil's message. Men must live together in no superficial way, but by sharing in a common love. Only in the community can one avoid the dangers of the solitary life and practise brotherly love and true humility. Only here can one grow towards fullness of love and life in the Holy Spirit. The health of the monastery depends upon the proper use and co-ordination of the many gifts which the Spirit has given. The second commandment, like all God's law, simply cultivates and grows the innate abilities which are planted in us like seeds. 'Who does not know that man is a tame and sociable animal, and not a solitary and fierce one? For nothing is so characteristic of our nature as to associate with one another, to need one another, and to love our kind.'[17] The implanted seed of love must grow as must the love of God which is implanted by the Holy Spirit. The intention of man is

---

[15] *L.R.* 3.
[16] See G. M. Cossu, 'Il motivo formale della carita in S. Basilio Magno', *Bollettino della Badia Greca di Grottaferrata* (1960), pp. 3–30, and 'L'amore naturale verso Dio e verso il prossimo', *ibid.* pp. 87–107.
[17] *L.R.* 3. Basil's reasons (*L.R.* 7) for the superiority of the cenobite over the anchorite are summarised by W. K. L. Clarke, *St. Basil the Great* (Cambridge, 1913), pp. 85f.: we are not self-sufficient in provision of bodily needs, solitude goes against the law of love, we need someone to correct our faults, we have duties to others, we are members one of another, we have different gifts, we are in danger of thinking that we have arrived at perfection.

there, but the achievement of such love is only possible through rigorous discipline and painful obedience. The unity of Christians in the body of Christ is a unity of love. Christ loves and gives, Christ receives and is loved. The spiritual union of Christ with believers is the basis of the love of the brethren.[18]

The community must still have its rules. To avoid disorder there must be a way to bring disputes before the brotherhood or the superior.[19] The idle man must either be brought to diligence or treated as a persistent sinner.[20] Through the common life the individual is able to recognise and overcome his sins.[21] Basil reformed but did not abandon the system of Pachomius. Basil's scheme is more humane and more intimate than the earlier form of community life. He also sees an important place for the community of monks in the life of the whole church, which should be ordered like a community.[22]

Basil declares his work to be that of restoring the laws of ancient love and the peace of the fathers.[23] The 'brotherhood' is another name for the church.[24] He speaks of 'the good old times when God's churches flourished, rooted in faith, united in love, all the members being in harmony, as though in one body'. Then Christians were truly at peace and the loss of this peace is the saddest feature of his day.[25] The first Christians shared a common life, common thoughts and sentiments and ate from one table. They showed brotherhood without division and love without pretence. They were one body in outward solidarity, and in inward unity. For Basil the monastic community is a renewing of the primitive church of Jerusalem. The need is sadly urgent. Love is cold, 'brotherly agreement is destroyed, the very name of unity is ignored, brotherly advice is heard no more, nowhere is there Christian pity, nowhere falls the tear of sympathy.' Christians have no concern for one another and are worse than animals who at least herd together. 'But our most savage warfare is with our own people.'[26]

The whole of Basil's moral teaching is drawn together by his account of love. 'For Basil charity is the first of the virtues, and the monastic life has only one end – charity and union with God.'[27] The first and

---

[18] See D. M. Nothomb, 'Charité et unité', *POC*, 4 (1954), 321.
[19] *L.R.* 49.   [20] *S.R.* 61.
[21] *L.R.* 26, 28, 29: see Vischer, *Basilius der Grosse*, p. 44.
[22] Church and community react on one another: Vischer, *op. cit.*, p. 49, 'Er gestaltet die Kirche nach dem Bild des Klosters.'
[23] *Ep.* 70.
[24] *Ep.* 133; *Ep.* 255; *Ep.* 266.1. See Vischer, *op. cit.*, p. 54.
[25] In her persecutions, the church found true peace and real unity, *Ep.* 164.1. See Vischer, *op. cit.*, p. 53.
[26] *S.* 30.78.
[27] Amand, *L'ascèse monastique*, p. 295.

great commandment is to love God, the second is to love one's neighbour,[28] and a proof of our love for God and for his Son is that we keep
his commandments. These we keep even to death, bearing all suffering
and tribulation for love of him.[29] The love of God moves us to fulfil
his commandments. Basil explains how this works, the love of God is
implanted in our souls and it responds to the need of our hearts. The
first motive which inspires us to love God is God's unspeakable beauty.
The second reason is that we are rational creatures and are therefore
obliged to love a creator who is infinitely good. The third reason is the
consideration of the many blessings we have received from God. God
has ordered the whole creation for the benefit of men. He made man
in his image and when man fell he did not desert the human race.
Through the old and new dispensations he has loved man and wrought
man's redemption, through Jesus. We are moved also by the fear that
we might neglect the love of God and of Christ, and so give to the
devil the opportunity to triumph on our account at the terrible day of
judgement.[30]

Basil's ethics are of permanent value. As an account of Christian living
they possess clarity and imagination. He is sensitive to later Platonism;
but the most ardent index-maker could hardly deny his main impulse
to the New Testament. As the first expositor of the ascetic way he
illuminates the subsequent course of Christianity. His account of
justice shows tendencies to legalism. He is fond of rules and prolific
in producing them. His rigorism runs to literalism. His greater
righteousness involves keeping rules more carefully; yet there is a strong
strain of individualism and an extended plea for freedom as essential
to morals. He is an advocate of natural law and sees beauty in natural
order; yet he pleads for violence and excess in storming the kingdom.
His chief danger would seem to lie in the ascetic extremes. Clement's
right use of the world and care of the body for the good of the soul
have both disappeared. The body is whipped or starved, not tended.
The path of renunciation is so demanding that it can easily become
an end in itself. Basil is aware of this danger and declares no other
end than the glory of God. The opposite tendency to mystic contemplation is not far away. Origen had shown the way and Basil is ever
ready to follow. Yet the sheer mass of practical prescription and the
prevalence of the theme of following maintain the sovereignty of the
Lord over his disciple. Faith is tied to creed, firm and exact. Yet Basil
has even more to say on the faith that trusts through adversity 'trusting most in God when we need him most'. Freedom never becomes

---

[28] *S.R.* 163.   [29] *M.* 3. 1–2.
[30] Amand, *L'ascèse monastique*, pp. 296–303.

licence. Love is certainly threatened by fraternal duties but these also form a check against vague sentiment. The notion of reward supplants sovereign grace. He who gives to the afflicted gives to the Lord and will be rewarded by the Lord. The common life springs from enthusiasm.

In each section there is tension and sensitivity. The great retreat lies in the attitude to the physical world. Basil could enjoy natural beauty when its quietness soothed him; but he could not see how the way of righteousness might be trodden by body and soul together or how the path of discipleship could lead into the world of people and daily work. Work was a curse on man consequent to the Fall.

Basil poses two insoluble problems. First, there is the question of a double standard for monk and layman. In fact there was a single standard but only the monk could achieve it. Basil meant to unify Christian morality so this point has to be handled very carefully. The asceticism of the monk was simply the continuation of the life of every believer. 'The monk is the authentic and courageous Christian who strains to live out his Christianity to the full, and to practise with greater fidelity all the virtues of the Gospel.' Basil did not want to put a barrier between the simple believer and the monk nor to divide Christian ethics into two parts. 'There is only one morality, that of the Gospel. But only the monastic life in community reaches the perfection, ...of the ideal of the Gospel.'[31] At the same time Basil expected an élite, a Christian nobility,[32] and he could not tolerate mediocrity. As an enthusiast, he wanted the fresh movement of the Spirit to stir a sluggish church. When, by placing asceticism in the centre of the church, he made a double standard inevitable, it was the opposite of his desire. History does not give men unlimited choice. Clement had to choose between a closed fatalist amoral élitism and an open, ethical élitist optimism of grace. Basil had to choose between an élite estranged from the church and an élite within one community and one gospel.

The evidence remains ambiguous. Christianity cannot approve a plurality of moral standards. Yet from early days there was a distinction between a path of perfection and a lower way. This distinction between 'precepts' and 'counsels' existed in the second century and the *Didache* described two ways.[33] Yet the opposition to Gnosticism maintained the perfection of baptismal faith and denied the predetermined categories of spiritual and carnal Christians; the passing of the Gnostic threat made it easier for later writers like Ambrose to distinguish clearly precepts and counsels. 'Every duty is either ordinary or perfect.'[34] Porphyry had used the customary distinction between the

---

[31] *Ibid.* pp. 12f.
[32] Cf. Jerome's commendation of a 'holy arrogance'. *Ep.* 22.16.
[33] *Didache* 6.   [34] *De officiis* 1.36.

philosopher and the common herd. Things are permitted to the many
which are not permitted to the best of men. The philosopher follows
divine laws.[35] Whenever Christianity drew on the philosophic ideal,
as it did in Clement and Basil, some trace of this distinction lingered
on.[36]

Basil remains unclear at this point because as an enthusiast he put
no limits on the spread of perfection. He wanted the whole church to
follow the way the monks had shown.[37] The transformed life of those
few who follow the one way of Christ is the best way to preach and
to change the world.[38] He never saw the monks as an enclosed order;
they were the beginning of a reformation for the whole church.[39] So
Basil deliberately tried to discard the two ways or double standard of
Christian living. Too many Christians chose the easy way, selecting
the convenient commandments. Basil demanded total renunciation
and total obedience for all who would enter the kingdom. Did this
mean that all should be monks? No, but it would be very difficult for
those who live in the wrong environment. Speaking carefully he says
it will be most difficult, not to say wholly impossible.[40] When less careful he claims that pleasing God[41] is impossible for one surrounded by
the distractions of the world. There is some distinction between the
three great demands.[42] Obedience and poverty are required of all.
Poverty means the dedication of one's wealth, not necessarily ceasing

[35] *On Abstinence* 4.18.
[36] That it was there is indicated by evidence brought against it in
discussions of the early church. Basil could not, as a bishop, restrict
perfection to monks, in the opinion of K. Holl (*Ueber das griechische
Mönchtum*, p. 278). But Vischer comments, 'Dabei übersieht Holl jedoch,
dass Basilius der Meinung ist, die Kirche müsse nach dem Vorbild
des Mönchtums gebildet werden' (*Basilius der Grosse*, p. 50).
Reluctance to admit non-Christian elements in monasticism is typified
by the comment of R. N. Flew, *The Idea of Perfection in Christian
Theology* (Oxford, 1934), p. 159, 'The soil for the plant of monachism
may have been prepared by many movements of the mind ... but the
seed itself is easily recognizable, and it is sown by those at work within
the garden of the Church.' The same writer however, does not hesitate
to say of Basil, 'It is clear that we have to do with the Stoic ideal of
apatheia': p. 176.
[37] Vischer, *Basilius der Grosse*, p. 167.
[38] J. Gribomont, 'Le renoncement au monde', *Irénikon* (1958), p. 475.
[39] J. Gribomont, 'Les règles morales', p. 417. Gribomont goes on to
describe the historical setting of Basil's rules in the conflict between
Eustathian enthusiasm and the rest of the church, p. 423.
[40] *L.R.* 6.
[41] *S.R.* 263.
[42] See J. Gribomont, 'Le monachisme au IVe siècle en Asie-Mineure: de
Gangres au Messalianisme', *Studia Patristica* II (Berlin, 1957), 400–15.

to be its legal owner. Chastity in the sense of celibacy or married
abstinence is put forward as good but not obligatory; but Basil continues to regard his disciples as a celibate élite.[43] The general conclusion remains that, in opposition to sectarian asceticism, Basil
directed his teaching to the church as a whole; but on this point it is
better to understand his inconsistency than to fight for his consistency.

However much we may admire the spirit and heroism of Basil and
the early ascetics, we should remember that their contribution was
neither distinctively Christian nor ultimately harmless. Asceticism was
everywhere. The community at Qumran was strangely similar to that
of Basil in spite of their separation in time and space. The harmful
aspects of asceticism are important because 'much in the traditional
ascetic disciplines is morally objectionable at just the points where it
is not true to Christian theism'.[44]

This points to a second insoluble problem: the right assessment of
asceticism in general and monasticism in particular. It is wise to see
Basil in his historical setting where he stands as a moderator, and
reformer. There is an ascetic tendency in most virtue. 'What has the
man of virtue learnt?' asks a modern philosopher; 'He has learnt to
conquer the obscuring effects of passion upon his judgements of good
and evil.'[45] It is unlikely that we might achieve an assessment of final
praise or blame in the matter. There can be general agreement that
Basil, by largeness of mind and sensitivity of spirit, gave to the ascetic
movement a tendency which lifted and held it higher.[46] On the
negative side, critics of the monastic movement will find many
unhappy elements in its varied development. One unbalanced verdict
ran: 'A hideous, sordid, and emaciated maniac, without knowledge,
without patriotism, without natural affection, passing his life in a
long routine of useless and atrocious self-torture, and quailing before
the ghastly phantoms of his delirious brain, had become the ideal of the
nations which had known the writings of Plato and Cicero and the
lives of Socrates and Cato.'[47] Historians are never kind to enthusiasts
and the monks have been blamed for disrupting the unity of the
church and for ensuring the later triumph of Islam.[48] Christian ascetic-

[43] Ibid. p. 413.
[44] D. Cupitt, Crises of Moral Authority (London, 1972), p. 47.
[45] G. H. von Wright, The Varieties of Goodness (London, 1963), p. 147.
[46] Amand, Fatalisme et liberté, p. 349, 'le grand réformateur du
    cénobitisme oriental'. W. K. L. Clarke summarises Basil's work as the
    organisation of asceticism, the moderation of austerities, the introduction
    of the common life and the bringing of monasticism into the service of
    the church. See St. Basil the Great (Cambridge, 1913), p. 115.
[47] W. E. H. Lecky, History of European Morals (1884), 2, 107.
[48] N. Zernov, Eastern Christendom (London, 1961), p. 80.

ism has long been an object of 'widespread and constant moral repugnance'.[49]

But an equally forceful statement may be found on the opposing side. Basil shaped Christian asceticism which in turn shaped later Christian morals. The originality of the life of faith was 'its reverence for the lowly, for sorrow, suffering, and death, together with its triumphant victory over these contradictions of human life'.[50] In his moral theology of the cross,[51] we may find 'the root of the most profound factor contributed by Christianity to the development of the moral sense, and contributed with perfect strength and delicacy'.[52] Later centuries were to go wrong as this insight changed into 'an aesthetic of spiritual agony and raptures over suffering'. There had always been some tendency of this kind. 'Yet, however strongly we feel about the unsightly phlegm of this corruption, and however indignantly we condemn it, we should never forget that it represented the shadow thrown by the most profound and at the same time the most heroic mood of the human soul in its spiritual exaltation; it is, in fact, religion itself, fully ripe.'[53] This is too much. Ripeness and consistency were not to be found in Basil. But he saw clearly where it should all lead: through the desert, to God. For Basil as for the New Testament, ethics point beyond themselves to religion and finally to God, 'das Wunder in den Wüsten, das Ausgewanderten geschieht'.[54]

[49] D. Cupitt, *Crisis of Modern Authority*, p. 30.
[50] A. von Harnack, *Mission and Expansion*, I, 217.
[51] The centrality of the cross comes out most clearly in the final sections of *Morals*. The mark of a Christian is to be cleansed in the blood of Christ, to eat in memory of him who died, to live for him who died for them and to love as Christ loved: *Morals*, 72.22.
[52] Harnack, *Mission and Expansion*, p. 218.
[53] *Ibid.*
[54] R. M. Rilke, *Stundenbuch*.

4

JOHN CHRYSOSTOM

John was born at Antioch towards the middle of the fourth century. His father was a military commander; his mother, left a widow at the age of twenty, was a devout Christian who gave all her attention to her son. John showed exceptional intelligence and studied to be a lawyer under the great teacher Libanius, who when dying named as his successor, 'John, if the Christians had not stolen him from us'.[1] John's eloquence was extraordinary; but he gradually turned from his first goal towards a life of renunciation. He could not bring himself to take a fee for arguing a false case. He was baptised and then ordained as a reader. His desire to become a monk was resisted by his mother, who pleaded that he should not make her a widow a second time. So he stayed at home; but he lived an ascetic life. He ate little, slept on bare ground, prayed, and lived in almost unbroken silence. Later, he went into the mountains south of Antioch, where he followed the guidance of an old Syrian monk. Finally he lived in isolation in a mountain cave where he slept and ate so little, that at the end of two years his health was broken and he had to return home to Antioch. These years left their mark on his body and mind. Back at Antioch he was ordained as deacon in 381, and as priest five years later. He preached his first sermon in the presence of the bishop and the great congregation hailed him as the preacher of the day. He preached at least twice a week, on Saturday and Sunday, and sometimes even five days in succession. The congregation were enthusiastic and noisy, applauding when they felt like it. The preacher indicated that moral obedience was the better way to show their approval. He also warned them not to bring their money to church because the packed congregation, hanging on the words of the preacher, invited the attention of pick-pockets. By the sixth century he was referred to as 'Chrysostomos' or 'goldenmouth' and the name has stuck. In 397 the bishop of Constantinople died. In front of many eager candidates, the emperor chose the great preacher, John of Antioch. With some difficulty he was brought to Constantinople and was consecrated as bishop in February

1 Sozomen, *H.E.* 8.2.

398. Almost from the beginning, John struck trouble with his clergy. The luxury of the great capital had entered the life of the church. Banquets which had been given by his predecessors were stopped. He lived alone in simple poverty. He attacked some priests who had taken a religious sister to care for them in their house, and dismissed other priests on grounds of murder or adultery. He fought against the continuing menace of the Arian heresy. Yet he was loved by the people, and the emperor and the young empress were his friends. He established missions to remote countries and cared for foreigners in Constantinople. One of his sermons was preached when Eutropius, who had held great political power, was dislodged from office. Eutropius took refuge in the church, the sanctuary of which he would have denied to others. John preached on 'Vanity of vanities, all is vanity', and went to the emperor to obtain an order of banishment for Eutropius, thereby saving his life for a time. But the seeds of trouble were already sown. Disorder broke out in the church at Ephesus, and John left Constantinople for about five months. In his absence, forces had formed against him. His deputy had been Severian of Gabala, who attracted the favour of the court and encouraged the luxury of the wealthy. John told Severian and his colleague Antiochus that they had been play acting and were flatterers and parasites. He preached a vigorous sermon about the table of Jezebel. Priests must choose whether they sat at the table of Jezebel or the table of the Lord. Everyone identified Jezebel with the empress Eudoxia and John was eventually forced to leave the city. There was an earthquake on the evening of his departure, and the people loudly demanded his return. The sentence of banishment was revoked, and John returned to the city in triumph, being welcomed with torches and shouts of joy. The peace did not last. John could not reconcile himself to the ambitions of the empress. Again he preached a dangerous sermon. This time the subject was 'Herodias' who demanded the head of John on a charger. Once again John was banished. This time he refused to go unless expelled by force. Soldiers dragged him from the cathedral on Easter Eve, scattering and wounding those who were waiting for baptism. Another two months dragged on before the emperor finally signed a decree for John's banishment. In the end John received the sentence calmly, and, to avoid a disturbance, left quietly. Shortly after he had sailed, his church went up in flames and trouble broke out in the city. This time John did not come back. His exile was to a lonely village in the mountains on the border of Armenia. After recuperating in Nicaea, he left to cross Asia Minor in mid-summer. He travelled through the poorest villages. He lived on black bread and foul water. In spite of illness he was forced on and given no chance of recovery. Yet when

he finally reached the place of his exile, he found friendship and rest. He had time to write, and many asked his help. His letters show the extent of his influence. The climate was unpleasant with extremes of heat and cold. Yet his enemies were still not satisfied. They chose another place of exile further east, on the bleak shores of the Black Sea. He was to travel there by foot. The towns which might have given him rest and refreshment were to be avoided. His guards were instructed to give him no chance to recover his strength. He died on the journey in the year 407, his last words being the theme of his life, 'Glory to God for all things.'[2]

John sees ethics as a pastor. In his account of righteousness he stresses the need for changed lives and attention to conscience, the comfort of man's immunity from external harm and the high place of daily work in the purposes of God. Discipleship is personal nearness to Christ and untiring effort to win life's race. Yet personal improvement is secondary to the taking of the gospel to all nations. Faith is an adventure which saves men from the twin destroyers of despair and pride; it ensure's man's freedom and self-determination. Love is the fervent life of Christian community which can transform the worst of men. None of the early fathers speaks with more directness to distant times. As a pastor, John was close to people and his rhetoric still conveys a deep sensitivity to human problems. 'If only we were the kind of Christians we should be, there would be no pagans left.'[3] Instead there is little to distinguish a Christian from a pagan life and no one will be interested in an ineffective faith. On the other hand, the raising of the dead does not convert as does the example of a virtuous life.[4] John's zeal for the gospel produces his ethical concern. True prayer is purity of soul and good works.[5] Among the gospels he turns most to Matthew, and in Paul he finds morality on every side. His sermons are still readable today, 'because they are so ethical, so simple and so clear-headed'.[6] While Clement spoke mainly to an inner circle and Basil to a separated community, John speaks to the whole of his society. He is not a metaphysician. As a moralist he is at once original and profound.[7]

---

[2] Chief sources for the life of John are: *Dialogue of Palladius, Histories* of Sozomen, Socrates and Theodoret, together with John's own writings.

[3] *Hom. on 1 Tim.* 10.3.

[4] *Hom. on Matt.* 43.5.

[5] *Hom. on Psalm 4*, cf. A. Puech, *S. Jean Chrysostome et les moeurs de son temps* (Paris, 1891), p. 217.

[6] H. von Campenhausen, *The Fathers of the Greek Church* (London. 1963), p. 157.

[7] Puech, *S. Jean Chrysostome et les moeurs de son temps*, p. 325.

RIGHTEOUSNESS

(i) *God must be just*

John preached in Constantinople as a moral reformer. Reform was necessary in a church where three deacons stole the archbishop's cloak. The sisters who kept house for many of the clergy were a cause of scandal. The extravagant luxury of many clergy was inconsistent with the gospel. It was claimed that John did not understand the time in which he lived. His biographer replied, 'Then neither did Moses, Elijah, Micah, Daniel, John the Baptist, Isaiah, Peter and Paul understand their times...Guided by the Spirit, Paul distributed praise and blame.'[1] A deacon told John that he could not rule over his flock unless he used a whip on them.[2] He attacked extravagance, telling the rich that private property was a result of the fall and that they would be better Christians if they looked after the beggars in the streets instead of furnishing their toilets in gold. He shocked married men by claiming that wives had as much right to expect fidelity from husbands as husbands had to expect it from wives. John also cleaned up the church at Ephesus where the bishop had misappropriated funds and sold episcopal consecration to the highest bidder.[3]

God, said John, is a righteous judge who scrutinises sins and good deeds. His justice balances man's sin; it is foolish to choose sin which will earn unending punishment at his hand.[4] The torments of hell cannot be fully imagined; men covered by shame, with heads bowed, are dragged to the fire, tortured on the way by evil powers and knowing that those who have by good deeds earned eternal life are being presented before the royal throne of God.[5] The last judgement will reveal God's justice to all.[6] Justice is entailed by the existence of God. If there is a God he must be just, otherwise he would not be God. God gives to each the due reward of his actions. God would not allow the wicked to flourish unless there were another life in which the balance would be redressed and justice ensured.[7]

The judgement of God stands over all. A priest must give account of the souls in his care. In prescribing penance he must be careful to

---

[1] Palladius, *Dialogue* 18 (65–7). For a careful account of the variety of vices which confronted John see J. M. Vance, *Beiträge zur Byzantinischen Kulturgeschichte am Ausgang des IV Jahrhunderts aus den Schriften des Joh. Chrysostomos* (Jena, 1907), especially chapter 9.

[2] Socrates, 6.4.   [3] Palladius, 14 (48–50).

[4] *To Theodore* 1.10.   [5] *Ibid.* 1.12.

[6] *That demons do not govern the world*, 1.8.

[7] *On the statues*, 1.18; *Hom. Matt.* 13.6; *Exp. on Psalm* 47.3.

avoid further damage. If he punish a sinner harshly, the priest will
share responsibility for that man's future sins.[8] When sins stand up
against us, the name of God is our helper, so we pray not to be led
into temptation but to be delivered from evil.[9] When we enter the
arena to fight against evil, the president of the contest does not ask
whether there is any charge against us, but he declares that although
we have committed all kinds of crimes, he is here and now prepared to
receive us. God is both just and justifier. In an earthly contest the
president is impartial; but he who presides at our contest for holiness
fights beside us against the devil.[10] God never turns from a sincere
penitent and does everything to restore the vilest sinner. He does not
require complete repentance, but when he sees the first sign he comes
to meet man with his love. When Ahab repented and put on sack-
cloth, he received the mercy of God, and was spared the evil which
he deserved.[11]

(ii) *Natural law, conscience and order*

In John we meet a developed Christian doctrine of natural law. There
is a divine law which rules over all things.[12] Man has within him a
natural law and conscience. 'When God created man at the beginning
he gave to him the natural law. What is this natural law? It shapes
and corrects conscience within us, and it provides knowledge which is
capable by itself of distinguishing what is good from what is not
good.'[13] Conscience teaches man in advance what is wrong. This innate knowledge of virtue was shown in Adam, who, when he had
sinned, hid himself in shame. When God speaks another commandment which is not known through conscience, he gives a reason for it.
The commandment concerning the Sabbath needs to be supported by
the reason that God himself did not work on the Sabbath.

As law-giver God has established the order of the universe. In
winter he makes the nights long, that seeds may grow in the cool-
ness; then he gives longer days that plants might grow in size, and to
ripen the fruit the days are longest. God arranges the seasons in a
harmonious way. Sudden changes to opposite extremes can cause great
harm, so God brings spring between winter and summer, then autumn
between summer and winter. Everything is planned in an orderly
manner. Eyelashes are arranged to keep dust away from eyes and to
prevent eyelids from being disturbed. Eyebrows stop perspiration from
running into eyes; yet, serving as eaves, they are not so big as to obscure

---

[8] *On priesthood*, 3.18.   [9] *On the statues*, 17.15.
[10] *Instructions to Catechumens*, 2.3.   [11] *To Theodore*, 1.6.
[12] *On priesthood*, 3.9.   [13] *On the statues*, 12.9.

the vision of eyes. God who ordered the visible universe has ordered the moral structure by which man is judged. Each sin brings its own penalty, and God has ordered penalties in various degrees.[14]

Order points to moderation. Timothy is encouraged to use a *little* wine. Timothy didn't need to be told this, but we do, so that our drinking should have measure and limit. Immoderate use of wine produces diseases of body and soul. The health of the body requires moderation. Wine was given to make the heart of man glad, but its immoderate use brings sadness.[15] Disorder holds great perils. Antioch had been a dignified, well ordered and quiet city, when sudden riots broke out. The disorderly madness of those who rioted must be restrained, for it points to a deeper disorder which has already shown itself in the church. There have been those who blasphemed and insulted God. Now it is possible to see what mad disorder can do, and the church must be ordered in a fitting way.[16]

Slavery is hard to reconcile with God's order. It is the result of man's sin, of his insatiable greed and envy. There is no need for a lot of slaves; at least some should be freed and all should be treated with humanity and kindness.[17]

(iii) *No one can harm man*

Man knows good and bad through his conscience and the natural law which God has implanted in him. He learns true happiness when he sees earthly life as a passing show. Many things are falsely claimed to be good or bad. John describes virtues and vices in detail. There are natural passions and artificial passions. There are passions which trouble particular ages of man's life. Both wealth and poverty can bring vice. Kindness and indulgence must be distinguished, as must pride and resolution, or humility and degradation. The body plays an important part. If it is soft, it softens the soul. Idleness is a great danger, and shamefulness is an outrage to God. Women who decorate themselves improperly are acting wickedly. Anger is a common fault. Man should never feel vindictive. Those who insult others are weak and sick. Envy has no place, nor has greed which looks to empty riches for satisfaction which it never finds. Wealth must be shared. The Christian shares not only his material wealth, but also spiritual goods. He does not despair in time of distress, but fixes his hope on the love of God. Duties have to be learnt in the school of virtue. In this school one makes progress and learns from virtue herself. Little faults bring

[14] *On the statues*, 10, 11, 12.   [15] *On the statues*, 1.11.
[16] *On the statues*, 2.2 and 2.11.
[17] *Hom on 1 Cor.* 40.5 and *Hom. on Eph.* 15.3f.

great ones in their train, and everything that leads towards sin must be avoided. Instead the Christian must visit the afflicted and will even find visits to the cemetery a moral benefit. Duties to one's neighbour include caring for the poor. Duties to God include fasting and persistent prayer. Particular people have special duties. The monk follows his ascetic vocation. Those who are married have duties of which he does not know. Parents have a duty towards their children, and citizens have a duty to their country. Masters have a duty to their slaves, and men are bound together within a framework of obligation.[18]

The treatise which maintains *That no one can harm the man who does not injure himself* depends closely on an argument of Plato in *Republic X*, that the soul, like everything else, can only be destroyed by what is evil for it. This argument will seem strange, says John, to those who see nothing wrong with man's present disorder. As iron is subject to rust and wool to moths, and flocks of sheep to wolves, so there is one thing that destroys man's virtue and harms his nature. That one thing is not poverty or sickness, but sin. You may take from a man his wealth, freedom, and native land; but since these do not constitute *the virtue of man* he is not thereby harmed. He alone can harm himself as he harms his moral state, the condition of his soul. For example, those who were thrown into the fiery furnace were unharmed because they did not desert their loyalty to God. Elsewhere John writes to Olympias, telling her not to be distressed or dejected by misfortune:

> Therefore do not be discouraged. For there is only one thing, Olympias, which needs to be feared, only one real test, and that is sin; and I have not stopped continually repeating this point; but everything else is fiction, whether you speak of plots, hates, deserts, slanders, insults, accusations, confiscation, exile, sharpened swords, the danger of the deep sea, the whole world at war. For, whatever these things be, they do not last but perish, and happen in a mortal body without harming the watchful soul in any way at all.[19]

This writing combines Stoic and Platonic themes. Plato insists in the *Apology*[20] that the good man cannot be harmed, and in the *Gorgias*[21] that it is better to suffer than to inflict injustice. *Republic* x[22] contains the essence of the argument. The invulnerability and incorruption of the good man is expounded by Chrysippus.[23] This immunity brings

---

[18] See P. E. Legrand, *S. Jean Chrysostome* (Paris, 1924), parts 2 and 3.
[19] *To Olympias* 1.1 (7.1).
[20] *Apology* 41.   [21] *Gorgias* 469.   [22] *Republic* 608f.
[23] *SVF* (1903), 3, 567, p. 150 and 3, 578, p. 152.

freedom.[24] Strangely, John's work makes no mention of faith in God or love for him. The name of Jesus occurs once. There is no recasting of Stoic-Platonic ideas in a Christian mould.[25] In this late work John seems to return to the studies and tastes of his youth.[26]

(iv) *Don't be ashamed of work*

John defends the importance and dignity of work; man belongs to the material world in which he has been placed, or rather this world, the whole creation, belongs to man, and is given for his nourishment and service. Man shares the destiny of the world; made in the image of God, he has dominion over all other works of God; even after the fall, his dominion and rule continue. There were those who denied the dignity and importance of work. John insisted on the nobility of working with one's hands, after the example of Christ and his disciples, and of Paul. Even God himself has given an example of work, for God created the world and made it, and the work of providence shows that he is active in the world where we too must work. In the garden of paradise man worked as a privilege, without pain and suffering, as a help to his moral life. After the fall, pain was linked with work. This pain was to train, teach and heal. Work and burden or suffering (*ponos*) are different things, but since the fall of man they have been tied together. At present man is called to the duty of work. The apostle Paul has given this instruction. Only by work have we an opportunity of showing our love for others.[27] Work is a law of nature, and the will of our creator. It preserves us from the dangers of idleness. It is shown in the activity of the animals who are lower than man. After work comes rest, and only by work can man gain the rest he needs. Arts are arranged in a variety of forms. They are concerned with the exercise of the mind, and with the transformation of the world. Man works in the presence of God. His temporal occupation must never draw him from thoughts of God; but his spiritual activity and detachment can

---

[24] Epictetus, *Diss.*, 1, 1, 21–5.
[25] See E. Amand de Mendieta, 'L'amplification d'un thème socratique et stoïcien', *Byzantion* (1966), pp. 353–81. Amand is critical of Puech's general position that John is, of all the fathers of the fourth century, 'le plus détaché de l'hellénisme', but Puech has distinguished this general assessment from his account of this particular work. On John's extensive use of Greek literary forms and culture see A. Naegele, 'Joh. Chrysostomos und sein Verhältnis zum Hellenismus', *Byzantinische Zeitschrift* (1904). pp. 73–113, especially p. 100, and H. M. Hubbell, 'Chrysostom and Rhetoric', *Classical Philology* (1924), pp. 261–76.
[26] A. Puech, *Histoire de la littérature grecque chrétienne*, 3 (Paris, 1930), 521.
[27] *Salute Priscilla and Aquila* (Rom. 16:3), 1.5.

make his work holy. God joins with man in man's work, for except the Lord build the house, they labour in vain that build it.

So John gives the first developed Christian theology of work. He points to the image of God which man bears and the work which man shares with God in the world. He shows that the burden of suffering, which is now joined to work, has redemptive qualities.[28]

DISCIPLESHIP

(i) *To imitate our master, to be his true disciple, we must follow him*

Nothing is more important than fellowship with Christ. To be estranged from him would be a more terrible fate than all imaginable punishments.[1] A thousand hells could not be so dreadful as to hear the words of Christ, 'I do not know you.' It would be better to be flattened by a thousand thunderbolts than to see his meek face turn from us and his quiet eye unable to look on us.[2] A direct relationship to Christ is presupposed in all that John says. In a letter to Theodore, a lapsed monk, he insists that the service of Christ pulls a man out of life's stormy billows and establishes him on firm ground. For, in contrast to the confusion of his previous life, he now has only one care – 'How ought he to please God?' As he must stand before the judgement seat of Christ, so he follows now this one pursuit. In following this one pursuit he is like an athlete, who, once he has withdrawn from a contest, cannot be permitted to re-enter.[3] He turns from this world's glory to the true glory of God.[4] For vain glory will quickly enslave him[5] and alienate him from his brothers.[6]

When God made man in his own image, he made him as a ruler because 'the image of government is meant, and as there is no one in heaven superior to God, so let there be no one on earth superior to

---

[28] See L. Daloz, *Le travail selon S. Jean Chrysostome* (Paris, 1959), for a lucid and comprehensive treatment.

[1] *On Compunction to Demetrius*, 1.9.

[2] *Hom. on Matt.* 23.8.

[3] *To Theodore*, 2.5.

[4] A. M. Malingrey, *Lettres à Olympias, SC* (1947), p. 13, 'Toute la vie morale de l'antiquité s'appuie. . .sur la gloire qu'une bonne action rapporte à celui qui l'a faite. Si le mot *doxa* est un des plus usuels du vocabulaire grec, celui de *kenodoxia* prend, dans la langue des Pères, une importance qu'il n'avait jamais eue. Autant la *doxa* forme, pour un païen, l'atmosphére où il aime vivre, autant la *kenodoxia* est, pour un chrétien, la tentation qu'il faut fuir avant tout.'

[5] *Hom. on Eph.* 13.4; *Hom. on Heb.* 28.5.

[6] *Hom. on Matt.* 62.5; cf. F. Leduc, 'Le thème de la vaine gloire chez S. Jean Chrysostome', *POC* (1969), pp. 3–32.

man.'[7] Like the imperial icons which are sent to the cities of the empire, man bears the royal image. Made in the image of God, he was made to rule, but the scars of sin have weakened his kingly power. Reason distinguishes him from animals and makes him like God. By virtue he preserves the dignity of the royal image which is in him.[8] Man shows his likeness to God as he works and transforms the world. Work must be done for God, and in the consciousness of his presence. Jesus Christ stands as the pattern for all Christian behaviour. His acts exemplify his teaching. The pictures of his earthly life make virtue a possibility. From him we may learn detachment, austerity, patience, meekness, charity and zeal. John is keen on historical models and concrete examples. He points to saints of the Old and New Testaments, especially to his hero Paul. He writes of the first Christians, and especially of the martyrs. The monks are contemporary examples, visible models of the way of Christ. He encourages the faithful to visit monks in their solitude and encourages monks to live in the cities that their example might be an inspiration to many.[9] The disciples of Christ were simple men, fishermen, tax-gatherers, tent-makers, but their discipleship was more effective than all the teaching of philosophers. Philosophers in a lifetime managed to win over a few to their opinion, but the disciples won the world over to truth within a few years, and the gospel grows and flourishes all the time.[10] Paul shows the great change which came to him when a former persecutor became a follower of Christ. He exhorted others to be imitators of him as he was an imitator of Christ. 'He imitated the Lord, and will not you, who have been educated in piety from the first, imitate a fellow servant, one who by conversion was brought to the faith at a later period of life.'[11]

We are granted the opportunity to know God, to philosophise concerning the future, to become angels and to join in the choir of the powers of the most high. Such knowledge of God enables us to 'become like God in the measure which it is possible for man to become like him'.[12] The knowledge of himself is the first knowledge for man to gain. Without self-knowledge he cannot judge correctly.[13]

---

[7] *On the statues*, 7.3.

[8] *On the virtue of the soul*, cited by L. Daloz, *Le travail selon S. Jean Chrysostome*, p. 26; see also pp. 132ff.

[9] L. Meyer, *S. Jean Chrysostome, maître de perfection chrétienne* (Paris, 1933), chapter 4. On the importance of biblical examples for the young, see *Hom. Eph.* 21.

[10] *On the statues*, 19.5.

[11] *Ibid.* 5.6.

[12] *Hom. on Matt.* 18.4. Cited J. Dumortier, 'Les idées morales de S. Jean Chrysostome', *MSR*, 12 (1955), 2.

[13] *Hom. on Psalm* 9.9. Cited Dumortier, *ibid.*

The ideal of Christian perfection is that of the true philosopher, of the angel or of one who is like God. God himself set this ideal before man from the beginning, that man should be in his image, and that man should be holy as he is holy. The ideal of likeness to God is renewed by Christ. Within this perspective all virtue is included, but love is best able to make man like God.

John's asceticism aims to show the superiority of the Christian to the pagan philosopher. In the New Testament the word 'philosophy' carried bad associations of a world-denying temper; but the Apologists took the word as descriptive of their whole message.[14] Justin finds in the gospel the only safe and worthwhile philosophy.[15] Clement widens the notion to include devotion to truth as incarnate in Christ.[16] John takes over both pagan and Christian uses of the word and modifies them again. While he shares the philosophy of Gregory of Nazianzus (inner conversation with God) and that of Gregory of Nyssa (spiritual interpretation of scripture), he finds the highest philosophy in the life lived in the world.[17] Christians claimed to have access to a truth which placed them among the intellectual élite of the day.[18] They claimed that they could make better, more genuine philosophers than other sects. John proudly quotes the impression made by his mother's example on his pagan teacher, 'heavens, what women there are among these Christians'.[19] John's poor opinion of Greek philosophers derives from their alleged ineffectiveness, ignorance of God, obscurity, and even their external appearance.[20]

(ii) *We must walk by the same way as he went, the way of the cross*

John followed the way of self-denial from the beginning. A Christian is called to fast but does not achieve merit for it. Fasting must be supplemented by good works.[21] On arriving at Constantinople John cut expenditure harshly and made many enemies. Inefficiency and dishonesty in management of church property were quickly discovered

---

[14] A. M. Malingrey, *Philosophia* (Paris, 1961), p. 128.

[15] *Dialogue* 8.

[16] Cf. Malingrey, *Philosophia*, pp. 156f.

[17] L'incarnation de la foi chrétienne avec toutes les exigences qu'elle comporte, indépendamment d'une forme de vie particulière', *ibid.* p. 288.

[18] *Ibid.* p. 294.

[19] *To a young widow*, 2. When Antioch was in trouble, the pagan philosopher ran away; but the monks came to the rescue. *On the statues*, 17. 3–5.

[20] See P. R. Coleman-Norton, 'St. Chrysostom and the Greek Philosophers', *Classical Philology* (1930), pp. 305f.

[21] *On the statues*, 4.12.

and corrected. John did not give the great banquets which his pre-
decessor had given, for it was robbing the temple to use church money
in this way. He was like a monk on a bishop's throne.[22] John, 'the
fiercest adversary of wealth and luxury',[23] attacked every form of
extravagance, including elaborate funerals.[24] He who would be worthy
of Christ must take up the cross and follow him. Bearing the cross
does not mean that we should have a piece of wood on our shoulders,
but that we should keep death before our eyes, and, like Paul, die
daily, laugh at death and despise the present life.[25] John encourages
Olympias in the face of possible threat of death. She has already anticipated death. 'Or do they threaten death? This also you have constantly practised by anticipation, and if they should drag you to
slaughter, they will be dragging a body which is already dead.'[26]

The way of discipleship is a way of *askēsis*, of discipline and of training. The word of God cures men, sometimes by cutting, sometimes by
searing. Medicines and painful treatment may be necessary to the
body. In the same way, the word does not hesitate to heal with power.[27]
All that John says about the way of the cross is ruled by the axiom
that all should be done to God's glory and to show forth his majesty.
'Glory to God for all things.' We fight for and beside the king of
heaven. An earthly king cannot permit all his soldiers to be at his side;
but the heavenly king wills that all should stay near his throne.[28]
Those who are preparing to be baptised are like athletes in a training
school. In a wrestling school the bouts are hard but not serious, for one
wrestles with friends; but then the great contests come when one must
wrestle with enemies. Training for baptism is a preparation of Christian
athletes to wrestle not with friends, but with the evil demon.[29] Christian
athletes must strip off worldly cares before they wrestle.[30] Afflictions
should not grieve us, but should move us to thank God that he has
stirred us out of our torpor and sluggishness and made us diligent in
the honour of his name.[31] Theodore is told that he has fallen like a

[22] Palladius, 12, 13. See C. Baur, *John Chrysostom and his time*
(London, 1960), 2, 59.
[23] A. Puech, *S. Jean Chrysostome et les moeurs de son temps*, p. 141.
[24] *Hom. on John* 85.5.
[25] *On the statues*, 5.14. For an extended treatment of John's account of
life under the cross, see Peter Stockmeier, *Theologie und Kult des Kreuzes
bei Johannes Chrysostomus* (Trier, 1966), pp. 160–91.
[26] *To Olympias*, 17.
[27] *On priesthood*, 4.3.
[28] *Hom. on Matt.* 54.5. Cited J. Stiglmayr, 'Zur Aszese des heiligen
Chrysostomus', *ZAM* 4, (1929), 32.
[29] *Instructions to Catechumens*, 1.4.
[30] *On the statues*, 3.7.
[31] *Ibid.* 6.3.

wrestler in a fight. There is nothing wrong in falling, but there is a great deal wrong in staying down. Suppose, says John elsewhere, there is one opponent. Two men wrestle against him. The first is weak through gluttony and unprepared for the contest, while the other is fresh from the wrestling school and thoroughly fit. Everyone knows who will win. In the same way the Christian who is fighting fit will win his contest, while the weaker, lazier and unprepared Christian will be beaten.[32] The presence of the devil on earth makes the Christian athlete stronger. The contest is harder, but without the rigour of contest, the Christian would not earn the lustre of overcoming the enemy.[33] The kingdom of heaven does not come to the weak or the insipid, it belongs to the violent who take it by storm. 'Lay hold of Christ who praises you for it.' If one plots to seize an earthly kingdom by violence, one is rightly punished, but if one strives to gain a heavenly kingdom by violence, one earns the praise of Christ.[34]

Martyrdom is a contest and the supreme way of serving God. The martyr is like a wrestler who, when he has defeated all his opponents, comes out to receive the prize. He is raised on the shoulders of cheering spectators. Ignatius was celebrated as a champion wherever he visited on his way to Rome. As he went, he laughed the devil to scorn and encouraged all the churches.[35] John further argues that martyrdom is not restricted to those who disobey the command to sacrifice to the gods and then die as a consequence. 'But he is also a martyr if he observes any commandment which is able to lead to his death. This is obviously martyrdom.'[36] In one letter John consoles a young widow. During the life of her husband she had known the honour, affection and care which were due to a wife; but now in the place of her husband she has God who is Lord of all. He has protected her in the past, and will do so in the future. John advises the young widow to consolidate her property by investing it all in heaven. Let her give up all possessions, deposit her goods in another world, and from such a deposit she will draw tranquillity and peace.[37] On earth man is a stranger and a pilgrim and must look to the heavenly country for final reward.[38] Olympias may look forward to the eternal glory which her light afflictions have earned.

In a special work John describes virginity as a physical and spiritual consecration to Christ.[39] It springs from faith and is formed by love, lifting the virgin to angelic life.[40] John lists the miseries of marriage[41]

[32] *To Theodore* 2.1; *On the devil,* 2.2.   [33] *Ibid.* 3.2.
[34] *On Eutropius,* 2.6.   [35] *On Ignatius,* 5.
[36] *Against the Jews,* 8.7.   [37] *To a young widow,* 7.
[38] *On the statues,* 2.17.   [39] *On virginity,* 5, 6.
[40] *Ibid.* 10f.   [41] *Ibid.* 49–58.

in a series of common platitudes. Some parallels have been noted. A rich wife will humiliate and dominate her husband.[42] The wife suffers constant torture and anxiety through the amorous misbehaviour of her husband.[43] When seen in the confines of eternity the benefits of marriage are insubstantial shadows.[44] John never loses a wistful preference for virginity.[45] Marriage is a cloak of servitude.[46] From the beginning he insists that the heretics (Marcionites, Valentinians and Manichees) gain no virtue from their virginity. Since it is given in service to the devil, they get the worst of both worlds; the pagans can at least enjoy themselves now. This is the weakest point of a wavering argument. Virgin heretics are less pure than adulterers, defiling both body and soul.[47] Paul and Plato are quoted to show that marriage is honourable (Heb. 13:4!) and the creator is good (*Tim.* 29). It is wrong to denigrate marriage in order to praise virginity.[48] On the other hand those who despise virginity are running a grave risk since God showed his hand in such matters when he sent the bears to kill the children who were rude to Elisha.[49] Marriage is for the weak, not for those who are capable of virginity.[50] The virgin has no need of what is beyond her power[51] and lives in tranquillity.[52] God wants us to be without care so he tells us to care only about him and not about the world of which a wife is a part.[53] No woman who cares about temporal things can be a virgin.[54]

The way of celibacy is freely chosen for God; but it is not the only way.

> You hear this word virginity – a concept which contains within itself much trial and struggle. Do not be afraid of it. It does not deal with a precept, nor does it have the compulsion of a commandment. It concerns only those who freely, and of their own free will, choose it in hope of reward. For the rest, those who hold back and do not wish to choose it will not be punished in any way, nor will they be compelled to observe it against their will.[55]

John argues against the followers of Marcion that 'Whoever condemns marriage also despises with it the true virginity.'[56] Celibacy is not for all. Wives are given as helpmates and not as snares. The prophet Isaiah had a wife, as did also Moses. Christ himself was born of a

---

[42] *Ibid.* 53f.
[43] *Ibid.* 56; cf. Sophocles, *Trach.*, 147–9.
[44] *Ibid.* 58; cf. Pindar, *Pyth.*, 8, 96.
[45] See A. M. Malingrey, *S. Jean Chrysostome, La virginité, SC* (1966), p. 60.
[46] *On virginity*, 14.5.
[47] *Ibid.* 1–6.   [48] *Ibid.* 10.   [49] *Ibid.* 21f.   [50] *Ibid.* 25f.
[51] *Ibid.* 60; *ta ouk eph'hēmin.*   [52] *Ibid.* 68; *ataraxia.*
[53] *Ibid.* 74.   [54] *Ibid.* 77.   [55] *Ibid.* 41.   [56] *Ibid.* 10.

virgin; but he was present at a marriage and made water into wine to honour the feast.[57]

A wife can bring harmony to the life of her husband and shape his whole outlook; the duties of the home give women a chance to be better philosophers than men.[58] John was not insensitive to the beauty of women in whose eyes, hands, teeth, cheeks, lips, brows and necks he found ground for comment;[59] but such beauty will fade away while spiritual loveliness endures for ever.[60] Elsewhere John distinguishes true virginity from physical virginity. He tells Olympias that she should not be sorry for her sins, for in fact she has no real sins. She has followed the way of true virginity. She has lived in patience, self-control and all virtue. It is in these things that true virginity lies, and it is something supremely great. God has required of men many difficult things, but not virginity. John insists that the heroes of old, like Moses, Abraham and Job were great men of God, who showed heroic virtue although they did not practise physical virginity.[61] John's wavering reluctance to restrict perfection to an élite has the same disharmony which was found in Basil. He sets the standard of celibacy for all Christians, and while he insists that he does not condemn marriage, he has to regard it as inferior.[62] On the other hand he has a strong sense of the value of the Christian family. When the family returns from church, the father goes over the sermon with them. Every Christian home should be, like that of the Philemon, a church. 'Make your home a church.'[63]

(iii) *Let your light shine before men*[64]

John does not propose solitary individualism. At baptism a Christian is born into the body of Christ. All who believe are united to Christ and to one another. Union with Christ is union with Christ glorified, and leads to the life of an angel. Union with Christ is union with Christ suffering and Christ serving, which leads to constant imitation of Christ in his earthly way. Union with Christ takes place in the eucharist and

---

[57] *Hom. on Vision of Isa.* 4.2–3.

[58] *Hom. on John* 61.3.

[59] *Hom. on 1 Tim.* 4.3, and *Hom. on 1 Cor.* 30.3; 31.3. See *St. John Chrysostom's Picture of His Age* (n.a., S.P.C.K., London, 1875), pp. 174f.

[60] *Hom. on Resurrection of Dead*, 5; *Hom. on Resurrection of Jesus Christ*, 5.

[61] *To Olympias*, 2.4ff. *Hom. on Matt.* 78.1f. and *Hom. on Heb.* 28.7.

[62] A. Puech, *S. Jean Chrysostome et les moeurs de son temps* (Paris, 1891), p. 97: 'il est fort vrai qu'il ne le condamne pas, mais il le méprise, et je ne vois pas ce que le mariage y gagne.'

[63] *Hom. Gen.* 6; see A. Puech, *op. cit.*, p. 156.

[64] *Hom. 1 Tim.* 2; see I. Maur, *Mönchtum und Glaubensverkündigung* (Freiburg/Schweiz, 1959), p. 148.

in the whole life of liturgy. Union with Christ who is head of the church shows itself in love and zeal for the church, while union with Christ our judge brings trust, assurance and confidence. These gifts come through our incorporation into Christ as we grow in spiritual grace.[65] Theodore, who has fallen from his vow, is reminded of a young Phoenician who left worldly goods and grandeur for the solitude of the mountains, there to become a Christian philosopher. He fell from this life and returned to the world, bringing shame upon those with whom he had been associated; but certain holy men continued to hope, watched for him and greeted him regularly in the market place, so that in the end he returned to a solitary life and with great penitence and sorrow honoured Christ.[66] John has provided a battleground for supporters and opponents of the monastic ideal. This has become clear in a series of controversies over the last hundred years. Ambiguity and ambivalence remain. It were better, says John, for those who retire from the world to remain within that world and to suffer its dangers. 'How much better were it for you to become less zealous and to profit others, than, remaining on the heights, to look down upon your dying brothers. For how shall we overcome our enemies if one part of us pay no heed to virtue, and those who pay heed to it withdraw far from the line of battle.'[67] The monk is like a ship which is always in port, while the layman must sail his ship through the storms of life. He is always on the deep striving against the mountains of waves.[68] We have been told to let our light shine before men, not before mountains, deserts and inaccessible places.[69] Yet on the other hand John defends the monks against their opponents and compares a monk favourably with a king. Those who are not monks should live in obedience to God in all things except their celibacy. Most who are saved are in fact married. Only a few are called to the way of celibacy. These too are saved.[70]

In the confusion one important point stands out. Because John was concerned with the inner renunciation of the monk, and because he saw that God's supreme will was that all men might be saved, he joined together the life of the monk and the work of the missionary. His words are striking: 'Therefore it is my wish that all lights should stand and shine on the lampstand, so that much brightness may come

---

[65] L. Meyer, *S. Jean Chrysostome, maître de perfection chrétienne*, chapter 2, part 2.

[66] *To Theodore*, 1.17.

[67] *Hom. on 1 Cor.* 6.

[68] *Hom. on Eph.* 21.

[69] See I. Maur, *Mönchtum und Glaubensverkündigung*, pp. 148f.; *Hom. on Matt.* 7.8; *Hom. on Heb.* 7.

[70] See Viller and Rahner, *Aszese und Mystik in der Väterzeit*, pp. 281ff. and Puech, *S. Jean Chrysostome et les moeurs de son temps*, p. 262.

to us. Let us therefore kindle this fire, that we should see that those who sit in darkness are freed from error.'[71]

> It is certainly better and more useful to journey in this way to foreign countries than to sit at home and to stay at rest, for when you are far away you can have everything which you have now. You can still fast, you can still watch through the night, you can still practise your other philosophic virtues; but if you stay sitting at home, you cannot then gain what you could achieve if you had gone away, namely the salvation of so many souls, the reward for so much danger, the credit for such preparedness.[72]

This original and important step is argued carefully. The one thing after which the monk strives is undivided dedication to God. Because his activity is grounded in the will and purpose of God, he must be involved in mission. God wills that all men should be saved and has established one church for all nations. Heretics, Jews and pagans, all had a claim on the care of John, who sent missionaries to all nations in his part of the world. The activity of the missionary is inspired by the spirituality of the monastic movement. John followed tradition in making a few monks into priests and bishops; but he did something new when he organised the sending of monks on missionary work. This, he saw, was the significant part which they could play in the history of salvation.[73]

FAITH

(i) *A noble and youthful mind*

The knowledge of faith has for its object the word of God which includes such truths of reason as that there is one God who created all things, as well as the mysteries of the trinity and of Christ's salvation. Faith sees over a wide range of truth, but its knowledge is limited. To believe is not to see as with the eyes, but to depend like Abraham upon the word of God.[1] Faith is freely chosen as man is free. The evidence does not force man to believe; but he has a moral obligation to believe. Those who do not believe are responsible for their unbelief. Obstacles to the decision of faith are sin, passions, heresies and other forms of falsehood. Sin blinds and paralyses the soul. The knowledge of faith is more than natural knowledge, and is crowned by practice. Faith is not

---

[71] *Hom. on Matt.* 43.5.   [72] *Ep.* 54.
[73] See Maur, *Mönchtum und Glaubensverkündigung*, pp. 180–2 for a summary of his sound and illuminating exposition.
[1] E. Boularand, *La venue de l'homme à la foi d'après S. Jean Chrysostome* (Rome, 1939), chapter 1.

just dependence upon God but a rule of faith which guides that dependence, especially in face of heresy. Faith is precious when it comes from a heart and soul on fire with love. Only faith can make is wise, for reason cannot comprehend the deep things. The heathen make no discoveries, yet the fishermen and tentmakers, the untaught simple Christians, by their faith have found greater understanding than all the philosophers. '*The work of faith calls for a noble and a youthful mind,* which rises above visible things and leaves behind it the weakness of human understanding, for no-one can have faith unless he soar above the normal level of man's thought.'[2] God has given more goodness than our understanding can grasp, and therefore he also gave faith. Christian doctrines go beyond human reason and require faith: the God who is nowhere and yet is everywhere, the God who was not begotten and yet did not create himself, the God who is spirit. 'See how great is the darkness and how it gathers round us, and how necessary in all things is faith. Faith is our fortress.'[3] Unbelief shows weakness in the soul. Faith is not guess-work, but an act in which the mind enters a world which had been closed to it.

(ii) *What perseverance was there if he did not fear?*

John's account of faith does not cover all that his hero Paul had said; but the two derivative virtues of steadfastness and humility are always under consideration. Faith which endures sufferings, fears, doubts, temptation, and faith which is ever humble in the presence of God's sovereign grace, such faith is, after love, the greater part of Christian living.[4] John refers to his own experience as a preacher. To him the proclamation of the word is a sacred trust which he cannot deny even when there is no response. As long as God gives him breath and life he will fulfil the duty and commandment of God. Even if his words do not decisively move anyone, they may make the sinner less sure of himself, and the good man keener about his goodness. What has not been achieved today may be achieved tomorrow, and if not tomorrow then at some future date. A fisherman may fail to catch anything, and, at the last cast of his net, catch the fish that he has been wanting all day. A farmer may have to neglect his farm for two or three days in bad weather, and the captain may have to delay his voyage because of storms: neither farmer nor sailor gives up his work. 'Should we stop just because no one listens to what we have said?'[5]

The woman of Canaan who asked help of Christ is an example of

---

[2] *Hom. on Heb.* 22.1.   [3] *Hom. on Col.* 5.
[4] *On priesthood*, 3.7 and 3.17.   [5] *Concerning Lazarus*, 1.1–3.

persevering faith. Christ who had compared her with a dog, praised her faith. 'At first he did not answer her request but when she came a second and a third time he granted it and thereby taught us that he postponed the gift not to refuse it to her, but that he might show to us all the perseverance of the woman.'[6] Paul boasted of weakness and dangers. 'Although he was Paul he was still a man.' He feared death and flogging, but fear did not make him act unworthily.

> Those who say that he did not fear the lash not only do not honour him, but they greatly detract from his merit. *For what perseverance, what self-control was there in facing danger if he did not fear?*
> I admire him because he feared, and not just because he feared, but because he actually trembled in dangers yet victoriously over-came them all and never gave in, cleansing the world and sowing the seed of the gospel everywhere on earth and on sea.[7]

John here shows profound insight into Paul's account of faith. The recognition of fear and trembling is strikingly different from the Stoic and the Socratic ideals.

The solitary, who shuts himself away, undergoes conflict and toil, but his exertion cannot be compared with that of the priest. The terrors of the priesthood are compared with those of a young country lad who is placed in charge of an army. Before the command is given to him he is shown the whole army, its equipment, the power of the enemy, the rugged nature of the country and all the terrors of war.[8] Whatever else we do, we must not grow weary and give up. Under the pressure of tribulation most of the wrong in us has been cut away. Now we only need to persevere a little longer and we shall be able to rejoice two or three times as much.[9] The word of Christ must dwell in us richly because we must stand firm on every side against all attacks. It doesn't matter how well a city is guarded, if there is a weakness in any one part of its defences.[10] The need for endurance cannot be stressed too often. When Eutychus fell from the window he showed how long he had listened to the preaching of Paul. Paul preached in every place night and day.[11]

The faithfulness of his people was a source of joy to John. When he returned from Ephesus he said that Moses was only away for forty days from the people of Israel, and in that time they had left him to go and follow idols. 'I was away more than one hundred and fifty days and I found you rejoicing, living as true philosophers and persevering

[6] *Hom. against those who misuse this saying of the apostle* [Phil. 1:18], *and on humility*, 12. Cf. also *Hom. Matt.* 52.2; *Hom. Gen.* 38.4 and 44.3.
[7] *Hom. on 1 Cor.* 6.   [8] *On priesthood*, 6.12 and 13.
[9] *On the statues*, 15.6.   [10] *On priesthood*, 4.4.   [11] *Ibid.* 4.7.

in the fear of God.'[12] To see the church living in Constantinople where heresy has raged around it is as wonderful as to see a beautiful olive tree in the middle of a furnace, a tree covered with leaves and fruit.[13] Steadfastness can be corporate. John knows that he is part of the true church of Christ which cannot be overcome.

> Nothing is more powerful than the church, O man! Stop the war lest you destroy your strength. Do not wage war against the heavens. When you go to war against a man you may either conquer or be conquered, but when you go to war against the church, you cannot win, for God is more powerful than all else.[14]

The paralytic, who after thirty-eight years was still meek and gentle, is an example of patience. He could easily have replied rudely to the inquiry of our Lord, 'Do you want to be made whole?': but he humbly replied, 'Yes, Lord.' Long illness makes people unreasonable and hard to please. Here was a man who after long suffering still preserved a quiet spirit. When man suffers a sickness of this kind it is a sign of the love and care of God. Just as the refiner of gold leaves the piece of gold in the fire until he sees that it has become purified, so God allows men to be tested by distress and trouble until they have become pure and better through their trials.[15]

Even banishment gave John his chance to write fervently about the need for patience in a letter to Olympias. Patience is always a necessity, and the heavenly reward is to be considered. The good must always suffer. We are in the end the only people who can hurt ourselves, and no misfortune can harm the soul if we bear life's misfortune in the right way.[16] Passive despair, hopeless passivity is unbalanced and satanic. Self mastery shows itself in freedom from passion.[17] John's final words, 'Glory to God for all things', showed the triumph of his own perseverance and patience. He died, said Palladius, as a victorious athlete.[18]

[12] *On the return of John*, from the surviving Latin version, *PG* 52, 421–4.

[13] *Against Anomoeans*, 11.1.

[14] *Sermon before exile*, 1. Cited Stiglmayr, 'Zur Aszese des heiligen Chrysostomus', p. 39.

[15] *On the paralytic*, 1.   [16] *To Olympias*, 1.

[17] *To Olympias*, 8 and 10. Cf. Malingrey, *Lettres à Olympias, SC* (1947), p. 84. 'En les écoutant, Jean apprend à cultiver la maîtrise de soi, la patience, le courage, mais surtout à placer la vie morale tout entière sous le signe de l'intelligence et de la volonté.'

[18] Palladius 11 (39). Cf. Malingrey, *op. cit.*, 'Elles enseignent sans doute à lutter contre les épreuves, contre le découragement, mais aussi à reconnaître avec une joie sans cesse émerveillée la grandeur, la puissance et la bonté de Dieu, et à lui offrir la souffrance même, un tribut de louanges et d'actions de grâces.'

(iii) *Concerning humility*

John has a special sermon on humility, and it is a constant theme. The Pharisee and the publican show the danger of pride and the greatness of humility. The Pharisee with all his virtue failed because of pride. He was like a ship which in a storm rides out wave after wave but is overwhelmed by one final wave. If we have achieved the peak of perfection we must consider ourselves the lowest and least of all, for pride can bring anyone down from heaven while humility can raise up anyone from the abyss of sin. 'Humility is the foundation of our philosophy.' We may have built up a whole fabric of good works, of prayer, of fasting, of every kind of virtue; but unless humility is the basis of it all, it will collapse like the building set on sand. In humility Paul was always thinking about others. When he was imprisoned unjustly by Nero he wrote a letter to the Philippians. He saw his imprisonment as a means to the extension of the gospel. Because of his bonds several of the brethren spoke the word more fearlessly. They might have said to Paul, 'Physician, heal yourself.' If you, Paul, cannot keep yourself out of trouble, how can you claim to bring us blessing. However, Paul's fellow believers knew that the power of Christ is made perfect in weakness. The demons fled because they saw Paul bound in body but free in speech. His word went out more swiftly because of his imprisonment. The humility of Paul is further shown by his reaction to heretics who were preaching Christ from envy and strife. They thought they would make his bonds heavier, but in fact Paul rejoiced that Christ was being preached, in any way at all. The humility of the woman of Canaan who asked that she might pick up crumbs is a sign of her faith.[19]

(iv) *Free will and freedom*

All moral activity begins with free choice. 'The faculty of the will is natural to us and comes to us from God; but the choice of evil is our doing and follows from our decision.'[20] Responsibility should not be evaded. 'Therefore do not accuse external things, but always accuse your own will.'[21] The sinner has only himself to blame. 'It is not circumstance which causes sins, but the wills of sinners.'[22] God is never the cause of evil for, 'All evil is the product of man's free will and

---

[19] *Against those who misuse this saying of the apostle* [Phil. 1.18], *and on humility,* 1–13. There are more than fifty explicit references to humility in John's works. The stories of the Canaanite woman and of the Pharisee and publican are recounted many times.

[20] *Hom. on Rom. 13.2.*   [21] *Comm. on Psalm 148.4.*

[22] *Comm. on Psalm 140.7*

choice',[23] and he has not loaded the universe against us. 'The ruler of the universe made our nature free...He does not impose any necessity upon us. He places appropriate remedies at our disposal and leaves to the sick man the decision to take them.'[24] Knowledge of good and evil is given by nature. We decide to follow good or bad desires. Sin comes from reflection on bad desires and is linked with mental blindness.[25] If we choose the good, God works in us to will and to do his pleasure.[26] Grace comes to those who will receive it and we may accept or turn from God's help.[27] Man is neither self-sufficient nor corrupt. John tries to avoid the notion of a constraining grace. Without free will the call of Christ could not have been answered even by Paul.[28] John stands in the tradition of Clement and Origen; in turn Pelagius looks to him as an authority.

John attacks those who use their supposed lack of freedom as an excuse for sin. Some argue from a blind irresistible fate, others from the power of evil spirits. John denies both views.[29] In the same way he refutes predestination, claiming that the doctrine was introduced by Satan who wants to destroy the freedom which God has given to man and to persuade man that evil is part of his nature.[30] There is no natural necessity which compels man to do evil, 'For nothing stops any man who desires to be good from becoming good, even though previously he may have been one of the most wicked of men'.[31] Fools ascribe their sins to evil spirits and to evil hours. There are no such things as evil hours, and evil spirits have no effect unless man allows himself to fall under their attack. The trials and temptations of the world give no ground for the dualism of the Marcionites or the Manicheans. Our Lord wrestled in prayer, and knew weakness of flesh and agony of choice. For our sakes he said, 'Nevertheless not as I will but as you will.' His will was one with the Father's but he wanted to teach men in their distress and in their trembling. He wanted to show the way of submission to the will of God.[32]

Free will belongs to all; but true freedom can only be found by him who belongs to Christ. Discipleship and freedom go together. 'For there is no man free except he who lives for Christ. He stands superior to all troubles, and if he does not choose to injure himself no one else

---

[23] *Hom. on Rom.* 19.6; *Hom. on Acts* 23.3.
[24] *Hom. on Gen.* 19.1.
[25] *Hom. on Rom.* 5.1; cf. *Hom. on 1 Cor.* 11.3f.
[26] *Hom. on Phil.* 8.1. [27] *Hom. on Heb.* 34.2.
[28] *Hom. in praise of Paul*, 4.
[29] Cf. Amand, *Fatalisme et liberté*, pp. 497–532.
[30] *Hom. on Matt.* 62. [31] *Hom. on 1 Cor.* 22.7.
[32] *Hom. on 'Father, if it be possible'*, 4; *Hom. on John* 4.5.

will be able to do this, but he is impregnable.'[33] We should thank God who gives us this freedom, and we should strive that we may never fall back into the slavery of sin. If a friend should fall back into such slavery, we must help to break his chains so that his soul may be free to soar aloft to heaven.

LOVE

(i) *Creator of every virtue*

Paul lived with such fiery vigour, because he knew that love was the head of all good things, their root, spring and mother. Metaphor is piled on metaphor to make this point.[1] Love is 'the creator of every virtue'.[2] All is to be done from love and all endured to the glory of God.[3] Love comes from faith, shows itself in good works and is the goal of perfection. It is a fire in the heart of every true Christian. Heavenly goodness is a great love for Christ, a love greater than all heavenly powers, without which one has nothing.[4] From love come all good things, like friendship which is true and firm, and unity which can only exist where virtue is supreme. 'Virtue is born from love and love from virtue. They engender one another.'[5] Love is power. 'Miracles have converted the world because love broke up the way for them; without love their effect would not have lasted.'[6] Love makes us like God[7] as our love answers his. God's loving kindness is such that he can never turn from one who is sincerely repentant, but always welcomes and restores. When Ahab repented, God did not bring evil in his day. No man, however passionate, has loved physical beauty as intensely as God longs after the salvation of the souls of men.[8] God's love shown in creation never ceases. 'God watches over us in no ordinary way. He does it with love, with an infinite love, a love without passion but fiery and intense, a love sincere, and indestructible, a love which can never be quenched.'[9] One can and one must do all for the glory of God.[10] There is strength and joy in the love of God.[11]

---

[33] *To Theodore*, 2.5. Cf. E. Käsemann, *Jesus means Freedom* (London, 1969), p. 145, 'The disciple will never be free from him without at the same time losing all freedom.'

[1] *On the incomprehensible*, 1. Cf. *On perfect love.*

[2] *Hom. on 1 Cor.* 33.9.

[3] Cf. Stiglmayr, 'Zur Aszese des heiligen Chrysostomus', p. 30. Chrysostomus', p. 30.

[4] *Hom. in praise of Paul*, 2.

[5] *Hom. on Eph.* 9.3.

[6] *Hom. on John* 72.4.

[7] *Hom. on Eph.* 7; *Hom. on 2 Tim.* 6.

[8] *To Theodore*, 1.13.

[9] *To those offended by adversities*, 6.

[10] *Hom. on calends*, 3–5.

[11] *Hom. on Rom.* 9.3f.

Paul cared for nothing in heaven or in earth so long as he found Christ. 'Being strong in love, the most excellent of all good gifts, he burnt brighter than any flame, for as iron when thrown into the fire becomes fire itself, so Paul animated by the fire of love became love itself.'[12] John like other members of the school of Antioch drew from Paul the theme of pure disinterested love of God. We look for no reward, but we seek to please God who is greater than any reward. When the righteous suffer, we must not doubt the providence of God. We simply hold on to the will of God, no matter what events may come.[13] Through love work finds its true meaning before God. Apart from love, man's work is a struggle to gain his independence on earth, an independence of God; but the purpose of work is to give to those in need, and it is more joyful to give than to receive. Love for a neighbour means to give to him, instead of receiving from him. John is not concerned to help his people perform a loving gesture to soothe their conscience. They must have true compassion towards those who are weak, and give of the fruit of their toil and hardship. Work binds human society together, and sustains its life. It is transmuted in its purpose and practice by the presence of love, which touches it with eternity and makes it a sign to lead man to faith.[14]

(ii) *The power and love of the church*

The sermon, 'Vanity of vanities, all is vanity,' which John preached with Eutropius clinging to a column of the altar, turns to the theme of love,

> To you it does not seem right that he should be able to take refuge
> in the church whose rights he always denied. Yet surely we should
> glorify God to the heights for allowing him to be driven to such
> dire necessity that he came to know the power and the love of the
> church – her power since he suffered this great disaster because
> he attacked her, her love in that she whom he attacked now holds
> her shield before him and takes him under her protecting wings.
> She makes him quite safe, forgets all resentment for past wrongs
> and lovingly receives him in her embrace.[15]

Yet John laments the state of the church. There was a time when all met together and sang psalms with one heart. Now the custom is pre-

---

[12] *Hom. in praise of Paul*, 3.   [13] *Hom. on 1 Cor.* 33.

[14] See L. Daloz, *Le travail selon S. Jean Chrysostome*, pp. 108–14. People believe less now than in the days of the apostles, because Christians don't preach with their lives and hands.

[15] *On Eutropius*, 1.3.

served, but inward unity of heart and soul is no longer there. John speaks of the controversy over the date of Easter. He says to those who insist upon their special time that he himself and those with him once fasted at that time. 'But we preferred unity to the observance of times.'[16]

We should pray for peace. 'Pray for peace in all your undertakings, peace for today, for all the days of your life, and for a Christian end. Commend yourselves to the living God and to his Christ.' This is the prayer to be said for the congregation, and we ask them then to bow their heads so that in the blessing that God gives they may understand that their prayers have been heard.[17] As a preacher John spoke with the fire of love. 'I know no other life', he said to his congregation, 'except you and the care of your salvation'. His one care was that they should become holy and perfect.[18] Love makes preaching a source of strength rather than a ground of exhaustion. 'As soon as I begin to talk all my weariness is gone. As soon as I begin to teach, all fatigue disappears...Therefore neither sickness nor a thousand other obstacles would be able to separate me from your surrounding love.'[19]

God has so ordered the world that man must live together with his neighbour. Because he wanted all men to be bound together he made the advantage of our neighbour the same as our own advantage. Though you may have reached to the highest point of the ascetic life, if you do not care for others who are perishing, you can have no assurance before God.

> Do you see how many chains of love God has made? These he has planted in our natures as pledges of concord. Our both being the same substance leads to this, since every animal loves its kind... Do you see in how many ways he has bound us together? Yet even this was not enough for him, for he made us to need one another since mutual need does more to create friendship than anything else.[20]

Love is a uniting force. Neither time nor space nor anything else like that can break the affection of the soul. A young widow is told to fix her love upon her husband and to know that through all eternity they will enjoy fellowship together.[21]

[16] *Against the Jews*, 3.3.
[17] *Hom, on 2 Cor.* 2; *Hom. on Col.* 3. See Neander, *Chrysostom* (ET), 1, 425.
[18] *On the statues*, 9.1.
[19] *Hom. after the earthquake.*
[20] *Hom. on 1 Cor.* 34.4.
[21] *To a young widow*, 3. 'For such is the power of love, it embraces and unites, and fastens together not only those who are present and near and visible, but also those who are far distant.'

(iii) *Deliver him into the hands of love*

Discussing Romans 8, John speaks of the power of the love of Christ. Man cannot separate Paul from the love of God which is in Christ, nor can angels nor all the powers of heaven.

> And were I for the sake of Christ to lose the kingdom of
> heaven, were I for the sake of Christ compelled to sink into hell,
> even this would not be dreadful to me!. . .He says this not as if
> angels would seek to separate him from Christ; but he supposes for
> the moment things which are impossible in order to present and
> make clear to all the powerful love which he had. For such is the
> custom of those who love. They cannot bear in silence to restrain
> their love. To every friend they impart the flame, calming their
> souls by the constant expression of their desire.[22]

Priesthood is clear evidence of one's love for Christ. This was the proof which Christ indicated to Peter when he asked him, 'Lovest thou me?', and then gave the commandment, 'Tend my sheep'. Our Lord asked Peter concerning his love, not because he wanted information, but because he wanted to show the importance he gave to the care of his sheep. Caring for his sheep is the greatest proof of a love for Christ.[23] The power of love to change men's hearts can hardly be measured.

> Love is the great teacher. She has the power to free men from
> error, to form their minds, to take them by the hand and to lead
> them on to wisdom. Yes, she may even make men out of stones. Do
> you want to find her power and know it? Bring me a man who is a
> coward, a man who is fearful at every noise and who trembles at
> shadows. Let him be violent, let him be rude, more of the brute
> than a man, let him be wanton and lustful, but *deliver him into
> the hands of love*, lead him into her school and you will soon see
> the coward change into a man of high spirit and of a fearless heart.[24]

The Christian life is an upward path as the believer struggles toward perfection, and perfection has different stages and different ways. *Faith and love join together to show the Christian way.* Not even martyrdom, which otherwise is the highest of all good things, is greater than love. 'For love makes us even without martyrdom to be disciples of Christ, while martyrdom without love cannot do that.'[25] The philosophers had conceived an ideal character which they were unable to realise. The Christian sets a similar ideal before him and is

---

[22] *On compunction to Demetrius*, 1.8.   [23] *On priesthood*, 2.1.
[24] *Hom. on 1 Cor.* 33.8.   [25] *Hom. on S. Romanus, martyr*, 1.

able to realise it. His philosophy means letting go the inferior goods of the earth and mastering himself. Where pagans have failed, the Christian succeeds. Christian perfection may be achieved in the monastic life, in the life of the priest, and in the life of the layman within the world. The preacher of perfection of the laity insisted that the goal of perfection is accessible to all.[26] Through perseverance, the monastic life achieves the perfect philosophy, the perfect life of angels, and even the divine life of love. John could never see the monk as solitary. His life should be apostolic and sent for the salvation of others. The priest performs heavenly duties and practises love. Yet priesthood may bring some to perdition by its difficulties and demands. The priest needs a higher holiness if he is to be the mediator, teacher and pastor of those who come to him. Finally, perfection is the goal of the layman. The commandments, the beatitudes, the counsels and the means of perfection are set down for all to follow. Perfection is possible within the world. It shows itself in the life of philosophy which is perfect, and the life of love which is the higher part of perfection.[27]

John has both a contemplative ideal and a higher, more practical ideal. Christ himself is the complete ideal of the Christian. His example illustrates his teaching and makes virtue possible. The final goal of all moral endeavour is rest or *anapausis*, where all will be peace, goodness, joy, blessedness, sweetness, order and love. There will be no more hatred, illness, no more death to body or to soul, no more shadow and no more night, but all 'will be day, light and rest'.[28] Already the Christian spends his whole life in one continuous festival, which he keeps not with the leaven of malice and wickedness, but with the unleavened bread of sincerity and truth. 'If, therefore, you have a pure conscience, you celebrate a continuous feast, being nourished by good hopes and rich in expectation of good things to come. But if your heart condemn you and you be guilty of many sins, you will be no better than a mourner in the midst of a thousand feasts and festive assemblies.'[29]

Love remains the more excellent way. Compromise is out. There can be no 'half-Christians'. The value of the human person is always guaranteed. Never say that someone is only a runaway slave, a thief or a derelict. 'Consider that Christ died for him too. That is enough to justify your entire concern.'[30] Enemies must be loved. Heresies

[26] M. Viller and K. Rahner, *Aszese und Mystik in der Väterzeit* (Freiburg, 1939), pp. 281 and 284.

[27] L. Meyer, *S. Jean Chrysostome, maître de perfection chrétienne*, chapters 4 and 5. See also A. M. Malingrey, *Philosophia* (Paris, 1961).

[28] *Hom. on Heb.* 6.4.   [29] *Hom. on calends*, 2.

[30] *Hom. against those who misuse this saying of the apostle* [Phil. 1:18], *and on humility*, 5.

should be abhorred, but heretics should be loved.[31] Love must always glow with fervour. 'It is not enough that love should be sincere. It should be violent, hot and boiling. What use is a love which is sincere, but still lacks fire.'[32] 'The measure of love is that it never stops.'[33] 'The debt of charity is the only one which knows no end. The more one does to fulfil it, the greater it increases.'[34]

John's exposition of the four patterns is filled with imaginative insight and practical detail. Less philosophical than Clement, more balanced than Basil, he generally impresses by enthusiasm and sanity. He has little legalism but a great deal of natural law. More explicitly than his predecessors he links divine law with natural law and conscience. Natural law shapes the conscience and tells man what he should do. The order of creation has the same moderate and harmonious aspect as it had for Clement, if not for Charles Darwin some time later.

The way of discipleship is not blocked by asceticism, which is extreme but subordinate to the purpose of following and inner obedience. The body is not an enemy to be weakened but a mortal thing whose death may be anticipated. Harm done to his body is not real harm to man. Ascetic virtues are still virtues but they are not central. It is more important to preach the gospel in every land because God wants all men to be saved. John here sees that asceticism by itself is wrong because it does not go far enough. The monk should be a missionary. True virginity or dedication is something different and superior to mere physical virginity. Concrete example and precedent protect John from mystical absorption. He has a strong visual imagination and finds virtue a possibility chiefly through pictures of the earthly Jesus. The influence of the gospel springs from the constant stream of new examples which it produces. The light of Christian perfection should shine before men and not on mountains or deserts. John saw faith as a central simplicity, a light in darkness and a strong defence. His account of the noble, youthful mind of faith which soars above man's normal ways anticipates the claim of Aquinas, that faith is the courage of the spirit. The steadfastness of faith perseveres in face of fears and conflicts. Love is seen with the same undistorted clarity. It cannot be tied up in good works for it has to be violent, hot and boiling. Christian perfection in love excels the goal of the philosophers and is practicable. Youth, priest and layman can all achieve it. John tries to

---

[31] *Hom. on anathema*, 3; *Hom. on 1 Cor.*, 33; *Hom. on Col.* 2.6.1; *On priesthood*, 2.5.

[32] *Hom. on Rom.* 21.10.   [33] *Hom. on Phil.* 2.1.

[34] *Hom. on the words spoken by the apostle, 'We know that all things work together for good'*, 1.

reclaim full discipleship from any monastic monopoly. His respect for the contingent made him an unpopular reformer, a great pastor, and a preacher who related daily work to faith. His enthusiasm for perfection is as endless as it is practical. For love is not a mystic ecstasy but a reforming power. Love teaches and liberates. The coward and the brute are transformed when they have been delivered into the hands of love.[35]

[35] Contradictions remain, chiefly through ascetic tensions. Asceticism was one reaction to the slackening of moral discipline in a world church. When Christianity conquered the world, the astonishing thing was the mediocrity of the result. The world remained the world. So the only way to preserve the rigour of Christian morals was to leave the world; this was a difficult choice for most people. Basil and John combined in different modes the best of both ways, (cf. Puech, *S. Jean Chrysostome et les moeurs de son temps*, pp. 250 and 314ff.); but they did this at the cost of their own consistency.

5

AUGUSTINE OF HIPPO

Augustine was born in 354 at Thagaste in North Africa. His pagan
father was Patricius and his Christian mother was Monica. Through the
generosity of a rich man of his town, he was able to go to Carthage in
370 to study. It was there in 371 he took a mistress and in 372 his son
was born. He found Carthage attractive in all kinds of ways. Here he
could study, here he could enjoy himself. Here at the age of eighteen
the first great point in his intellectual life was reached. While reading
a dialogue of Cicero he was inspired with a love of truth. He writes,
'Every vain hope at once became worthless to me and I longed with an
incredibly burning desire for an immortality of wisdom, and began
now to arise that I might return to thee.' The journey of the prodigal
to the father's house was to take many years yet; but the intellectual
fire never left Augustine and it was his mind as much as his heart that
brought him home to God. He found the Bible barbaric and incomprehensible after the literature of the schools. He joined the Manichees
because they were always talking about truth and their dualism made
some sense of the problem of evil; but he never went far in their
religion and remained an 'auditor' for nine years. He returned home
in 373 and became a teacher in Thagaste. The following year he
returned to Carthage where he remained until 383, when he left for
Rome with hopes of high appointment and more agreeable students.
All this time Monica had been praying that her son would become a
Christian. Reassured by a saintly bishop that the son of her tears could
not be lost, she was desolate when Augustine slipped away from
Carthage one night while she prayed in a chapel by the sea. During his
short time in Rome Augustine was not happy. At Milan, he became a
professor of rhetoric. He was deeply impressed by the preaching of the
Bishop Ambrose, and by the sonorous liturgy of the Psalms. The study
of Platonism answered many questions and determined the future
shape of his thought.[1] The climax of his inner struggle came in July

---

[1] Possibly after a Stoic interlude (*Conf.* 7.1 and 5). See C. Baguette,
'Une période stoicienne. . .de S. Augustin', *REA* (1970), pp. 47-77.
P. Courcelle, in *Recherches sur les Confessions de saint Augustin*

386 when in his garden he heard the voice of a child shouting, 'Take up and read.' He took up the New Testament, and read verses which exhorted him to put on the Lord Jesus Christ and make no provision for the flesh. 'I neither wanted nor needed to read further: for instantly at the end of this sentence a light, as it were, of serenity infused into my heart. All the darkness of doubt vanished away.' With his mother, who was now in Italy, and some friends, he went into seclusion.[2] He was baptised in the following April and decided to return to Africa and to establish a community in which through piety, friendship and industry he might serve God. On the journey back to Africa Monica died. At

(Paris, 2 ed., 1968), has shown how much Platonism Augustine must have met in the preaching of Ambrose. A. Lenox-Conyngham has indicated serious weaknesses in Courcelle's argument on this point. Courcelle (p. 138, n. 2) argues that Augustine came across Plotinus through certain sermons of Ambrose in 386, in spite of Augustine's reference to the man 'swollen with the most presumptuous pride' (*Conf.* 7.9). Courcelle also argues, in a circle, that these sermons could not have been preached after 387 because this would imply that Ambrose learnt about the *Enneads* from Augustine. See Lenox-Conyngham, Cambridge dissertation, 'St. Ambrose's Attitude to the Concepts of Church and State' (1972), p. 103, n. 4. Christian Platonism was strong in Milan through the presence of Simplicius and Theodorus. It would have been hard for Augustine not to become a Platonist and a Christian, if he had any inclination either way. See J. J. O'Meara, 'Augustine and Neoplatonism', *RA* (1958), pp. 91ff., for the view that Porphyry was a stronger influence than Plotinus on Augustine; see R. J. O'Connell, *St. Augustine's Early Theory of Man* (Harvard, 1968), for a recent statement of the case for Plotinus.

[2] His conversion is a 'conversion to philosophy', to the life of contemplation and celibacy. Cf. R. J. O'Connell, *St. Augustine's Confessions, The Odyssey of a Soul* (Harvard, 1969), pp. 92–4. O'Connell cites A. D. Nock, *Conversion* (Oxford, 1933), pp. 164–86, and H. I. Marrou, *S. Augustin et la fin de la Culture Antique* (4 ed., Paris, 1958), pp. 161–86 for the importance of philosophical conversion. P. Brown, *Augustine of Hippo* (London, 1968) (henceforward *AH*), p. 106, 'The ideal of philosophical retirement was as stringent as any call to the monastic life: it would mean breaking off his career, his marriage, all forms of sexual relations; while the renunciations which the Catholic church demanded in its mysteries of baptism, were also thought of as heroic, as nothing less than the death of an old life. Augustine's friend, Verecundus, for instance, would not be baptized as a Christian, just because he was a married man, even though his wife was a Christian.' (*Conf.* 9.3.5). Augustine's attitude to philosophy differed from that of Ambrose, who was bound to the past, and from that of the monks of Egypt, who had broken decisively with classical culture; he believed that the philosophical mind could and should think creatively within the framework of belief. P. Brown, *AH*, pp. 112f. He had early hopes of philosophic vision, which he later abandoned, setting severe limits on what sinful man may come to know on earth: *ibid*. p. 147.

Ostia in the days before her death Augustine shared with his mother a sense of nearness to heaven and a mystical exultation which he describes in Platonic language. He established a house of quiet retreat with his friends at Thagaste; but in 391 by the will of the people he was made a priest at Hippo, and in 395 he became a bishop. When he died, thirty-five years later, the city of Hippo was already in the third month of its siege by invading Vandals. He had lived through days of great change. He had written letters, sermons and discourses of vast scope. He left behind him an inheritance to which the western world is still indebted. Few lives have the same fascination as does the life of Augustine. There is an openness about him, a lack of camouflage, genuine weaknesses and a real complexity. He has had many critics. He has been called, 'the destroyer of Christian morality', and many other things besides. The power of his literary style has carried his ideas over the centuries. He wrote Latin with vitality and strength, expressing clearly what he felt so deeply. His physical health was never good but he achieved a great amount of work. His intellectual fire was matched by a warm humanity, a love of beauty and a humble confidence in prayer. He has within him so much that most biographers have shaped him in their own images. When they have done all, his authority stands intact, for the story of his pilgrimage can be read in his own *Confessions*.[3] His account of Christian morals builds together earlier ideas into a final synthesis of early Christian ethics.[4] As Clement and

---

[3] Not that the *Confessions* may be taken as history without question and qualification. Boissier, Harnack, Loofs and Alfaric raised serious difficulties. It is not easy to reconcile the philosophical dialogues of Cassiciacum with the radical conversion story of the *Confessions*. When the strong replies of Boyer and others have been considered, there is still ground for concluding that Augustine was able to 'remember with advantages'. The converted will always have difficulty in assessing the effects of their conversion. See, for a summary of discussion, J. J. O'Meara, 'Augustine and Neoplatonism' *RA* (1958), pp. 91–5. P. Courcelle, *Recherches sur les confessions de S. Augustin*, pp. 29–48, has shown the varying degrees of credibility which may be given to different parts of Augustine's recollections. His account of infancy has no historical value, and incidents in childhood, which have strong emotive content, may be discounted. The record of events in Milan may be taken as reliable, although Augustine acknowledges his inability to recall certain details of important events. 'Nous avons bien affaire à une oeuvre historique de valeur', p. 40. See also pp. 247–58, where it is noted that Augustine's concentration on the hand of God in the events of his life leads him to omit some human agencies.

[4] This is maintained forcefully by E. Troeltsch, *Augustin, die christliche Antike und das Mittelalter* (München u. Berlin, 1915), against Harnack's judgement that Augustine is to be linked rather with the beginning of the Middle Ages. It is not easy to decide between these views and Augustine's

Origen had fused the Platonic account of good with the Pauline account of grace, so Augustine develops this theme in an all-embracing system. To this ethic of the supreme good he adds vitality and universal scope.[5] Grace is active in every move of God to man and man to God. There is no division between natural and supernatural. Augustine's ethic should therefore be set in contrast with the Aristotelian and scholastic account. He presents, for all his untidiness, the first great Christian ethical system. Elements lasted on but his synthesis was lost.

RIGHTEOUSNESS

(i) *Righteousness comes from God; law and order*

There is an objective justice which does not depend upon human custom. It is wrong to lie, not because men say so, but because lying goes against the eternal pattern of right behaviour. Eternal law is 'the divine mind or the will of God, commanding the observance of the natural law and forbidding any disruption of it'.[1] Law and order go together. Fallen man lives in confusion, but '*order is that which, if we hold it in our lives, leads to God*'.[2] Good things are not obligatory unless required by the right order of the world.

The eternal law commands us to preserve the natural order which a divine creator has imposed upon all that he made and which man may follow by faith.[3] Order is truth as eternal law, raised by its power above space and by its eternity above time. It is the primal unity of the Father and the divine wisdom, by which all was created, and by which all is governed.[4] A spiritual power never has the right to constrain any other spiritual power. Almighty God respects the souls of men,[5] but God, soul and body stand in a descending scale, and it is proper for the higher to rule the lower.

Happiness is the fulfilment of human nature, and 'Man finds a happy and peaceful life when all his impulses agree with reason and truth.'[6] Happiness brings all human impulses to a state of rational order so that desires are fulfilled in a rational way. Augustine adds, 'Only he is happy who has all that he wants and who wants nothing that is

influence is readily seen in subsequent centuries. However, there has been too much of a tendency to read Augustine in terms of his posterity, and Troeltsch's case seems stronger. 'Er ist in Wahrheit Abschluss und Vollendung der christlichen Antike, ihr letzter und grösster Denker', pp. 6f.

[5] Troeltsch, *op. cit.*, p. 77.
[1] *Against Faustus*, 22.27.　　　　[2] *On order*, 1.9.27.
[3] *Against Faustus*, 22.27 and 30.　　　　[4] *On true religion*, 43.81.
[5] *On immortality of soul*, 13.21 and 22.
[6] *On Genesis, against Manichees*, 1.20.31.

bad.'[7] Augustine defines virtue, after the manner of Cicero, as 'a mental disposition consistent with nature and reason'.[8]

Conscience makes judgements according to the eternal law of God. All inner commands of conscience and all exterior acts of public legislation derive finally from God's eternal law. So law may be adapted to meet changing circumstances, but never be altered.[9] As a child grows up, he discovers, by the use of reason, the law which is in his rational soul, and which is his conscience.[10] Human ideas of justice are images or impressions of the truth and righteousness of God.[11] Through sin man lost his righteousness and defaced the divine image within him; but the image is renewed when righteousness returns. So Augustine links the natural law of the Stoics, which since Philo had been identified with the law of Moses, with a Platonic theory of values and gives it a future reference.

One must begin by knowing oneself. 'Go not outside yourself, but return within yourself, for truth resides in the inner part of man.'[12] Augustine helped to turn the attention of western philosophy from the world to the soul.[13] God's law 'while always remaining fixed and unshaken in him, is, as it were, copied into wise souls; so that they know that their loves are better and higher, in proportion to the perfection of their contemplation of this law in their minds, and to their zeal in its observation in their lives'.[14] For Augustine natural law is always a goal of aspiration.

The law of grace restores in men justice and the image of God. It fulfils all previous law, crowning it with love in the two commands of Christ. Man's righteousness comes from God alone.[15] With Christ, Paul is nailed to the cross and no longer lives; Christ lives in him. Paul's righteousness is not gained through obedience to the law but

---

[7] *On the trinity*, 13.5.

[8] *On 83 diverse questions*, 31.1.

[9] Cf. E. Gilson, *The Christian Philosophy of Saint Augustine* (London, 1961), p. 130.

[10] *Ep.* 157.15.   [11] *On the trinity*, 14, 15, *passim*.

[12] *On true religion*, 39, 72.

[13] See, P. Archambault, 'Augustin et Camus', *RA* (1969), pp. 195–221, esp. p. 221. Camus was attracted by the 'hard' parts of Augustine: universal and original sin, predestination, grace and freedom, non posse non peccare, the damnation of unbaptised infants. Camus wanted to stress his deep disagreement with 'this other African'; but he shows the influence of Augustine. 'Dans la richesse impressionnante de la sensibilité de Camus, ou encore, dans sa conviction que toute démarche philosophique doit commencer par un reditus in intima mea, serait-ce là que réside l'apport permanent d'Augustin à l'oeuvre de Camus?'

[14] *On order*, 2.8.25.   [15] *On Psalm 118*.

comes from God alone. God's actions are always just, especially when man cannot see his justice. Man is apt to err in his judgement. He cannot even be sure concerning the innocence or guilt of fellow creatures who face him in the courts. In his just providence God sees that all things work together for good. The course of the world, like a poem, gains in beauty through the clashing elements in it.[16] God's perfect righteousness is shown in his decree of predestination. This mysterious power which determine's man's destiny is neither blind nor arbitrary, but is justice and truth.[17]

Only by God's grace is it possible for man's need to be supplied. This grace cannot be earned but is to be received by faith. Against Julian the Pelagian, Augustine insists that all good comes from God, and that therefore grace is indispensable. So Augustine finds it hard to find a place for heathen virtues. He calls them 'splendid vices', and admits both the effect of conscience and a form of piety amongst the ancient Romans. But since true virtue cannot exist without true piety, in the end the Romans have merely achieved an inadequate morality based upon glory. Epicureans look for satisfaction of flesh, while Stoics look for satisfaction of soul. In contrast to both, the Christian seeks to hang upon God. Even Plato has not found true piety, for he cannot see man's moral dependence upon God. The individual virtues of the heathen count for nothing without divine grace which alone can make man good. Yet Augustine places positive value on created things in general and sees moral conditions for their use. Civilisation is based materially on the tension between poverty and wealth; but it is a real unity and the state has moral significance. Because they are under one God, powers of spiritual and physical being should work together. Man may be completely devoted to God and still work for a secular end. He acknowledges the standards and the requirements of his work and his culture but through his inner obedience to God he lives a life which is positive and fruitful. The man who merely serves himself in the service of culture lacks a sense of direction and this lack infects his whole morality.[18]

All righteousness springs from God as *fons justitiae*,[19] *sol justitiae*,[20] *summa justitia*.[21] The 'righteousness of God' has both objective and subjective meaning. It is that by which God himself is said to be just and also that by which a man is justified.[22] But there is a relative

---

[16] *C.D.* 11.18 (*C.D.* = *City of God*). This was a Stoic theme.
[17] Cf. Gilson, *The Christian Philosophy of Saint Augustine*, p. 156.
[18] See J. Mausbach, *Die Ethik des heiligen Augustinus* (Freiburg/Br., 1929), 1, 316 and 350; 2, 260–99.
[19] *C.D.* 1.21.   [20] *C.D.* 5.16.
[21] *C.D.* 20.2.   [22] *C.D.* 22.2.

righteousness[23] in this world which states may achieve[24] and which man may perceive and possess.[25] This rational and original righteousness has survived the fall of man.[26] So while true righteousness is found only in the City of God, and may be anticipated here among believers, there is for pagans and their political organisations a real human righteousness to be found on earth.[27] This righteousness is closely related to peace and concord.[28]

(ii) God's righteousness is always the same; measure, form and order

The chief good is the supreme and original being who exists without change or corruption. The Manichees ask where evil comes from. Augustine insists on a prior question, 'What is evil?', 'Does it exist?', 'Has it being?' Only God exists in his own right, and other substances are derived from him. The Manichees maintain that evil is a nature and substance; but God is the cause of all natures and substances, and God is not the cause of evil. Evil is corruption, negation or privation, not a substance. The Manichee stories about the powers of good and evil have neither consistency nor credibility. God is the highest good. It is absurd to think he could change.[29] The conduct of Manichees is inconsistent with any acceptable moral standard. The conduct of Catholic Christians, even allowing for the unworthy ones, is far superior to that of the Manichees.[30]

Justice is unchangeable and must be God himself. As God who is life grants us to share in life, so God who is justice imparts his justice. 'We are more or less just according as we are united to him in greater or lesser measure. . .This supreme God is clearly true justice, or, this true God is supreme justice.' We must not assess God in terms of our own justice, but think of ourselves as growing more like God the more just we are and the more we share in his grace.[31]

The goodness and justice of God are seen in the work of providence. Evil is simply the absence of good. A wound deprives the body of health, but itself has no positive nature. 'All natures then are good, seeing that the author of absolutely all natures is supremely good. But because, unlike their supreme author, they are not supremely and unchangeably good, the good in them can decrease and increase.'[32]

[23] See V. Hand, Augustin und das klassisch-römische Selbstverständnis (Hamburg, 1970), pp. 55f.
[24] C.D. 19.24ff. [25] C.D. 19.27. On Spirit and Letter, 27.47.
[26] On Spirit and Letter, 28.48.
[27] V. Hand, Augustin, p. 63. [28] Ibid. pp. 63ff.
[29] On morals of Manichees, 3.5–7.11.
[30] On morals of Manichees, 20.74f.
[31] Ep. 120.4.19. [32] Encheiridion, 12.4.

In creation God has placed things in proper order. Trees are superior to dead things, and among living things, animals are superior to plants, and man is superior to animals. Immortals are above mortals, as angels are above men, for 'these are placed first by the order of nature'. However, the value placed on these things is as different as is the use to which they may be put, 'For who would not rather have his pantry full of meat than of mice, or possess pence rather than fleas?'[33]

There is order and variety everywhere. An ape may be beautiful, but it is not as beautiful as a man. The beauty of the ape is a lesser good than the beauty of man. God orders all things, beginning from formless matter, which is not evil, but is potential and not actual. God himself is not subject to measure or limitation, but shows these qualities in his activity. The fall of the angels was due to their sin, and was not the work of God. God turns to a good end what men have done wrong. The eternal fire which tortures the wicked is not evil nor is it eternal in the way that God is eternal. No one can suffer any harm except by the just will of God.[34]

The righteousness required by God consists in keeping one's place in the order of things, serving under him and ruling over all else.

> The lover, then, whom we are describing will get from justice this rule of life, that he must with perfect readiness serve the God whom he loves, the highest good, the highest wisdom, the highest peace; and, as regards all other things, must either rule them as subject to himself, or treat them with a view to their subjection. This rule of life is, as we have taught, confirmed by the authority of both testaments.[35]

God is served by harmony, form and order. The drive towards being is the same as the drive towards unity. Perfect unity is found only in God, who is perfect being, and the whole creation is involved in an imitation of unity through a harmony of its various parts. The soul has a high degree of unity, for it is a simple substance. Existence is always linked with unity or order. Things which exist are united in an ordered way, while corruption produces disorder.[36] All nature is good, and receives from God the qualities of measure, form and order. 'These three things, therefore, measure, form and order, are as it were universal goods in all spiritual or physical things made by God.' A nature that sins is punished to restore the right order of things.[37] Order brings peace. The human body, human society and the whole universe

---

[33] C.D. 11.16.   [34] On nature of good, 22.33.40.
[35] On morals of Catholic Church, 24.44.
[36] On morals of Manichees, 4–6.
[37] On nature of good, 3 and 9.

find their good in a common peace. The appetites of the irrational part and the knowledge of the rational soul must be ordered. Body and soul must live at peace. A society seeks peace which depends upon the proper ordering of its parts. As a healthy body has its many organs in agreement, so a healthy society has its parts ordered. Peace is the tranquillity of order. In its harmony all may rest from striving, all living things are united. Ordered tranquillity does not end on earth, but finds fulfilment in eternal peace with God.

Peace of mortal man and God is ordered obedience in faith under the eternal law. Peace between man is ordered agreement, peace of a family an ordered agreement of form and obedience among its members, peace of a city an ordered agreement of command and obedience among the citizens, peace of the heavenly city a most orderly and harmonious society in enjoyment of God and of one another in God; peace of all things is tranquillity of order. For order is disposition of like and unlike things, allotting to each its place.

The creator of all things, the parent of man, who is the first wonder of creation, gave to man good things in this life, 'health and safety and human fellowship'. With this peace God gave light, air, water, food and drink and clothing, so that man, who uses creation rightly, may know peace, immortality, glory and the full enjoyment of God and of his brother in God.[38] Traces of God which reveal the creator in his creature are not used as proofs of God's existence, but rather as incentives to raise the soul to God. In the beginning God created all that is. Everything was germinally or causally existent in his first creation. The Stoics had used the notion of seed to describe the part played by reason in the world; there are seminal or rational causes in all things. Augustine writes, 'All the normal course of nature has its own natural laws, according to which every living creature has its own fixed tendencies.'[39] Seminal reason is linked with the idea of natural law; 'the world itself is heavy with the causes of things yet to be.'[40] Reason and natural law show man's goal and not his starting point. God rules over all things by the power of his wisdom, so that what seems a miracle to us is not a miracle from his point of view. After all, there is no greater miracle than the world itself, and the God who marvellously made all things is well able to act now in a miraculous manner. God is free to

---

[38] *C.D.* 19.13.
[39] *On Genesis ad litt.*, 9.17.32.
[40] *On the trinity*, 3.9. On seminal reason, see G. Verbeke, 'Augustin et le stoïcisme', *RA* (1958), pp. 81f. See also my *Justin Martyr* (Tübingen, 1973), chapters 2 and 11.

act within nature as he wills, for nature is subject to his divine sovereignty and freedom.[41]

(iii) *Man's righteousness varies*

Virtue, the art of living well and honourably, is not a gift of nature,
but something to be acquired. Virtue is an art or harmony between
extremes. It may be identified with right reason, 'Right reason is virtue
itself',[42] or with the love by which what should be loved is loved.[43] 'A
concise and accurate definition of virtue is: the order of love.'[44] While
God is unchangeably good, the good in his creatures may increase or
decrease. Human wills are changeable and imperfect because they
were created from nothing. They had only to turn from creator to
creature for the disorder of sin to break out.

In the Sermon on the Mount, Augustine finds 'as regards the highest
morals a perfect standard of the Christian life', and a foundation on
which man may build to survive floods and storms. The sermon is
given on a mountain, which indicates its pre-eminence over former
teaching. It is concerned with 'the greater precepts of righteousness'.
Our Lord requires that we should fulfil not only the least precepts of
the law, but those which he himself has added as he comes to fulfil
the law.[45]

The living of the good life is further complicated by degrees of merit
or failure. To begin with, there is a difference between precepts and
counsels. To disobey a precept is sin, while to disobey a counsel is to
lose an opportunity of gaining merit. There is a difference between
mortal and venial sin, between those sins which cannot be forgiven
and those which can. Venial sins are daily or trivial sins without which
one cannot live. Goodness also is not of one order. 'Incipient charity
is incipient righteousness; advanced charity is advanced righteousness;
outstanding charity is outstanding righteousness, and perfect charity
is perfect righteousness.' In heaven, glory will be awarded according to
obedience on earth, and in hell, punishment will be proportionate to
one's sins.[46]

The Stoics maintain that all virtues are equal, and that there are no
degrees of virtue or vice. It is true that love fulfils the whole law, and

---

[41] *C.D.* 10.12. See R. A. Markus, *Cambridge History of later Greek and Early
Medieval Philosophy* (ed. A. H. Armstrong, Cambridge, 1967), pp. 399f.;
Markus provides (pp. 341–419) the best short account of Augustine's
thought on philosophical themes.
[42] *On usefulness of believing*, 12.27.
[43] *Ep.* 167.15.   [44] *C.D.* 15.22.
[45] *On Sermon on Mount*, 1.9.21.
[46] *On nature and grace*, 70, 84. *Encheiridion* 31, 111ff.

when one sins against one commandment, one sins against love. However this does not mean that all sins are equally serious. Sins may be assessed according to gravity and frequency. Moral problems need careful analysis. A liar is one who holds back truth, or speaks falsehood. There are eight different degrees of gravity in this offence.[47] The question of war is complex. In war man kills in obedience to law and not from passion. John the Baptist did not tell the soldiers to give up their profession but he told them not to use violence. One should render to Caesar what is rightly Caesar's, and the paying of tribute involves support of wars. The centurion is praised for his faith and not told to desert from the army. How can war be right? The natural order implies that a prince has power to declare war. God may command war to test the righteous or to destroy the proud, but a war of conquest is nothing but wholesale brigandage. War is sometimes necessary to assure the triumph of justice, and it can be a good thing when compared to the rule of wicked men. The fear of war keeps a nation from corruption and from civil war. War can be a sad necessity. Brave soldiers deserve honour, but more glorious are those who by peaceful words destroy war.[48]

Augustine establishes the ban on suicide which has dominated Christian thought ever since. Suicide is wrong because it involves killing a man. This prevents a man from gaining wisdom and virtue, or if he should already possess them, it deprives society of what he has. Augustine disposes of the various grounds which are given for suicide, such as suffering, falling into the hands of enemies, threat of martyrdom or dishonour. We are told that when persecuted in one city we should flee to the next. Suicide is forbidden to the worshippers of the one true God.[49] The horror of suicide was not of Jewish or Christian origin.[50] In the Roman world there were two moralities: a refined way for the nobility and a simple way for the people.[51] Roman law protected the refined morality, while the institution of slavery guarded the second. When the church suddenly received the entire population of the Empire both moralities were preserved.[52] Those who ruled in church and state had different duties from those who were ruled, although the church never dropped her claim that the message was the

---

[47] *On lying*, 14.25.
[48] *Ep.* 189.6, 229.2, and *C.D.* 1.1 and 2. R. Gosselin, *La morale de S. Augustin* (Paris, 1925), p. 147.
[49] *C.D.* 1.22.
[50] See A. Bayet, *Le suicide et la morale* (Paris, 1922), Part 2, chapters 1 and 2.
[51] *Ibid.* p. 307.
[52] *Ibid.* p. 319. 'La haute Église adopte une morale nuancée, un peu incertaine, qui ressemble de façon frappante à celle de l'aristocratie païenne; la foule garde, sous de étiquettes neuves, l'antique morale d'en bas.'

same for all. Yet it was the popular pagan morality which came to dominate the attitude to suicide. Sextus had forbidden suicide but approved non-resistance to a murderous attack.[53] Ambrose and Jerome reject suicide as a Christian option.[54] Lactantius rejects suicide as the worst of crimes even if it be practised by philosophers through their false belief that the soul is immortal.[55] Augustine's argument takes up the account given by Lactantius. No one has the right, as an individual, to kill either an innocent or a guilty man. The prohibition, 'Thou shalt not kill', is absolute against suicide. It is nobler to endure rather than to escape difficulty by death. It is foolish to kill oneself to avoid temptation and sin, because thereby one commits a certain sin to avoid a possible sin.[56]

While Augustine's views are set in opposition to philosophy and echo the sentiments of the simple people, it is only the Stoic and Epicurean view which is rejected. Plato is strongly on Augustine's side.[57] Plotinus is equally firm that one should not take life into one's own hands nor prevent the soul from further progress before it leaves the body.[58] Plotinus saved Porphyry from suicide so Porphyry's opposition to suicide is no academic affair.[59] Apuleius rejects suicide because it takes from divine law a prerogative which does not belong to man.[60]

One may acknowledge that the widespread acceptance of the ban on suicide which followed Augustine was largely due to the disappearance of the aristocracy and the triumph of what had been the popular pagan morality.[61] However, in Augustine's case, Platonism must have played the dominant role.[62]

Augustine wrote extensively on marriage and virginity.[63] He sees marriage as the first form of human society. It possesses a holiness of its own, and is based on natural law. Marriage is concerned to propagate the human race, and to realise the natural society of man

---

[53] Sextus, 321; cf. H. Chadwick, *The Sentences of Sextus* (Cambridge, 1959), p. 100.
[54] Bayet, *Le suicide et la morale*, pp. 323f. Ambrose, *On virgins*, 3.32ff. Jerome, *Comm. Matt.* 4.27, and *Ep.* 39.3.
[55] Bayet, *op. cit.*, p. 324. Lactantius, *Div. Inst.*, III. 18.
[56] *C.D.* 1.17–27. See Bayet, *op. cit.*, p. 324f.
[57] *Phaedo* 61, *Laws* 873C. See Bayet, *op. cit.*, p. 284.
[58] *Enn.* 1.9.
[59] *On Abstinence*, 2.47.
[60] *De Plat.* 2.254. See Bayet, *Le suicide et la morale*, p. 328.
[61] This is Bayet's case, p. 372.
[62] For the very late emergence of the English word and the background of thought, see D. Daube, 'The Linguistics of Suicide', in *Philosophy and Public Affairs*, 1, 2 (1972), 387–437.
[63] *On continence, on the good of marriage, on holy virginity, on the good of widowhood, on adulterous unions.*

with woman. The authority or power over a wife's body belongs to the husband, and the power over the husband's body belongs to the wife. Augustine insisted, as had John Chrysostom, that the same standards of marital fidelity were required of husbands as of wives.[64] Marriage for Christians is a sacrament, yet celibacy holds a higher place because it means consecration to God alone. The virgin shares with angels and anticipates, in this flesh, the incorruption of eternity. Augustine returned to the subject of marriage on several occasions and concluded in his *Retractationes* that, although he had shown their complexity, he had not achieved a full statement of the issues involved.[65]

Augustine wrote *Concerning the industry of monks* at the request of the bishop of Carthage. Many monks did no work and claimed that it was inconsistent with their profession. Augustine attacks their position and defends the dignity of work. Against the motto of some monks, 'Only pray and read', Augustine proposes: 'Work and pray.' This theme, anticipated in the East by John Chrysostom, is to be the ruling principle of western monasticism. Augustine's teaching influences first Benedict, and then the whole Christian attitude to work in the middle ages and in the modern world.[66] Augustine laid down his own monastic rule for those who lived at Hippo with him. Just as he had followed an elaborate moral code in his days as a Manichee, so he had tried to find a discipline which would fit in with the spirituality of Platonism.[67]

[64] *Sermons* 9.4 and 392.4 and 6. See P. Brown, *AH*, p. 248.

[65] *Retract.*, 2.53. See M. F. Berrouard, 'Augustin et l'indissolubilité du mariage', *RA* (1968), pp. 139–55. It is impossible to give a complete account of Augustine's opinions here. After a spirited, if optimistic defence of Augustine against dualism, F. J. Thonnard writes, 'On y trouve bien le dualisme biblique "chair-esprit" inspiré de saint Jean et saint Paul; mais il est pleinement surmonté grâce à la méthode personaliste et en s'appuyant sur la toute-puissance de la grâce du Christ; – de telle sorte que la morale conjugale y est intégrée à une spiritualité du mariage où la sanctification des époux chrétiens est pour ainsi dire placée sous la lumineuse attraction des conseils évangéliques': 'La morale conjugale selon S. Augustin', *REA* (1969), p. 130.

[66] *On the work of monks*, passim. See A. Zumkeller, *Das Mönchtum des heiligen Augustinus* (Würzburg, 1968), p. 112.

[67] On Augustine's monastic beginnings it is important to separate fact from fiction. R. J. Halliburton has indicated 'the errors of the theories that St. Augustine resolved to become a monk at his conversion and that he consciously prepared for the monastic life while at Cassiciacum...They are after all but the echoes of an earlier polemic, which is in turn the echo of a medieval legend', 'Fact and Fiction in the Life of Augustine', *RA* (1968), pp. 39f.

(iv) *Sin is opposite to righteousness*

'Sin is the will to keep or seek what righteousness forbids.' Sin violates the justice of God because it harms the soul in which he dwells and disrupts the order of his world. 'You offend him with your mischief; when you injure yourself you injure him, for you do injury to his grace and to his dwelling place.'[68] While angels naturally excel men by the law of righteousness, good men are placed above bad angels. Evil is not natural, but is a result of free choice.

Man does not possess innate righteousness, for if this were the case, the death of Christ would have been superfluous.[69] Sin may take many forms. It is wrong to act against nature, even with good intention, for ends do not justify means. A work which is clearly bad cannot be an act of love, because love works no evil. Sin can grow; anger can become a word which expresses anger and merits the greater judgement of the council and hell fire. The greater righteousness requires that one should not merely obey the law concerning adultery in a literal sense, but should obey it from the heart. Sin is made of three components: suggestion, pleasure and consent.[70]

Fallen man is marked by self-love, greed, love of power and glory, and lust. Nature is good, but evil men have made this evil world. From his earliest years Augustine was troubled by the power of sin. He writes with rhetorical power: 'Behold with what companions I walked the streets of Babylon and wallowed in its mire, as if in a bed of spices and precious ointments! And that I might hold the closer to its very centre the unseen enemy trod me down and seduced me, for I was easy to seduce.'[71]

There is the dramatic account of how he, with his friends, stole some pears. He wanted to steal, not because he was hungry, nor because he was poor; but because he was sick of doing what was right and because he was pampered by sin. 'It was foul and I loved it. I loved to perish, I loved my own fault, not that for which I was faulty, but my fault itself. Foul soul falling from your sky to utter destruction, not seeking anything through the shame but the shame itself.' Augustine dwells on this apparently trivial fault because it shows the deep roots of sin, his ignorance of inner righteousness and of the right law of God.[72] He is brought to suffering because of sin. God breaks his

---

[68] *On two souls, against Manichees* 11, 15; *Sermon* 9.10.
[69] *Against Julian*, 4.3.17.
[70] *On Sermon on Mount*, 1.12.33 and 34.
[71] *Confessions*, 2.3.8–2.4.9.
[72] For further possible meaning, see L. C. Ferrari, 'The Pear-Theft in Augustine's "Confessions"', *REA* (1970), pp. 233–42.

bones with the staff of correction. When he passes the age of thirty he says, 'My evil and abominable youth was now dead and I was passing into early manhood.'

DISCIPLESHIP

(i) *Blessed is he who has God*

All men desire the happy life, or the blessedness of the Beatitudes. Augustine defines simply: 'Blessed is he who has God.' Participation in God is the chief end of man's life. Man's good is found in the exercise of his contemplative mind and the purification of his soul for the vision of God. The soul comes before the body. Yet the body benefits from the virtuous soul because it is ruled in a better way. Soul and body are like a coachman and horses. If Augustine tells his coachman to look after the horses and rewards him, 'Can anyone deny that the good condition of the horses as well as that of the coachman is due to me?' The highest good remains in God himself. 'Following (*secutio*) after God is the desire of happiness; to reach (*consecutio*) God is happiness itself. We follow after God by loving him. *We reach him not by becoming entirely what he is, but in nearness to him and in wonderful and intelligible contact with him.*' Love makes us like God, and this may be called our conforming to God, and our circumcision from this world. These ideas are in the Old Testament as in the New for the psalmist says: 'It is good for me to cleave to God.' The word 'cleave' says what the apostle Paul has said about love. The saints who love God live in perfect continence and in amazing indifference to the world.[1]

Happiness is both the motive and the result of knowledge. 'Man has no reason to philosophise except for the sake of happiness.' By wisdom man sees and possesses the supreme good. Man's likeness to God must be a matter for mind and soul, because God has no body. God is the source and Christ is the centre of all morality.[2] God, who is perfect being and goodness is known as 'holiness working on the will in the form of omnipotent love'. Two principles of Augustine's ethics are 'Nothing is good except a good will', and 'None is good but God.'[3] Augustine believes just as much in the end of happiness as does the

---

[1] *On morals of Catholic Church*, chapters 3–30, including 11.18.
[2] J. Mausbach, *Die Ethik des heiligen Augustinus* (Freiburg/Br., 1929), **I**, 51–127.
[3] Cf. A. von Harnack, *History of Dogma*, 5 (E.T. 1898), 118f., 'It belongs just as essentially to God to be grace (*gratia*) imparting itself in love, as to be the uncaused cause of causes (*causa causatrix non causata*).'

Platonist Antiochus, but he does not believe that this happiness can be found on earth or apart from God. The good are those who live 'according to God'. Those who live 'according to man' are bad, even when they claim to follow the path of virtue.[4]

Augustine's account of man's chief end moves through four main phases. In the first phase, at Cassiciacum, he shows close affinity with Stoicism and Neoplatonism: life must be lived according to reason. The second phase is found in the works concerning the morals of the Catholic church and the morals of the Manichees; life must be lived according to God. In the third phase, the phase of *Concerning Christian doctrine*, his moral theory is organically related to his whole Christian system. In the fourth phase, the city of God shows the moral problem on the scale of world history[5] and happiness is communal in its nature.

Happiness is fullness of joy. Joy in truth, *gaudium de veritate*, is found only in God. Beatific joy, truth and sovereign good unite in the vision of God. Like Plotinus, Augustine looks for the image of God in the inner shrine of the soul. Only by ascent through mind and soul can one know God. However, Augustine's conversion leads to a crucial difference between him and the Platonists: 'he knew his heart to be his worst possession and the living God to be his highest good.'[6] So while, for Plotinus, union with the One is a conquest for man to achieve, for Augustine, union with God is God's gift in Jesus Christ.[7] Yet Augustine's account of God as the supreme good, the object of man's love and the source of man's blessedness, has been severely attacked. In one place he is described as the 'destroyer of Christian morality'.[8] In another it is claimed that his account of love is egocentric, and turns God into the source of man's enjoyment. For Augustine, love still retains some of the character of *erōs*. It is desire, yearning or *desiderium*.[9] But God never becomes relative to man. He is always the supreme good, supreme being and good in himself. Other things exist and are good in dependence upon his being and goodness. The soul is the life of the body, and God is the happy life of the soul, 'For just as the whole life of the body is the soul, so the blessed life of the soul is God.'[10] As for Plato the ideas or forms participate in the Form

---

[4] *C.D.* 15.1.   [5] R. Holte, *Béatitude et sagesse* (Paris, 1962), pp. 194ff.
[6] A. von Harnack, *History of Dogma*, **5,** 64.
[7] See M. Comeau, 'La vie intérieure du Chrétien', *RSR*, 20 (1930), 5–25, 125–49.
[8] K. Holl, *Der Neubau der Sittlichkeit, Ges. Aufsätze* 1 (1921), 139. Cited Holte, *Béatitude et sagesse*, p. 207.
[9] R. Holte, *op. cit.*, p. 208. For Nygren's account of Augustine, see *Agape and Eros* (London, 1953), Part 2, 2, chapters 1–4.
[10] *On free will*, 2.16.41.

of the Good, so for Augustine the good or blessed life is participation in God. As we cleave to the eternal creator, we are ourselves necessarily affected with eternity.[11] In this immortality we may be called divine: 'God wills to make you a god, not by nature as his Son is, but by his gift and adoption.'[12] To enjoy, possess or participate in God is to be formed in the image of God and made to live in obedience to the will of the creator. In his fallen state man wishes to be his own master and lives by pride. He does not see the order of things, until he turns to God. Then grasping the order of things in obedience and subordination to God, he finds freedom and happiness.[13]

The Christian is a servant of God who finds in God's service true and perfect freedom. He serves with a complete and ready will, in fellowship with others. 'The servant of God is the people of God, the church of God.' In Augustine the noun 'servant' occurs fifty times, the verb 'serve' occurs twenty-five times, and the abstract expression 'service of God' is often found. The words frequently express the special dedication of the monk; 'To hold his heart ready, to follow the will of the Lord, to do what he has decided for his servants, whether he strikes or spares'.[14] Yet service given to God is free service, for the monks are 'not as servants under the law'.[15] The community which Augustine establishes on his return to Africa displays a common life in loving and serving God. Platonic and Stoic influences unite in his ideal of the Christian ascetic, who is the Christian philosopher, the truly wise man.[16] The whole aim of philosophy was happiness or blessedness, and Plato identified that supreme good in which man may find happiness with God. 'And therefore he would have it that to be a philosopher is to be a lover of God.'[17]

---

[11] *On true religion*, 10, 19.

[12] *Sermon* 166.4.4. See comment of A. H. Armstrong, *St. Augustine and Christian Platonism* (Villanova Univ. Press, 1967), pp. 6ff.

[13] *On morals of Catholic Church*, 13.22. See R. Holte, *Béatitude et sagesse*, pp. 229–31.

[14] *Ep.* 243.12, cited Zumkeller, *Das Mönchtum des Heiligen Augustinus*, p. 159.

[15] *Rule for the servants of God* 12. 'These *servi dei* had owed their position in the Latin church less to any connexion with an organised monastic life than to the pressure of a fashion in perfection....a *servus dei*, a baptised, dedicated layman, determined to live, in the company of bishops, priests and noble patrons, the full life of a Christian', P. Brown, *AH*, p. 132. See also G. Folliet, '*Aux origines de l'ascétisme et du cénobitisme africain*', *SA*, 46 (1961), 25–44.

[16] *On morals of Catholic Church*, 17.31.

[17] *C.D.* 8.8.

(ii) *Put on the Lord Jesus Christ*

The turning point in Augustine's life was the command to put on the Lord Jesus Christ. The incarnation presents the divine law in the person of Christ, and gives an example of life in him.[18] 'The measure and test of all morality and all holiness is the inward surrender and complete orientation of the soul to God.'[19] To be a Christian is not just to accept divine truth and obey divine commands. To be a Christian is to be born again in the new man, which is Christ. 'Christ is my source, Christ is my root, Christ is my head.'[20] The good life is a quest for likeness to God. Man is made in the image of God, and by participation in the life of God, the image which is in man may be restored to God's likeness. 'Where understanding, mind, and the reason which discovers truth are, where faith, hope and love are, there God has his image.'[21] Man possesses divine life, so far as his soul partakes of the divine wisdom and becomes able to receive God. By faith, men are drawn to the sonship of God, not a natural sonship like that of the only begotten Son, but one of participation in wisdom.[22] The measure of our assimilation to God is the measure of our progress in love and in perception of God.[23] The renewal of likeness through the indwelling spirit of God leads to a deeper insight concerning God and eternal truth.[24] The indwelling Christ is the source of righteousness and life, 'For Christ is life and he dwells in their hearts for the present by faith, but hereafter by direct sight. For they see now through a glass darkly, but then face to face.'[25] Through him we learn the breadth and length and height and depth and his love which passes knowledge. The breadth is good works, the length is endurance and perseverance, the height is the hope of heavenly reward, and the depth is the hidden grace of God.[26]

The command to follow Christ is the second pattern which Augustine uses to describe the ascetic life. To follow or imitate Christ is his frequent theme. Matthew 11:29, 'Learn of me, for I am meek and lowly of heart', and 1 Peter 2:21, 'Christ has suffered for us and left us an example that we should follow in his steps', are often quoted. Augustine says, 'What does it mean to follow him except to imitate

[18] *On true religion*, 16.30. *Ep.* 11.4.
[19] K. Adam, *S. Augustine* (1932), p. 39.
[20] *Against Petilian*, 1.7.8.
[21] *On Psalm* 48.2, 11.   [22] *On Galatians*, 27.
[23] *On Psalm* 99.5. 'Quantum accedis ad similitudinem, tantum proficis in caritate, et tanto incipis sentire Deum.'
[24] See Zumkeller, *Das Mönchtum des heiligen Augustinus*, p. 210.
[25] *Ep.* 140.25.62.   [26] *Sermon* 53.14.

him. . .Everyone follows him in the respect in which he imitates him.'
The imitation of Christ may take many forms, as the beatitudes show
us,[27] and it expresses our love for him. 'If we truly love him, let us
imitate him. For we shall be able to produce no better fruit of love
than the example of imitation.'[28] Imitation is linked with the mystery
of the incarnation. His humiliation and death is that act of the son of
God, which brings true rest to those who try to imitate it.[29] Through
his lowliness and weakness Christ saves us from pride, nourishes us in
love, and becomes the way for us.[30]

In all men there is an image of the holy trinity, to be restored and
to become like, though not equal, to the original. There is a three-fold
structure in man's being, his knowledge and his love for being and
knowledge.[31] Man's soul is created like God, for the soul gives man
reason and understanding, and makes him supreme over other
creatures. God made man out of the earth and breathed his breath
into him to give him life.[32] Of the two great cities or societies of men –
those who live according to man and those who live according to God
– the second will be made like the image of the Son of God. As he was
made like us in mortality, we shall be made like him in immortality.
In the resurrection we shall rise again to be like him and to be with
him.[33] It is hard for man to know himself as one in the presence of
God. This self-knowledge leads to knowledge of God and to true
humility.[34] Christ is a teacher who produces inner transformation
rather than outward effects.

Shortly before Augustine's conversion, the call to discipleship in
Matthew 19:21 and the response of Saint Anthony and of the two
young imperial officials pointed to the contemplative life as a way of
following Christ.[35] The direction of discipleship was inward. Christ,
the inward teacher, is the truth. One should not wander abroad, but
should retire into oneself, for truth dwells in the inner man.[36] The soul,
the image of God, is able to see as God gives illumination. The ascetic

[27] Cf. Mausbach, *Die Ethik des heiligen Augustinus*, 1, 391–6.
[28] *Sermon* 304.2.2.   [29] *Confessions*, 7.9.14.
[30] *Confessions* 7.18.24.   [31] *C.D.* 11.26.
[32] *C.D.* 12.23.   [33] *C.D.* 22.16.
[34] *On Psalm 38*.8. See O. Schaffner, *Christliche Demut* (Würzburg, 1959),
    p. 206: 'humilior ex eo quod deest, quam elatior ex eo quod adest'.
[35] *Confessions*, 8.6.14 and 15.
[36] *On true religion*, 39.72. See P. Brown, *AH*, p. 181, 'It is this therapy
    of self-examination, which has, perhaps, brought Augustine closest to some
    of the best traditions of our own age. Like a planet in opposition, he has
    come as near to us, in Book Ten of the *Confessions*, as the vast gulf that
    separates a modern man from the culture and religion of the Later Empire
    can allow: Ecce enim dilexisti veritatem, quoniam qui facit eam venit ad
    lucem.'

life is free and rational, not driven by the compulsion of dualism. Manicheeism is inconsistent with Christianity. Love inspires all Christian living, both in the world and out of the world. Whether we serve God in our daily work or in the contemplative life, our whole life is guided and ruled by the same spirit. The love of God and one's neighbour includes all goodness.[37]

Discipleship is life in Christ and in the body of Christ. The Christian through the imitation of the poverty of Jesus becomes a member of Christ, the poor man. Christ prints on his follower the likeness of the new Adam, and the virgin dedicated to God is joined to Christ by spiritual marriage.[38] A Christian grows up in Christ. 'Christ will be formed in him who receives the form of Christ, but he receives the form of Christ who hangs on Christ in spiritual love. So it happens that through imitation he becomes what Christ is, within the limits of his position.'[39] Discipleship is a corporate thing. The church, in following Christ, declares him and his hope of salvation. The whole body in all its members follows Christ. All have their part in the life of Christ. All must deny themselves and take up the cross for Christ's sake.[40] Prayer is central because God is central, 'God and the soul I long to know. Nothing more? Nothing whatever.'[41] Prayer expresses this central loyalty to God, the love and yearning of man towards God and eternal things. In the eucharist is found the body and blood of the Christ who was incarnate, suffered and rose again.[42] Augustine speaks of present life in heaven, in contemplation of God, in freedom from passion, and in 'enjoying communion with God...most blessed in contemplation of his beauty'.[43] Mary, who sits at the feet of her Lord, is a picture of the heavenly church, and of that restful, blessed and eternal life, the holy leisure which finds its perfection in present participation of heavenly vision.[44] The religious community lives with one heart and with one soul in God. Such a community is the temple of God. The fellowship of saints are together and individually the temple of God because he dwells within them.[45]

---

[37] *Sermon* 350.2 and 3.
[38] *Ep.* 243.2ff. and *On virginity*, 2. This section is indebted to Zumkeller, *Das Mönchtum des heiligen Augustinus*, pp. 152ff.
[39] *On Galatians*, 38.
[40] *Sermon* 96.7.9.
[41] *Soliloquies* 1.27.
[42] See W. Gessel, *Eucharistische Gemeinschaft bei Augustinus* (Würzburg, 1966), pp. 175ff.
[43] *On Morals of Catholic Church*, 31.66.
[44] *Sermon* 104.3.4. 'Quod agebat Martha, ibi sumus: quod agebat Maria, hoc speramus'.
[45] *C.D.* 10.3.

(iii) *He who made you demands all of you*[46]

There can be no compromise between the love of God and the love of the world. A servant of God must be separate from those who love the world, 'I had left behind me all worldly hope.' 'I separated myself from those who love the world.'[47] Mortification of flesh and self-denial are obligatory for every Christian. Manichean and Neoplatonic dualism left some mark on Augustine. The body is a prison to the soul, because it is linked with punishment and with death. It is a heavy fetter, a grave and a burden. Yet on the other hand the body is the creation of God. The flesh is corruptible and, strictly speaking, it is this corruption which is a prison rather than the body itself. For the incarnation redeemed man's body and gave it new and higher value. The bodies of the saints are sacrifices before God, members of Christ and the temple of the Holy Spirit. But, for us, the harmony of the whole man, the union of body and soul without tension will be known first in the resurrection of the flesh.[48]

Renunciation works with a safety margin, giving up some things which are permitted. He who cannot deny himself what he is permitted, is already close to what is forbidden. Mortification expresses man's eternal longing after God, the angels and heaven. It gives up carnal joy, to receive in its place spiritual joy. It reunites men to the One from whom they were broken into many.[49] The example of Christ dominates; 'For this reason he was on earth dishonoured and crucified, that he might teach us to despise the good things of this world rather than to love them.'[50] His teaching points the same way. 'Listen to what he has said: "If one comes to me but does not hate his father, and mother, wife and child, sons, brothers and sisters, indeed even his own life, then he cannot be my disciple."'[51] We are joined to him in sacrifice. 'A true sacrifice is every work that is done in order to be joined to God in sacred fellowship.'[52] God does not want slaughtered animals but humble hearts. In such sacrifices there is realised the universal sacrifice of the church which was foreshadowed in the death of Christ upon the cross,

> that all the redeemed city, that is, the congregation and society of the saints might be offered as a universal sacrifice to God by that great priest who even offered himself in his passion for us...in the

[46] *Sermon* 34.4.7. [47] *Sermon* 355.2.
[48] *On Psalm 141.18*. See Zumkeller, *Das Mönchtum des heiligen Augustinus*, p. 259.
[49] *Confessions*, 10.29.40. [50] *Ep.* 220.1.
[51] *Ep.* 243.2. [52] *C.D.* 10.6.

form of a servant. This form he offered, and in this he was offered;
for in this he is our mediator, priest and sacrifice.[53]

Christian life is constant warfare. The Christian soldier fights against
Satan and bad angels, to triumph by the strength of Christ. While
every Christian is a soldier, the martyr or the monk fulfils the ideal
best. The monk has thrown off earthly ties and dedicated his heart
freely to the service of God. He is able to serve because he is not caught
up in this world's affairs.[54] The good life includes a moderate and
practical asceticism. Marriage is holy, but he prefers virginity to marriage, not as a good to an evil, but as the better to the good. Augustine
defends monastic and other vows.[55]

Continence or self-control, the subject of a special treatise, is concerned with control of the heart and not merely control of the lips.
Our Lord taught us to cleanse what is within, and the cleanness of
what is outside will follow.[56] To achieve this virtue involves a constant
battle of virtues against vices.[57] Another treatise argues the goodness
of marriage. The first natural bond of human society is that of man
and wife. Marriage requires continence which is always a virtue of the
soul rather than the body.[58] Virginity, the subject of another treatise, is
preferable to marriage. No fruitfulness of the flesh can be compared
with the holy virginity of the flesh.[59] It is a gift of God, to be guarded
and protected. Christ is the bridegroom of virgins and they are joined
to him in love. A treatise on the good of widowhood shows how those
bereft of husbands should find in their new state a way of serving God.
Abstinence from flesh and wine does not mean that these things are
evil; it aims to do three things – to check indulgence, to protect weakness and to avoid offence.[60] Fasting and abstinence, as far as health
allows, are valuable. Mortification is a life-long job; but if one has
attained perfection, then the time of struggle is over, for the flesh has
become spiritual and incorruptible, and is risen to an eternal life.[61]
Augustine puts no special value on the number or the extent of ascetic
practices.

In his early work *Concerning the morals of the Catholic Church*,
Augustine shows the influence of the Stoic ideal of *apatheia* or passionlessness. The passions are to be removed and avoided. Later, Augustine
comes to see that the affections of man are given by God. In the *City
of God* the passions are perturbations or affections such as desire and
fear, joy and sorrow. They become morally neutral and capable of

[53] *Ibid.*   [54] *On the work of monks*, 15.16.
[55] *On morals of Catholic Church*, 31.67. *Ep.* 150 and *Ep.* 211.
[56] *On continence*, 2.4.   [57] *Ibid* 3.8.
[58] *On marriage*, 22.27.   [59] *On virginity*, 8.8.
[60] *On morals of Manichees*, 14.   [61] *On fasting*, 1.

good or bad use, 'According to holy scripture and sound teaching, the citizens of the holy city of God are on the pilgrim journey of this life, and although they live according to God, yet they feel fear and desire, pain and joy. Yet because they possess the right love, all these affections are right.[62] The ideal of passionlessness comes to mean avoiding those passions which war against reason and the spirit. This high ideal cannot be realised on earth. If one interprets *apatheia* strictly in the manner of the Stoics, it is a *stupor* which Augustine regards as a curse. Such a state is in lasting contradiction to the love and joy of the Christian man. Yet another meaning for the ideal of *apatheia* is freedom from all pain and fear. This is an ideal state which the Christian does not achieve on earth but only in heaven.

Poverty is not a goal in itself, but a way of becoming free from worldly burdens in order to serve God better. 'Voluntary poverty' makes it easier to receive God and divine things. Such poverty is true wealth. Augustine says, 'Listen to me, you poor, what do you not possess if you have God? Listen to me, you rich, what do you possess if you have not God?'[63] Poverty is part of following Christ who was poor and humble. Happy are the poor in spirit who make themselves poor by an act of will. Poverty is humility in following the Christ who for our sakes became poor. Discipleship looses all earthly ties, the better to carry the cross, and wears no longer the image of the first Adam, but that of the second Adam who came from heaven.[64]

Augustine found the first great difference between Platonism and Christianity in the new fact of the incarnation. The Word had emptied himself, taken the form of a servant, and become obedient to the death of the cross. By his poverty the Christian points to the true poor man who can save mankind. The example of the son of God, the practice of world-denying virtue and the fellowship of the Church, protect the Christian against worldly sins.[65] Christ is 'the teacher of humility through word and example'.[66] He who would share eternal blessedness with Christ must follow him along the way of suffering and pain. 'Such great humility of so great a God!', says Augustine. The humility of Christ is without measure because of his infinite greatness. So all springs from Christ; 'Christ is my source, Christ is my root, Christ is my head.'[67]

[62] *C.D.* 14.9. See Zumkeller, *Das Mönchtum des heiligen Augustinus*, p. 262.
[63] *Sermon* 311.18.15.
[64] *Ep.* 243.10.
[65] See Mausbach, *Die Ethik des heiligen Augustinus*, I, 351ff.
[66] *Sermon* 62.1.1.
[67] *On faith and creed*, 4.8; *Against Petilian*, 1.7.8. See Schaffner, *Christliche Demut*, pp. 93–128. Augustine's insistence on the central place of humility in Christology and ethics had lasting effects. 'The type of humility

In his account[68] of glory as in that of virtue, justice and common-wealth, Augustine draws on and transforms the values of Roman culture. Glory is the *'iudicium hominum bene de hominibus opinantium'*.[69] The longing for this glory is an 'ingens cupiditas' which finds no lasting satisfaction on earth. The believer alone finds true glory[70] in the glory of God.[71] Augustine contrasts the true God with the gods of men 126 times in the *City of God*. He also speaks of true religion (25 times), true piety (20 times), true virtue (11 times), true happiness (10 times), true justice (9 times), true sacrifice (8 times) and true divinity (5 times). In each case the idea is seen to be redefined in a specific Christian sense.[72] It is agreed 'among all who are truly pious, that no one can have true virtue without true piety, that is, without the true worship of the true God, nor can that be true virtue which serves the glory of man'.[73] So the noble army of martyrs far excels the virtues of the great Roman figures like the Scaevolae.[74] Apparent virtues which do not depend on God are to be seen as vices.[75]

FAITH

(i) *Faith and knowledge*

Faith is where Augustine begins. He often quotes, 'Unless you believe you will not understand', never thinking of faith in general, but of Christian faith which works by love, frees the soul and produces good works.[1] We prepare for faith by reason. We believe in order that we may understand, and understand in order that we might believe. Faith is tied to morals, and does not separate illumination of mind from purification of heart, 'In its essence, Augustinian faith is both an adherence of the mind to supernatural truth and a humble surrender of the whole man to the grace of Christ.'[2] To believe in God means to love him and enter into him through love, being incorporated in his

---

exhibited in majesty – this it was that overpowered Augustine: pride was sin, and humility was the sphere and force of goodness.' A. von Harnack, *History of Dogma*, **5**, 131.

[68] See V. Hand, *Augustin und das klassisch-römische Selbstverständnis* (Hamburg, 1970), for the main argument of this paragraph.

[69] *C.D.* 5.12.   [70] *C.D.* 5.18.   [71] *Ibid.*

[72] See V. Hand, *Augustine und das klassisch-römische Selbstverständnis*, pp. 26f.

[73] *C.D.* 5.19.   [74] Cf. *C.D.* 5.14 and 18.

[75] *C.D.* 19.5 and 21.16; cf. Hand, *Augustine und das klassisch-römische Selbstverständnis*, p. 35.

[1] Isa. 7.9 (Latin version), *nisi credideritis, non intelligetis. On Gospel of John*, 29.6.

[2] E. Gilson, *The Christian Philosophy of Saint Augustine*, p. 31.

members. Faith ends in the knowledge of the beatific vision when the blessed no longer believe but have direct knowledge of the Father in the Son. The faith which understands is warm with zeal. We are to love with all our hearts to understand; to prove the existence of God, we must believe in him.[3] Faith is not just *doctrine*, but also *discipline*,[4] for the church is the fellowship of Christians united in living faith. Pledged to Christ alone, they are his virgin bride. The church is the mother of all Christians, a virgin who has brought forth virgins in devotion to the one Lord.[5] Those who live a dedicated life must always remember that they do not depend upon their own righteousness, but upon God, who alone justifies them.

(ii) *Freedom and grace*

Freedom from sin depends entirely upon God's healing grace. 'The misery of sin overcome by faith, humility and love – that is Christian piety. In this temper the Christian was to live.'[6] Sin springs from the will, and the will needs divine grace. Believers are renewed daily until their righteousness is perfect. Until then they are saved by hope, 'Full righteousness therefore will only then be reached when fullness of health is attained, and this fullness of health shall be when there is fullness of love. For love is the fulfilling of the law.'[7] Until man has been healed by the grace of God, he cannot be free. He wants to live happily, but cannot. Apart from the one mediator between God and man, everyone has needed forgiveness of sins.[8]

'Without the help of God we cannot by free will overcome the temptations of this life.'[9] Grace is a secret power. Prevenient grace comes first to initiate good thoughts and aspirations. Co-operating grace is that by which God helps what he has begun. Sufficient grace is that which Adam possessed before he fell. Efficient grace is possessed by all saints whom God has predestined to share in his kingdom, and who are enabled to will and to do what God requires. 'Grace gives merits and is not given in reward for them.'[10] A sense of disquiet is the first effect of God's prevenient grace, when the voice of the Saviour breaks hard hearts of stone. With disquiet comes desire for unity with God. Grace substitutes delight in good for delight in evil. That law which

---

[3] *Ibid.* p. 38.
[4] K. Adam, *Saint Augustine* (1932), p. 55.
[5] *On virginity*, 11f.
[6] A. von Harnack, *History of Dogma*, **5**, 72, 'Thus Augustine dethroned the traditional feelings of the baptised, fear and hope, the elements of unrest, and substituted the elements of rest, faith and love.'
[7] *On perfection in righteousness*, 3.8.
[8] *Ibid.* 21.   [9] *On Psalm 89.4.*   [10] *On patience*, 20.17.

fallen man cannot obey becomes an object of his love and his delight. The order of creation has been broken by the sin of man. To re-establish order, God himself must act; only the creator can be re-creator. God himself gives us grace, restores the will to its first strength, making it good and free. Free will now finds freedom. True liberty is the service of Christ. Liberty and charity come from the grace of God, and 'the law of liberty is the law of charity'.[11]

Augustine insists on two things in the complex matter of freedom and responsibility. First, those who reach their eternal destiny owe everything to God's mercy for God makes them righteous, and God enables them to persevere; second, those who have fallen into sin have only themselves to blame. Predestination and responsibility are two sides of a mystery which Augustine believes to be insoluble. He puts forward the Stoic view that a good man is free, although he may be a slave, and that a bad man is always a slave, even though he may sit on a throne. The mind of man cannot endure the light of God because it has inherited and fostered too many vices. Only faith can cleanse it and make it new. A man with freedom would be able to use his faculty of free will for doing good. He would be free from desiring or willing things which are in conflict with his true happiness. He would love that which he should love. Faith leads man towards freedom by giving him a higher truth than he could have without faith. Love gives man the power to love God.[12]

Man for Augustine is freed only by Christ, through whom he shares in the divine freedom. The gift of the gospel is nothing less than God's own freedom. Such freedom stands in clear distinction from the false freedom which man might imagine for himself as he follows a path of sin.[13] Augustine's concern for free will leads him to fight on two fronts – against Manichees and against Pelagians. On the one hand, those who want to excuse their sin by blaming it on fate are mad! 'This is that filthy madness of the Manicheans whose satanic schemes the sure truth readily overthrows, truth which confesses that the nature of God cannot be contaminated or corrupted.'[14] On the other hand, there are those who claim that grace cannot be active in man without destroying man's free will. Pelagians claim that one can, without help

---

[11] *Ep.* 167.6, 19. For recent discussion of the idea of freedom in Augustine, see M. Clark, *Augustine, Philosopher of Freedom* (New York, 1958); also note H. A. Wolfson, 'Philosophical Implications of the Pelagian Controversy', *Proceedings of American Philosophical Society*, **103**, 554–62. F. J. Thonnard, *REA* (1965), pp. 239–65, indicates the need for caution with some of Wolfson's generalisations.

[12] M. Clark, *op. cit.*, p. 131.

[13] *Ibid.* pp. 246f.

[14] *On continence*, 5.14.

of the grace of God, fulfil what God has commanded. This, says Augustine, would mean that one does not need to watch and pray, nor should one ask to be delivered from temptation in the Lord's Prayer. Temptation is a fact, and therefore, 'Let us seek that he may give, what he bids us that we have.' 'Therefore we do not undermine in any way the free choice of the human will, when we do not deny with ungrateful pride but affirm with grateful devotion that grace of God by which free will is helped.'[15]

The root of original sin lies in evil concupiscence or lust,[16] which grasps after what is not its own. Man desires the divine life which he lacks, and it is this pride and lust which brought the sin of Adam, 'in whom' all men sinned. As a slave to the powers of evil, lust and ignorance, man lives in a state of necessary sin.[17] Moral action derives from the will, which may choose either order and goodness, or disorder and negation. A good will acts in accordance with God's eternal law. The happy life consists in possessing what one wants, and wanting only what one has a right to possess. Moral action is contingent. In it a free will responds to the demands and to the invitations of God's eternal law. Every soul acts partly as ruled by the laws of the universe. A bad will does not point to an efficient cause beyond it. It is itself such a cause. Yet its efficiency is not real, for it is a deficiency, rather than a positive power to evil. Evil is a defect rather than an effect. Good will has its efficient cause in God, but the origin of sin springs from man's

---

[15] On widowhood, 17.21. 'The Pelagians deserve respect for their purity of motive, their horror of the Manichean leaven and the *opus operatum*, their insistence on clearness, and their intention to defend the Deity. But we cannot but decide that their doctrine fails to recognise the misery of sin and evil, that in its deepest roots it is godless, that it knows and seeks to know, nothing of redemption, and that it is dominated by an empty formalism', A. von Harnack, *History of Dogma*, **5**, 203. Much more, of course needs to said to present Pelagius' total thought. There are useful comments in R. F. Evans, *Pelagius: Inquiries and Reappraisals* (London, 1968). Pelagius' first concern was ethical. He aimed to prove man's natural capacity to choose and act, so that there would be no ground for lack of zeal in pursuit of virtue. See Pelagius, *Letter to Demetrius*.

[16] F. J. Thonnard, 'La notion de concupiscence en philosophie augustinienne', *RA* (1965), pp. 95–105. 'L'étroite connexion entre le dogme révélé du péché originel et la categorie morale classée sous le genre "péché" qui est la "notion de concupiscence" telle que nous l'avons trouvée chez Augustin . . .Mais il faut d'abord insister sur le *sens total* de la concupiscence qui définit ainsi pour Augustin le péché originel. Plusieurs ont tendance à exagérer le rôle de la "concupiscence" charnelle au sens strict', p. 96.

[17] See J. Mausbach, *Die Ethik des heiligen Augustinus*, vol, 2, for a full treatment of grace, sin and freedom. For the effect of the mistranslation of Romans 5:12 as 'in quo', see J. N. D. Kelly, *Early Christian Doctrines* (London, 1958), pp. 354ff.

evil choice of disobedience to God.[18] 'Further *all sin was against God*; for the created spirit had only one lasting relationship, that to God. Sin was self will, the proud striving of the heart (*superbia*); therefore it took the form of *desire* and *unrest*. In this unrest, *lust*, never quieted, and fear revealed themselves.'[19]

In the scale of freedom God stands at the top. He is absolute freedom and sovereign act. After him come the angels, who submit to him, and then come the saints and then other men. The lowest place in the scale of freedom is that of sinful man who is no longer able to choose against his lower desires.[20] One can still say that he has free will, but he is not able to choose what is good, nor without God's help to make his way to God. Yet of all creatures only man can be free in the sense that his actions are not subject to natural necessity. His love may be either a natural impulse or a deliberate choice which selects from impulses and shapes behaviour. Augustine speaks of the will as love and shapes a morality on this basis. Augustine's account of grace moves far beyond the ideas of predestination and freedom. As much as the Greek fathers, he insists on the divinisation of the believer; he speaks of a most intimate union with Christ within the church which is his body, and of a heavenly delight in which each is led by grace to ever greater heights of freedom.[21]

(iii)   *Blessedness begins from humility*

Augustine writes of the first need:

> To have a devout submission. . .to the God who has seen the uncertainty of our steps and who has himself traced our ways to him. . .
> The first is humility, the second is humility and the third is
> humility. . .It is not that there are no other precepts to be mentioned,
> but if humility does not precede, accompany and follow all our
> good undertakings. . .pride will tear all good from our hands.[22]

Humility is central for Augustine as it was for Paul. For both, a Christian has nothing which he has not received, and only when he is weak is he strong. Augustine, in his desire to know two things only – God and the soul – sees man's place in the divine order, under God and over earthly things. Pride is disorderly love of one's own excellence.

[18] R. Gosselin, *La morale de St. Augustin* (Paris, 1925), Part 2.1 and 4.

[19] A. von Harnack, *History of Dogma*, 5 (E.T. 1898), 70.

[20] R. Holte, *Béatitude et sagesse*, p. 291. Cf. also, F. J. Thonnard, 'La notion de liberté en philosophie augustinienne', *REA* (1970), pp. 243–70.

[21] See H. Rondet, 'La théologie de la grâce dans la correspondance de S. Augustin', *RA* (1958), p. 315.

[22] *Ep.* 118.22.

Humility is love of the glory of God. 'What is it to be humble? To be unwilling in oneself to be praised.'[23] Humility is not to be gained by mechanical means, but to be found in the presence of God with the help of his revealing truth. 'What I know about myself I know because you give me light.'[24] Humility is found in the person of Jesus, whose humility has 'brought something new into the world which must be seen in his person'.[25]

The divine humility which appears in Christ sees to it that the lowliness of men is brought to a saving end. Humility and gentleness in following the Lord are 'the first great gift of the spirit'.[26] With humility man stands in the presence of God. With humility he bears the troubles, temptations and sorrows of this world. True humility exhibits that 'holy childlikeness' to which the kingdom of heaven has been promised.[27] Humiliation which man has thrust upon him must be augmented by self-imposed humiliation. Celibacy and fasting are ways of humbling ourselves in the presence of God. Difficulty and dangers remain. 'Better a humble virgin than a humble married woman, but better a humble married woman than a proud virgin.'[28] Those who have taken the ascetic way may still be proud of their choice, and pride is always the opposite of humility, and the source of man's first sin. Pride says, 'I am, I and no one else.' Such pride is like smoke or snow, like a swelling, like a mountain, like birds, like the body of the devil, like the ninety-nine sheep. The raven and the unicorn and the tower of Babel, the mountain and the smoke are also symbols of pride.[29] Without humility no man can be holy, nor can he rise to be with God.

Christian humility determines relationships to God, self and neighbour. Before God the Christian is humble as a creature before his creator. He knows his insignificance and confesses his sin. He prays that God's will alone should be done. He wants to please God alone. He loves God and forgets himself. The humility of the creature before his creator is augmented by the humility of the redeemed sinner, 'Know what you are, know yourself as weak, know yourself as a man, know yourself as a sinner, and know that it is he who makes you just.'[30] As John 15:5 and 1 Corinthians 4:7 remind us, we can do nothing good except with God's grace, and this is a ground for humility. We are as

---

[23] *On Psalm* 33.2, 5. For this and following paragraphs, I am greatly indebted to O. Schaffner, *Christliche Demut* (Würzburg, 1959).

[24] *Confessions*, 10.5.7.

[25] W. Herrmann, article on 'Demut' in *Realencyclopädie für Prot. Theol.* (Leipzig, 1898), pp. 571–6.

[26] *On Galatians*, 45.   [27] *Sermon* 353.2.1.   [28] *On Psalm* 75.16.

[29] See Schaffner, *Christliche Demut*, p. 236.

[30] *Sermon* 137.4.4, cited Zumkeller, *Das Mönchtum des heiligen Augustinus*, p. 281.

beggars before God. We ask of him, we seek and knock. In relation to himself the Christian is turned by humility against vanity and boasting, against pursuit of honour and distinction and against self-confidence. He understands himself. Finally, humility inspires service and love towards one's neighbour. Each considers others greater than himself, and aims to be all things to all men. Christian humility needs a community where it can be practised. '*Caritas serviens*' is the essence of Christian living. The greater the building, the deeper the foundations must go. The foundation is always, for the Christian, humility, to support that which God has done for him. Augustine even says that perfection is humility. The pride, which, like that of the Pharisee, dwells upon acts of service done, and not on how much has been forsaken, will never receive the love of Christ.

Augustine is always turning to the second chapter of Philippians for a description of the humiliation and humility of Christ, and to the Sermon on the Mount for the blessing of the poor in spirit. The humility of the gospel is the goal of every Christian who wishes to advance in the kingdom of God. It is built around the example and the grace of Christ, his incarnation and his cross.

An evil world threatens the Christian, but Christian hope and confidence stand firm. Humiliation comes to the servant as it came to the Master. Many may fail but the house of the Lord stands sure. There is a positive value in temptation and adversity. They are the refining fire, the furnace of the goldsmith which purges away dross from gold: 'The world is the furnace, bad men are dross, good men are gold, tribulation is the fire, and God is the goldsmith.'[31] In God's whole plan of salvation, tribulation and temptation serve the final end of purifying and perfecting the good.

Life is a battle and a test. Augustine is not very optimistic about the battle against sin. He sees a continual opposition between man's sin and God's mercy. Two sets of opponents denied this opposition. Donatists claimed that the church must be holy in itself. Augustine maintains that all that is good in the church comes from Christ, and until the last day it is a 'mixed body'. The church is the poor man before the gate of the rich, and Christ too is poor in, with and for it. On the other hand, the Pelagian controversy saw Augustine in attack against those who claimed that man could be pure by his own strength, 'Against the Pelagians he was just what he had been against the Donatists. . .he was the defender of sin.'[32] Augustine was hardly a supporter of sin, but he considered that it could not be excluded without excluding man.

[31] *Sermon* 15.4.4.
[32] E. Mersch, 'Deux traits de la doctrine spirituelle de S. Augustin', *Nouvelle Revue*, 57 (1930), 399.

LOVE

(i) *No other precept*

Love should be seen in every part of life. Charity is shown in the way in which Christians eat, speak, dress and look. 'They know that it has been so laid down by Christ and the apostles; that if it is lacking all things are futile, if it is present all are fulfilled.'[1] Charity is the essence of all virtues. 'So that temperance is love keeping itself entire and uncorrupt for the beloved. Courage is love bearing everything gladly for the sake of the beloved. Righteousness is love serving the beloved only and therefore ruling well, and prudence is love wisely discriminating between what helps it and what hinders it.'[2] Augustine's understanding of love is both intricate and systematic.[3] Only through love is union with God possible, and in this union man realises his highest good or happiness. 'We move not by walking, but by loving.'[4] 'There is no surer step (*gradus*) to the love of God than the love of man towards man.'[5] Man is moved by will, affection or desire. This desire or unsatisfied longing points him to happiness in a life that is to come. 'You have made us for yourself, and our heart is restless until it rest in you.'[6] 'Oh love which ever burns and will never go out, love, my God, set me on fire!'[7] Further, love is a uniting force. It is that which joins the church together. 'Our life is love, and if our life be love, then hatred is death.'[8] Christ has loved us that we may love one another. 'The effect of his love for us is so to bind us to one another in mutual love that we become the body of which he is the head, his members linked together in such sweet slavery.'[9] So strong is this uniting force that the church becomes 'the one Christ loving himself'.[10] Finally, the distinction between means and ends or between using and enjoying shows that all else is instrumental to the love of God. Only God is to be loved for himself, while this world is to be used for life's necessities.[11]

The love of God is the centre of morality. 'Virtue is simply nothing but the highest love of God.'[12] Faith is important for ethical knowledge and growth, but the essence of morality is the direction of the will and

[1] *On morals of Catholic Church*, 33.73.

[2] *Ibid* 15.25.

[3] See J. Burnaby, *Amor Dei* (London, 1938). The remainder of this paragraph is indebted to chapter 4 of Burnaby's fine work.

[4] *Ep.* 155.4.13.   [5] *On morals of Catholic Church*, 26.48.

[6] *Confessions*, 1.1.1.   [7] *Confessions*, 10.29.40.

[8] *On Psalm* 54.7.   [9] *On Gospel of John* 65.2.

[10] *On Epistle of John* 10.3.   [11] *On morals of Catholic Church*, 20.37.

[12] *Ibid.* 15.25.

this is controlled by love. Love and fear of God are not exclusive. The more one fears the judgement of God in hell, the more one loves God. Love has a contemplative quality which finds expression in moral activity. The whole of life becomes the worship of God. Love must, like fire, first seize on the nearest thing and then extend to what is more distant. Love is love for righteousness, and this love brings all the virtues together. Love for God rules over all things. There is great variety in the following of the good life, but all centres around the supreme command to love. The whole Christian life is holy longing or desire. By this longing the soul becomes capable of attaining to God. In this world the faithful wander in the wilderness. 'If you do not want to die in that desert from thirst, drink love.'[13] Love unites man with God through good works and through contemplation which comes from faith. The soul ascends to truth and to contemplation.

Some kind of love provides the motive power for every human act. 'My weight is my love.' It is this which moves us wherever we go. As bodies tend to find their place, moving upwards or downwards, so love draws man up towards God, or draws man down away from God. The moral problem is not whether we should love, but how we should love. 'Are you told not to love anything? Not at all. If you are to love nothing you will be sluggish, dead, detestable, wretched. Love, but be careful what you love.'[14] Virtue means loving what we should love. The highest virtue is the highest love – charity by which we love what we ought to love. The love of God asks that we should give ourselves to God. We are to love God with all that we are. 'He who made you demands the whole of you.' Whilst this love has links with the desire for God in the philosophy of Plotinus, there is nothing in Plotinus to correspond to the prevenient grace of God which means so much to Augustine. 'Let us love because he himself first loved us.' It is a gift of God that we should love God. Further, Christian love is not a simple and undifferentiated desire. It looks to the whole of human life and includes the love of mind, heart and of the lower parts of the soul. The love of the mind is philosophic love, or *erōs*, which for Plotinus is the only kind of love. Augustine's love of the heart and of the lower soul for God emerge as the love of one's neighbour, and the love of oneself in the care of one's own body. These actions are referred to God and point to the beginning of the difference between enjoying and using.[15] When man in the obedience of faith submits to God and loves his will, he becomes an instrument of God's creative action, and his loves of utility mark an ascending instead of a descending path. Human love is both what

[13] *On Epistle of John* 7.1.
[14] *On Psalm* 31.2, 5.
[15] Cf. Holte, *Béatitude et sagesse*, p. 265.

regulates and what is regulated. Love must be ordered by reason, self-discipline and inward law. Augustine took the Stoic distinction between pleasant, useful and right, reduced the three categories to two and spoke of what is right or good for its own sake, and what is useful for the sake of something else. We enjoy what is good for its own sake, we use what is good as a means to something else. What is used should not be loved, and what is loved should not be used. There are things however which are to be 'enjoyed in God', and these are a special class. Our fellow men are in this category. Good men use the world so that they may enjoy God, while the wicked, in order that they may enjoy the world, would like to use God. A man's love is like the hand of the soul. If this hand holds one thing it cannot hold anything else, 'But that it may hold what is given to it, it must let go what it already holds.'[16] Augustine turns to the fourth gospel, to insist on the ethical character of the love of God. Those who do the truth come to the light. Love involves repentance, purification and a progress towards sanctification which lasts as long as earthly life. By keeping the Lord's commandments we remain in his love. The love of the world, which built Babylon, must be replaced with the love of God, which builds Jerusalem, the holy city. To be filled with good and emptied of evil, one must choose between the two loves, the love of the world and love of God. Preparation for the love of God involves purification, 'Make room for love to come in so that you may love God.'[17] God's word is offered to all. Those who can, should buy, and those who want to buy, must give themselves because this is the price to be paid for the word.[18] The love of one's neighbour is part of the love of God, and while it is second in precept, it is first in practice. Charity is not only the love of God, but the love of the good, of virtue, of order. 'Charity is known as good will.' To act well in any circumstances one must love God for 'without this love of the creator, no one can use any creature well'. 'All these precepts of love, that is of charity, are such great commands that if a man acts without charity none of the actions which he thinks he has done well are really good.'[19] Charity is that movement of the soul which aims at the enjoyment of God for his own sake, and the enjoyment of oneself and one's neighbour for God's sake.[20]

[16] *Sermon* 125.7.
[17] *On Epistle of John* 2.14.
[18] *Sermon* 117.2.
[19] *On Psalm 36.2*, 13; *Against Julian*, 4.3.33; *On Grace and Free Will*, 18.37. See E. Portalié, *A Guide to the Thought of St. Augustine* (London, 1960), pp. 276f.
[20] *On Christian doctrine*, 3.10.16.

(ii) *Be careful what you love*

In the order of love, external goods are lowest, but they are dear to Augustine. If we despise all the interests of natural man, we despise the creator who made him and the world in which he is placed. Love to God does not forbid that we should love these things, but forbids only that we should look for final happiness in the love of them. We are to make them a means of loving our creator. A man who loves the world more than God is like a woman who has become engaged and who loves the ring more than she loves her betrothed. 'God then has given you all these things; love him who made them.'[21] Second in the ascending scale of love is the love of self. He who loves God loves his neighbour as himself. A man who does not love God does not love himself. The love of self means that one should give oneself to God. This is the price of love or charity. Unless we give ourselves to God we lose ourselves. Love hears the words of wisdom, 'My son, give me your heart', for 'he who made you demands all of you'. 'Let us be what we receive' is a theme of Augustine's preaching concerning the eucharist.[22] The love of one's neighbour is next in order, and points to the necessity of the church, as a standing illustration of the truth of the gospel and a living sacrament. Augustine preaches to his congregation with all consciousness of the terrors of hell, and yet is able to say, 'I do not wish to be saved without you.'[23]

Finally, there is the love of God, or love for God. This means the love of him who is being and who is life, for God is life and gives life to all men. It means also love of truth and knowledge, for it is life eternal to know the only true God. The desire of knowledge for its own sake is always a thirst for that of which we have a part. The beauty and construction of the world point us to the greatness and beauty of the one who made it. We cannot behold God in his purity, and so he has put his work before our eyes. By looking at this work we love what we cannot see, and then one day because of our love we shall be able to see. Again, the love of God is the love of love. God is to be loved because he is love.

> God is love, why then should we go rushing off to the top of
> heaven or to the bottom of the earth looking for him who is with us,
> if but we would be with him. Let no one say, I know not what I am
> to love. Let him love his brother and he will love that same love.
> He knows the love with which he loves his brother, better than the

---

[21] *On Epistle of John* 2.11; cited Burnaby, *Amor Dei*, p. 115.
[22] *Sermon* 34.7 and *Sermon* 57.7; cited Burnaby, *op. cit.*, pp. 124f.
[23] *Sermon* 17.2; cited Burnaby, *op. cit.*, p. 128.

brother whom he loves. God may be held more known than a
brother, more known because more present; more known because
more inward; more known, because more sure. Embrace the love
which is God: through love embrace God. He is that very love that
links in the bond of holiness all the good angels and all the servants
of God, and that joins us and them to one another in obedience
to himself.[24]

The love of God may be seen in creation, for it was from love that he
created, and it is in love that he continues the goodness of his creation.
The love of God is seen supremely in man's redemption.[25] There was
one purpose for the coming of Christ and that was to prove the love of
God towards us, for there is no stronger invitation to love than to offer
love in advance. God proves his great love by sending his word. His
only son takes flesh upon him, is born and suffers for man's sake. In
this we come to learn 'How much man counts to God'.[26] For God
made man from dust, gave him life, and then did not hesitate to give
his only son to die for something which he had made. Such love can
never be fully explained, can never be worthily imagined. 'He who
made, remade.'[27] Holding to our eternal creator, we are affected by
the contagion of his immortality.[28] The end of all living is the reward
which God gives. God's reward is himself. 'He will give himself
because he has given himself.' 'When we see him as he is we shall be
like him, and being like him how should we fail, by what should we be
distracted? – Fear not that you will lack power ever to praise him
whom you will have power ever to love.'[29]

The challenge of perfection comes to those who recognise that they
have only begun. Perfection in wisdom is perfection in love. The
charity which fulfils the law is the goal of Christian living. 'Perfect
love is perfect righteousness.'[30] Christian perfection consists in continuous striving towards perfection rather than in freedom from sin, 'Let
us, who run perfectly, know this, that we are not yet perfect, so that we
may thereby be perfected whither we are still perfectly running.'[31]

If you say, it is enough, then you have already perished to
destruction. Ever onwards, ever forwards, ever further! Nowhere
on the way should you stay back, should you turn around, should

---

[24] *On the trinity*, 8.11f; cited Burnaby, *op. cit.*, pp. 160f.
[25] Burnaby, *op. cit.*, p. 168.
[26] *C.D.* 7.31; Burnaby, *op. cit.*, p. 169.
[27] *Ep.* 231.6. Burnaby, *op. cit.*, p. 170.
[28] See Burnaby, *op. cit.*, p. 179.
[29] *On Psalm 42.2; On Psalm 83.8.* Burnaby, *op. cit.*, pp. 246 and 250.
[30] *On nature and grace*, 70.84.
[31] *On perfection in righteousness*, 8.19.

you turn aside. He drops behind who does not push on, he goes backwards who turns back to that from which he has already broken free. He turns aside who is rebellious.[32]

(iii) *One heart and one soul*

Love is the key to history because two loves give rise to the two cities. Self love despises God and builds the earthly city. Love of God despises self and forms the heavenly city. The first love looks for glory from men, and the other desires God only as its greatest glory. The two loves are opposite; the first produces lust for power, while the second brings men to mutual service in love. One loves worldly virtue, and the other says to God, 'I will love thee, O Lord, my strength.'[33] In one place, the city of God is identified with the church scattered through-out earth and resident among nations.

> There shall the camp of saints stand, there shall the beloved city
> stand. There shall the fury of the persecuting enemy hem them in
> with crowds of all nations, united in one fury of persecution; there
> shall the church be hedged in with tribulations, oppressed and
> closed in on every side, yet shall she not forsake her warfare which
> is indicated by the word 'camp'.[34]

Christ is the founder of the heavenly city, but he is not adored because he has founded that city. It works the other way around: the church is founded because it adores Christ as God.[35] When Rome had been built, she adored Romulus who had founded her; but the heavenly Jerusalem adores Christ as her founder and by this faith and adoration she is built. Rome had an object for her love which she honoured with a false faith. The city of God has an object for her faith, 'which she is ever ready to honour with a true and rightly grounded love'.

The motto of Christian love runs through all that Augustine has to say concerning the monastic life. Love, eternal love, gives light to all. Love must shape the whole life of the monk.[36] The theme of the rule stands at the beginning, 'Before all things, beloved brethren, God must be loved, so then, the neighbour must be loved, for these are the chief commandments which have been given to us.'[37] The love of one's neighbour is again a special way of loving God.

[32] *Sermon* 169.15.18.   [33] *C.D.* 14.28 including Psalm 17:2.
[34] *C.D.* 20.11.   [35] *C.D.* 22.6.
[36] *On morals of Catholic Church*, 33.73.
[37] Rule for the servants of God, 1. Cited by Zumkeller, *Das Mönchtum des heiligen Augustinus*, p. 318. Zumkeller comments on authenticity, pp. 323ff. While it is true that, 'Son inspiration augustinienne n'a jamais été sérieusement contestée' (A. Sage, 'La règle de S. Augustin', *REA* (1968),

The monks in their community provide a living expression of the love which fulfils the law of Christ. They have *one heart and one soul.* They show the unity of the body of Christ; their life is one life and they belong to Christ alone. They share their Lord's poverty and make visible the poverty and virginity of his body, the church. Their honoured title is 'Christ's paupers' (*pauperes Christi*).[38] The body is the one Christ, loving himself. The pattern of the apostolic church, in its unity and sharing of goods, is always remembered. The eucharist, too, is a 'mystery of peace and unity', the sign of unity and the bond of love.[39] The Manichees never achieved a worthwhile community and this was an important factor in their decline. Wandering ascetics met imperial opposition; but Manichees could not move beyond this initial individualism.[40] On the other hand Augustine has a distinctive contribution here. Only through love of neighbour can one reach the vision of God.[41] The love of neighbour is the first word of natural law which God speaks to man through his conscience.[42]

(iv) *Love and do what you will*

The theme of one heart and mind in God runs through the whole of Augustine's theology, from his account of the trinity to his doctrine of the Spirit. Without brotherly love there can be no knowledge of self or God. He who does not love his brothers is closed to his brothers, to

p. 123), there are serious difficulties in this area. The most comprehensive treatment of the sources and the problems is given by L. Verheijen, *La règle de S. Augustin*, 2 vols (Paris, 1967). The four main rules associated with Augustine are classified by Verheijen as:

i. The *Regula recepta*, previously described as the *Regula tertia, the rule* for the servants of God.

ii. *Praeceptum*, which omits only the first sentence of *Regula recepta*, and which is found in feminine form in *Ep.* 211.

iii. *Ordo monasterii* (previously known as *Regula secunda*).

iv. *Praeceptum longius* (a combination of ii and iii). Since Erasmus, it has been widely believed that only (i) can be traced to Augustine, and that it is a masculine form of a rule (*Ep. 211*) written by Augustine for a convent of nuns directed by his sister. Verheijen argues for the priority of (i) over the feminine form in *Ep. 211*, and that (iii) is the work of Alypius. His comprehensive treatment requires careful assessment.

[38] *Ep.* 157.4.37.

[39] *Sermon* 272.1. *On Gospel of John* 26.13. Cited Zumkeller, *Das Mönchtum des heiligen Augustinus*, p. 176.

[40] P. Brown, *Religion and Society in the Age of St. Augustine* (London, 1972), (*RASASA*), pp. 114f.

[41] *On Gospel of John* 17.11.

[42] A. Sage, 'La contemplation dans les communautés de vie fraternelle', *RA* (1971), pp. 273 and 302.

himself and to God.[43] The saying of Augustine, 'Love and do what you will', grows out of his conflict with Donatism and his guilt over its suppression. From this specific origin, it speaks to a wider context of a rigour which he claims must go with brotherly love. Severity is a necessary part of love. Love is not restricted to particular attitudes and emotions. It may be angry; but because such anger is directed towards correction rather than to hatred, it is not sinful. Love uses and brings to focus different energies. In each case love makes a creative effort to find the appropriate and effective action. 'Once for all, then, a short precept is given you: Love, and do what you will: if you are silent, be silent from love; if you cry out, cry out from love; if you correct, correct from love; if you spare, spare through love; let the root of love be within, nothing but good can spring from this root.'[44] The Christian has simply to examine his heart in the presence of God. If he finds in that heart love for his brothers, then he may do what he will. The formula says something about Augustine. Confronted by perplexing problems in his work as a bishop, he made love the force which held his life together.[45] Nothing else can take the place of love, 'All may sign themselves with the sign of Christ's cross; all may answer "Amen" and sing "Hallelujah". All may be baptised, all may come to church and line the walls of our places of meeting. . .they that have love are born of God, they that have no love are not.'[46] Augustine grew more severe to heretics and schismatics as years went by.[47] Outside the church is the world of the damned.[48] Truth is to be loved for its own sake, and not for the man or the angel who brought it.[49] Whatever is contrary to truth must be put to death.

So the way was clear for Christian to persecute Christian and to do it all for love. There are few sadder, grimmer pages in Christian

---

[43] *Ibid.* p. 302.   [44] *On Epistle of John* 7.8.

[45] J. Gallay, *'Dilige et quod vis fac'*, *RSR* (1955), p. 555. It was better that some Donatists should be incinerated in their own church than that all of them should go to hell; and go to hell they would, unless force was brought to bear on them. *Ep. 204*, 2. See P. Brown, *AH*, pp. 335f.

[46] *On Epistle of John* 5.7.

[47] 'He is a sensitive and conscientious pastor up to his victory over the Donatists; but in 420, he can appear, for an instant, as a harsh and cold victor.' After quoting Augustine's callous reaction (*Ep.* 204.2) to the possible conflagration of a Donatist congregation in their church, P. Brown cites a letter (*Ep.* 95.3) written in 408 to Paulinus of Nola. Augustine shows his deep concern and the source of his guilt in these matters. 'What shall I say as to the infliction and remission of punishment in cases in which we only desire to forward the spiritual welfare of those we are deciding whether or not to punish?. . .What trembling we feel in these things, my brother Paulinus, O holy man of God!' See P. Brown, *RASASA*, pp. 277f.

[48] *Sermon* 96.7.8.   [49] *On Galatians,* 4.

history, all the sadder because Augustine knew the depth of human
deceit so well. Love is strongest, not in the splendid sweeping rule but
in the contingency of the cup of cold water and the particularity of the
cross.

Yet Augustine knew this when he gave up his holy leisure to be a
bishop out of the necessity of love. Nothing shows the particularity of
love better than a letter to a nun, Sapida, accepting the tunic of her
late brother and offering comfort from scripture.

> I have accepted the gift you wished me to have, made by the just
> and pious labours of your own hands, lest I should increase the
> grief of one who needs, as I see it, much rather to be consoled by
> me; especially because you said yourself that it would be no small
> consolation to you if I should wear that tunic, which you had made
> for the holy minister of God your brother; since he, already
> departing from the land of the dying, no longer needs things which
> perish. I have, therefore, done what you desired, and whatever kind
> and degree of consolation you may consider this to bring, I have
> not refused it to your tender affection for your brother. The tunic
> which you sent I have accepted, and have already begun to wear it
> before writing this to you. Be of good heart; but lay hold of far
> better and far greater consolations, in order that the cloud which,
> through human weakness, gathers closely round your heart, may be
> dispersed by words of divine authority; and, come what may, so
> live that you may live with your brother, since he has so died that
> he still lives.[50]

Augustine wrote so much on ethical matters and developed his ideas
over so many years, that a total assessment is difficult. His fixation upon
order and his Platonic hierarchical universe lasted on. His account of
discipleship loses the ground gained by John and reverts to Basil's unwilling distinction between monk and layman as first and second class
Christians. The sweeping verdict is given by a recent interpreter of
Augustine: 'And it was just this widening gulf between an ascetic élite
and a passive rank and file which brought the Christianisation of the
Roman world to a halt.'[51] He seems close to merging man with God
but specifically insists on limits to the identification.[52] Faith suffers
chiefly through the account of freedom. Man is not free and his free
choice is helpless without God's grace. This account is not remarkable,

---

[50] *Ep. 263.*
[51] P. Brown, *AH*, p. 248. Yet the same writer sees the establishment of
monastic communities as 'one of the most remarkable institutional
achievements of the early medieval period', *RASASA*, p. 79.
[52] 'God wills to make you a god; not by nature, as his Son is, but by his
gift and adoption', *Sermon* 166.4.4. See A. H. Armstrong, *St. Augustine*

but what distorts it is a view of man which anticipates Machiavelli and Hobbes, together with a view of God as a well-programmed if clumsy computer. Yet Augustine's account of predestination was not just a device to win a debate. He was convinced that Pelagius was fundamentally wrong in his estimate of man's ability and, when the bishops of Palestine supported Pelagius, he was genuinely alarmed. Like Paul, he saw that the piety of the pious meant the end of the gospel. His enthusiastic love has already been noted: the exhortation 'Love and do what you will' is as sinister as it is plausible. For Augustine knew the importance of practical kindness and above all he had given an ethical structure to love. Those who love must be careful what they love and must remember the order of love. This was exactly the kind of argument that had been needed to avoid antinomian mysticism. Augustine seemed to lose both ways. He worked out the order of love so badly that it was possible to persecute in love. He developed the notion of order and law so thoroughly that he lost the freedom which his plausible words suggest.

Augustine's importance may lie in the problems he did not solve and the contradictions he handed on. He was attached to the law, order and peace which the Roman world had given. The turbulence of his private and public worlds made him prize these things all the more. Like all Stoics he never trusted the passions and his own passions confirmed the mistrust. Yet he also knew both the ecstatic vision of the Platonist and the infinite mercy of the Christian's God. He saw life as love and hatred as death. His own mixtures of law and love, order and grace did not work. The 'order of love' sounded well but Augustine's doctrine of predestination and his 'love and do what you will' showed that neither God nor man could love by numbers. Doctrines devoid of consistency seem to last longer than others. The influence of Augustine has been largely due to the many sides of his thought and life. No one has been so revered by different people for such conflicting reasons; and in the history of ideas practical influence and theoretical incoherence have often gone together.[53]

and Christian Platonism (Villanova Univ. Press, 1967). Armstrong points out (p. 6) that *theos* meant 'immortal'. The fathers saw renewed man as a created divinity who participated in God with whom he was never identical.

[53] But there was a positive achievement as well. Augustine grasped more of the NT than did his predecessors. In him piety found its limit and his influence has rarely been rivalled: 'If we review all the men and women of the West since Augustine's time, whom, for the disposition that possessed them, history has designated as prominent Christians, we have always the same type; we find marked conviction of sin, complete renunciation of their own strength, and trust in grace, in the personal God who is apprehended as the Merciful One in the humility of Christ.' A. von Harnack, *History of Dogma*, 5, 74.

6

FOUR PROBLEMS

There are four questions which may be considered in the light of what has been learned. Each pattern has at least one problem. The account of righteousness raises the question of natural law, discipleship raises the problem of imitation and the Jesus of history, faith raises the question of how much non-Christian ethics can exist in a Christian ethic and love raises the problem of situation ethics. These issues have all been discussed during the last twenty years. Happily the study of patristic ethics illuminates each of these questions.

NATURAL LAW

Natural law, with its ambiguities,[1] dug itself into Christianity during the patristic period. During its long history the term has come to mean three main things – a universal system of laws, a rational foundation of ethics, and a theory of natural rights. The first two themes play some part in early Christian thought but are far removed from their development in later centuries. The Apologists appealed to a law which was sovereign over all men and to right reason as the guide to conduct; but they did not make the wide claims of Justinian or Aquinas under these headings.[2] Nature was subordinate to the central notion of Logos. The key move is made by Justin, whose scheme is dominated by the Christ who is both Nomos and Logos. Standing in continuity with Matthew's gospel, he speaks of the culmination of all divine law in Christ. 'Now I have indeed read, Trypho, that there would be a final law and covenant supreme over all, which now men should keep if they wish to pursue the inheritance of God...And Christ was given to us – an eternal and final law and faithful covenant, after which there shall be no law, no precept, no commandment.'[3]

---

[1] P. Delhaye distinguishes twenty possible meanings: *Permanence du droit naturel* (Paris, 1960), p. 21.
[2] A. P. d'Entrèves, *Natural Law* (2 ed. London, 1970), chapters 2 and 3.
[3] *Dialogue*, 11; see E. F. Osborn, *Justin Martyr* (Tübingen, 1973), pp. 159f.

Like the Stoics for whom he wrote, Justin knew that an eternal or universal law had no point unless it were brought down from heaven into human hearts. 'For those creatures who have received the gift of reason from nature have also received right reason, and therefore they have also received the gift of law, which is right reason applied to command and prohibition.'[4] So Justin's *logoi spermatikoi* made it possible to be a Christian before Christ. Lawgivers had spoken in partial apprehension, while the whole Logos had appeared in Christ.[5]

Philo had already spoken of the 'unwritten law' found in the lives of holy men. This eternal moral truth is expressed concretely in the decalogue, a theme which is common to Philo and Paul, not to mention the many who come after them.[6] In the early centuries there is simple spontaneous reference to the decalogue.[7] The new Israel inherits the essence of the law of the old Israel. The history of salvation culminates in the concentration of all the commandments in the double command of Christ which is, through the Spirit, a law of liberty[8] and an inward law.[9]

Lactantius[10] explicitly acknowledges Cicero as his source,

> We must therefore take up the law of God, which may direct us to this path, that sacred and heavenly law which M. Tullius describes in his *Republic* III with speech that is almost divine. . .: 'indeed there is a true law, right reason, in accord with nature, dispersed among all, the same, eternal, whose command calls to duty and whose prohibition keeps from wrong.'

---

[4] *De legibus*, 1.xii.33.
[5] 2 *Apol.* 10. See also *1 Apol.* 46 and 63, *2 Apol.* 8 and 13.
[6] See E. Troeltsch, *The Social Teaching of the Christian Churches* (London, 1931), 1, 188ff., for a concise presentation of the evidence.
[7] There is scope for disagreement on the place of the decalogue.
   G. Bourgeault, *Décalogue et morale chrétienne* (Paris-Montreal, 1971), sets out an extended case for the powerful place of the code, either through its inspiration of moral thought (p. 105), or through explicit references in apologetic works and in the anti-heretical works of Irenaeus and Tertullian (pp. 313, 357, 416ff.). He sets out different assessments in the introduction to his work. Dublanchy, Broillard and Delhaye find that the decalogue is suspect during this period, because it belongs to the Law of Moses which Christ has abolished. Grant sees the decalogue as expressing divine and natural law in a form suitable for catechesis. Röthlisberger insists that the decalogue is either ignored or discarded in early Christian ethics which are based on a Pauline Christology.
[8] Irenaeus, *Demonstration*, 89–96.
[9] Irenaeus, *Against Heresies*, 4.13. See Bourgeault, *Décalogue et morale chrétienne*, pp. 417f.
[10] *Divine Institutes*, vi.8.

The contrast between man's present capabilities and right reason could be explained by a Fall from a Stoic golden age or a biblical paradise, the two stories being blended together. Laws and institutions arose through man's unhappy decline; slavery was an example, *jure enim naturali ab initio omnes homines liberi nascebantur.*[11]

The chief use of the theory of natural law is as a rational foundation for ethics. It is not easy to see where the fathers went wrong, because they did not use the argument very much and when they did, they used it reasonably. For instance, John argues that work is a law of nature, the will of the creator saving man from the perils of idleness. The law is shown in the activity of animals who are below man.[12] The argument for natural law goes wrong chiefly in claiming to draw an observable and autonomous system from the highly ambiguous evidence of natural phenomena. Harmony with nature and with God was a welcome theme, because it declared God as creator and ruler of this world, and man as a creature whose earthly life was important to God. But natural law went further and claimed that nature can help men to read off propositions about good and evil, virtue and vice. Nowhere has reason been found for accepting this development, 'the logical jump from the facts of human nature to the values of morality'.[13]

Is the plucking of hairs, as Clement claims, a threat to God's arithmetic? If so, then the drawing of teeth and the trimming of hair are also wrong since God has counted and measured all organs of the body (Ps. 139:16). Basil goes further than Clement in listing examples in nature for man to follow or to avoid. His ground of discrimination is not clear. Why not follow the shiftiness of the serpent and avoid the obedience of the fish? Why follow the stork's care for the aged and the swallow's industry instead of rising above them as the patterns of inferior creatures? After all, a superman may wish to eliminate the unfit and the contemplative wants to live by prayer alone. Why live at peace like bees and ants, instead of whipping one's brother as if he were a charging bull? John draws less confidently than Basil on particular lessons from nature, stressing the general value of order and harmony. For Augustine, argument from particular natural phenomena is subordinate to argument from a universal conscience.

Clement sees the need to supplement the simple observation of nature. The ordered hierarchy of being, stressed in later Platonism, guides man to avoid acting like inferior creatures: because he is rational, man does not whistle, spit or snort in public. Even man's distinctive acts need rational definition: laughing is natural but man

[11] Justinian, *Institutes*, 1. 2.2.
[12] See above, p. 121.
[13] D. J. O'Connor, *Aquinas and Natural Law* (London, 1967), p. 81.

should not always be laughing any more than a horse should be always neighing. Moderation is natural, violence is not. The logos is not an impersonal order as he was for some heretics and philosophers but a living person who directs the course of the world. Even harmony and order are not enough, for the followers of Epiphanes base their immorality on a heavenly harmony.

Basil is less conscious of the need to supplement nature's example. Man may learn from some who are below him in the hierarchy. Basil draws many examples of harmony in nature; but he allows one which is violent: the body must be whipped by reason as one whips a charging bull. John sees moderation and order in all that is natural. The riots in Antioch had to be wrong because they were disorderly. The argument for work as a law of nature depends on hierarchy and order in two directions: man learns both from the animals below him and from God above. Augustine observes order in the universe as a hierarchy of being and goodness which culminates in God. Order brings peace which is God's will for his entire creation. Body and soul should reflect this peace.

We must begin by disowning arguments from observed natural phenomena. The law with which we are concerned is prescriptive, not descriptive. 'No one, on reflection, could seriously maintain that statistically normal behaviour is the model for good behaviour.'[14] An argument which has been used frivolously to prove that eating people is not wrong (1. People have always eaten people; 2. If we had not been meant to eat one another, we should not have been made of meat)[15] is too open to be useful. The best example by far is:

> 'Is dat right den, you paint yer boots?'
> 'True, it's the most economical way. Sometimes I paints 'em brown, when I had enough o' dat I paints 'em black again. Dat way people tink you got more than one pair, see? Once I played the cricket I painted 'em white, you should try dat.'
> 'Oh no,' said Murphy solemnly. 'Oh no, I don't like interfering wid nature. Der natural colour of boots is black as God ordained, any udder colour and a man is askin' fer trouble.'[16]

Further, natural law is a distortion of the pattern of righteousness, whenever it implies an abstract system, fixed in the heavens or in the depths, capable of justifying precepts without additional support. There is no such thing as an argument from natural law, when that law is considered as an abstract and autonomous system. The followers

[14] *Ibid.*
[15] Flanders and Swann, L.P. Record, *At the Drop of a Hat.*
[16] S. Milligan, *Puckoon* (Penguin Books, 1965), p. 16.

of Epiphanes had just as much evidence on their side as against them, when they insisted that the righteousness which was natural to men involved promiscuous intercourse. What is distinctive for man? There is no ground for selecting reason rather than making fire, sexual intercourse at any season, despoiling the environment or killing for fun. These are all distinctively human habits. Further, reason may be used for good or ill.[17]

A case may be made for the notion of natural law, when it is seen as hypothetical and exploratory. If, for example, human survival is accepted as a self-evident fundamental good, then certain principles will follow.[18] These principles remain exploratory, however ultimate they may seem, since they depend on human society remaining much the same, and since they need to be modified as society is better understood. Here again, the fathers went wrong in their vision of a universal autonomous system. Their error was again mitigated by their infrequent use of the scheme and the reasonable consequences which they drew from it. But the potential for future dogmatism was there.

In this connection we may note a present uneasiness about natural law.[19] Moral theology has to move from a classicist methodology to a historically conscious methodology.[20] This move will take it away from absolute norms.[21] Calvin is commended for neither neglecting nor overdoing natural law.[22] However, the difficulties of redefinition are considerable and the empirical content is asked to carry more than it can bear. The tensions of the problem are evident: 'Are the mental gymnastics of a *reservatio mentalis* necessary or even worthy of a grown man?',[23] while the cause of the tension is, 'How can one know inviolable values in this world?'[24] The confrontation of legalism and situationalism calls for an appreciation of the variety of attitudes which are held. Bonhoeffer and others propose an ethic of contexts with a soteriology of grace. Situation ethics propose a contextual ethic without a soteriology. Neocasuistry sets out an ethic of norms with a soteriology of grace, for the tables of the law were kept in the ark of the covenant of grace.[25]

---

[17] B. Williams, *Morality* (Penguin Books, 1973), pp. 73ff.
[18] This is the approach of Hart, *The Concept of Law* (Oxford, 1961), pp. 187ff., for whom it is 'entirely obvious' that 'the proper end of human activity is survival'. An analysis of Hart is given by I. T. Ramsey, *Christian Ethics and Contemporary Philosophy*, pp. 386ff. It is safer to regard the argument as hypothetical although Hart considers the basic premise to be self-evident.
[19] *Norm and Context in Christian Ethics* (edited by G. H. Outka and P. Ramsey, London, 1969), Part Two, pp. 139–264.
[20] *Ibid.* p. 166.   [21] *Ibid.* p. 173.   [22] *Ibid.* p. 196.
[23] *Ibid.* p. 222.   [24] *Ibid.* p. 223.   [25] *Ibid.* pp. 265–95.

The study of the fathers suggests that too much time has been given to the exposition and defence of natural law. The most to be expected here is that the social, humane and objective aspects of ethics will be reinforced. These points are not dependent on natural law but have greater strength in their own right. Christianity, as Clement saw it, meant living God's way in God's world. Harmony with nature was a necessary addition to the eschatological strain in New Testament ethics. The social aspect of Christianity was decisive for its impact on the world. 'We always stand in to one another', wrote Justin.[26] Christians had to deal with one another, with their neighbours and with the world. Clement shows that they could do this with some success, avoiding the errors of dualism and antinomianism. As often happened, the Gnostics had been there before him; they had found their own natural righteousness. Epiphanes[27] opposed the righteous order or harmony of heaven to any observance of laws on earth. God's righteousness pervaded all things and denied the moral rules which man made. Clement applies the principles of reason, harmony and nature to the whole of human life.[28] Basil, for all his aggressive asceticism, also loved the beauty of God's world. He learnt obedience from fishes and caring concern from storks.[29] 'Who does not know that man is a tame and sociable animal and not a solitary and fierce one? For nothing is so characteristic of our nature as to associate with one another, to need one another and to love our kind.'[30] John's theology of work guards against anti-social individualism. Work is a law of nature, the creator's will and our way of showing concern for one another.[31] Augustine saw the fulfilment of man and society in the peace which is 'ordered obedience in faith under eternal law', 'ordered agreement' among men and the right use of God's ordered creation.[32]

Living together in God's world brought the question of man to the centre and here again natural law played a role. However, those who reject an autonomous system of natural law do not reject the moral discernment of common men.[33] Jesus clearly appealed to the moral convictions of those who did not believe in him,[34] and placed a high

---

[26] *I Apol.* 67.1.

[27] See Clem. Alex., *Stromateis* 3.2.6f.

[28] See above, pp. 53–6.

[29] See above, p. 91f.

[30] See above, p. 107.

[31] See above, p. 121 and p. 138.

[32] See above, p. 151f.

[33] See A. N. Wilder, 'Equivalents of Natural Law in the Teaching of Jesus', *JR* (1946), p. 132.

[34] Wilder makes his case against Bultmann's definition of all value as obedience to God. He does not, however, find in Jesus' teaching what Bultmann calls 'an intelligible theory, valid for all men, concerning what should be done or left undone' (p. 128). The common man's discernment is not 'ultimate' (p. 134), nor is it 'one of the glories of Jesus'

estimate on man. The place of man in a hierarchy of being, above animals and below angels and God, became increasingly important under the influence of later Platonism. Throughout the patristic period the manhood of Christ was prized because it displayed the true manhood which had been lost in Adam. In the renewed manhood of Christ, the law of nature and of God could be discerned.[35] The link between humanity and natural law has permanent significance.[36] Clement sees that some people are more like pigs or dogs than men. Basil thought that, as a biped, man had the edge on quadrupeds, because man looked more easily to heaven. John saw man guided by inner law from the beginning, so that Adam hid himself in the garden when he had done wrong. Augustine sees the child growing to manhood with the discovery of the law within him. Today the same point comes out: 'The notion of human responsibility. . .implies an order which man does not create but which rather lays a demand on him.'[37] The question about man goes deeper and is far from academic. On the one hand, an eminent historian, who, after his own expulsion, chronicled the German opposition to Hitler, has claimed that the first need of modern Europe is to discover the picture of a man.[38] In the same university it has been shown convincingly[39] that the quality which distinguished the Jesus of the gospels was that 'he made co-humanity (*Mitmenschlichkeit*) possi-

---

teaching that it is thus fundamentally confident of man's native insight and free moral responsiveness' (*ibid.*). Wilder has answered one exaggeration with another. He shows again the wide ambiguity of the expression 'natural law'.

[35] Irenaeus, *Against Heresies*, 4.13.1 and 5.10.1 and *passim*. See F. Flückiger, *Geschichte des Naturrechtes* (Zürich, 1964), p. 359, 'In der Menschwerdung Christi erkennen sie die Offenbarung der wahren, ursprünglichen Menschennatur, von hier aus werden daher ihre Aussagen über die Natur und über die Gerechtigkeit bestimmt.'

[36] E. Troeltsch, 'The Ideas of Natural Law and Humanity in World Politics', published in O. Gierke, *Natural Law and the Theory of Society, 1500–1800* (translated by Ernest Barker, Cambridge, 1958). Troeltsch contrasted the German ideal of a group-mind inspired by anti-bourgeois idealism, with the classical and Christian ideas of natural law, humanity and progress. The latter he saw dominant in Western Europe.

[37] J. Macquarrie, *Three Issues in Ethics* (London, 1970), p. 103. See also the total approach of Hart, *The Concept of Law*, pp. 181–207.

[38] Hans Rothfels in *Aufstand und Widerstand*, an address recorded in *Staatsanzeiger für Baden-Württemberg*, 25 July 1964, p. 8. He cites a letter from Count von Moltke to an English friend, Lionel Curtis, in 1942.

[39] E. Käsemann, *Der Ruf der Freiheit* (Tübingen, 1968), ET of 3 ed. *Jesus means Freedom* (1969), p. 40. Cf. also H. Chadwick, *Some Reflections on Conscience* (London, 1968), p. 18, 'The old language of conscience. . .stood for the glory, for the misery, and against the trivialisation of man.'

ble and demanded it'. Christianity confirms the Stoic view that *homo sacra res homini.*[40]

Thirdly, natural law helped to stress the objectivity of moral judgements. In times of crisis, Christians want to point beyond their own revelation to the principles on which God's world is built and which man can not ignore with impunity. The church must 'bear witness to this aboriginal law of man's creation. The count against the great anti-Christian systems...is not just that they reject *our* ethic, the ethic we happen to prefer...It is that they repudiate the law of man's creation.'[41] While the fathers were more moderate in their claims, the same insistence on objectivity was important. For Clement the only real object of shame was wickedness and all it produces. For Basil there were no slight sins; all sins were serious. John made enemies at Constantinople, because he believed God and justice were inseparably linked. God must be just or he would not be God. Man learns what is good and bad from the natural law which God has planted in him. Augustine insists that man does not make things right or wrong. The divine mind commands the observance of the natural law.

Here as earlier, natural law was never the only way and is not the best way to preserve what is desired. The objectivity of ethical values has long been under attack, but it is best defended in isolation from natural law. An important defence shows that one cannot separate evaluation from facts. Right and wrong are not matters of personal arbitrary decision. 'It is surely clear that moral virtues must be connected with human good and harm, and that it is quite impossible to call anything you like good or harm.'[42] Of course, as the fathers saw, circumstances alter cases. The beginning of casuistry helped to preserve objectivity in ethics by showing that some things can be set down as right and others as wrong, but not as universally so. To use a modern statement, it is *prima facie* right to preserve life and *prima facie* right to tell the truth. That there can be times when other obligations are stronger, does not deny the tendency of these acts to be right. So, 'if we want to formulate universal moral laws, we can only formulate them as laws of *prima facie* obligation, laws stating the tendencies of actions to be obligatory in virtue of this characteristic or of that.'[43]

---

[40] Seneca, *Epistulae Morales*, 95.33.

[41] C. H. Dodd, *Gospel and Law* (New York, 1951), p. 82; cf. also, W. D. Davies, 'Relevance of Moral Teaching', in, *Neotestamentica et Semitica* (ed. Ellis and Wilcox, Edinburgh, 1969), p. 36, 'For Jesus there was an inward affinity between the natural and the moral, a kind of "natural law" in the "spiritual world".'

[42] P. Foot, 'Moral Beliefs', in *Theories of Ethics* (ed. P. Foot, Oxford. 1967), p. 92.

[43] W. D. Ross, *Foundations of Ethics* (Oxford, 1939), p. 86.

Christian use of natural law went wrong when patristic hints were built into a universal autonomous system. Here, as often, 'The pursuit of certainty is the enemy of the pursuit of truth.'[44] While in the early fathers the demands of a righteous God can be learnt from the renewed humanity of Christ, later developments claimed universality and autonomy for the moral insights of human reason.[45]

HISTORY AND DISCIPLESHIP

In the patristic period discipleship retains and even intensifies its focus on the person of Jesus.[1] Should this development, like that of natural law, be discounted? We know so little of the historical Jesus and the fathers were no better off. The literature on the question is vast, because it has been a flashpoint in theological discussion for more than a hundred years. Successive controversies found expression under this heading,[2] which still means different things in different countries. We shall consider only its effects on ethics and discipleship.

One approach to this aspect may be seen in an influential article which rightly challenged the description of certain parts of the gospels as 'eye-witness accounts' of Jesus, declared their value as direct accounts of the church, and then went on to say,

[44] D J. O'Connor, *Aquinas and Natural Law*, p. 84.
[45] F. Flückiger, *Geschichte des Naturrechtes*, p. 435. 'Das Naturrecht war die Ordnung der integren Natur, die allein im Licht der Gnade wieder erkannt und hergestellt wird. Bei den Autoren des dreizehnten Jahrunderts aber treten andere Auffassungen in der Vordergrund. . .Die natürliche Ethik, die im Anschluss an die antike Philosophie entfaltet, beginnt sich heimhaft als autonomer Bereich von der christlichen Sittlichkeit zu lösen.'
[1] In the interest of brevity I have drawn especially on these sources:
(i) my *Word and History* (Univ. of W.A., 1967), (ii) two articles by Ernst Käsemann: 'The Problem of the Historical Jesus', *ENT*, *EVB* 1, and 'Blind Alleys in the Jesus of History', *NTQT*, *EVB* 2, and
(iii) L. E. Keck, *A Future for the Historical Jesus* (London, 1972). The summary given by H. K. McArthur, *In Search of the Historical Jesus* (London, 1970), must be handled with care. The categories of minimal and maximal lives of Jesus obscure central issues. The number of facts admitted by each writer is not important. For instance, Käsemann, who has a low score on facts, gives central importance to the historical Jesus and claims that portraits tell more than photographs. Knox, who has a high score on facts, gives less importance to the historical Jesus and great importance to the early communities.
[2] See R. Slenzcka, *Geschichtlichkeit und Personsein Jesu Christi* (Göttingen, 1967), especially pp. 303ff., and L. E. Keck, *op. cit.*, pp. 209 and 249.

It is idle to deny that some real loss is involved in our conclusions. If they are right, then it is illegitimate to press the details, and many of the personal traits in the stories:. . .A question mark is clearly set against some forms at least of *imitatio Christi* devotion and also against the practice, which still largely governs the life of the Churches, of quoting individual sayings and incidents from the gospels as precedents.[3]

There is an initial logical weakness in this argument. The writer is concerned with two things – a positivist theory of history which depends on eye-witness accounts and the results of this method when applied to the gospels. Granted the lack of results from this method, there is no 'real loss' unless the method be a valid one. There is no reason given why the method should be considered valid. The writer in question nowhere argues for it. One may recall the alarm and sense of loss which the theory of evolution raised concerning the first chapters of Genesis. The result of that attack on literal understanding has been a deeper appreciation of the meaning of creation. For whom could the failure of this method be a real loss?

There is no real loss for Bultmann who rejected the relevance of the historical Jesus for faith. Jesus was a Jew, not a Christian.[4] Faith comes by hearing the word of God. Nor is there real loss for the opposing view of Jeremias whose historical investigation does not depend on 'eye-witness' accounts. The origin of Christianity is neither kerygma, Easter experience nor christology, 'but an historical event, namely the appearing of the man Jesus of Nazareth, who was nailed to the cross by Pontius Pilate, and his message'.[5] The only people for whom there should be a real loss are those fundamentalists for whom literal accuracy is all important. Yet here again, no loss could be acknow-

[3] D. E. Nineham, 'Eye-witness Testimony and the Gospel Tradition, III', *JTS* (1960), pp. 255ff. I. T. Ramsey considers the importance of the article in *Christian Ethics and Contemporary Philosophy* (London, 1966), p. 396. It is odd to regard this as a new problem. A. B. D. Alexander wrote in 1914, 'One cannot forget that the battle of criticism is raging today around the inner citadel – the very person and words of Jesus – we might have to give up some of the passages upon which we have based our conception of truth and duty', *Christianity and Ethics* (London, 1914), p.31. For Nineham's own approach to history see *London Quarterly and Holborn Review*, April, 1967, pp. 93–105.

[4] R. Bultmann, *Das Verhältnis der urchristlichen Christusbotschaft zum historischen Jesus* (Sitzungsberichte der Heidelberger Akademie der Wissenschaften, phil.-hist. Klasse, 1960), **3,** 8ff.

[5] J. Jeremias, 'Der gegenwärtige Stand der Debatte um das Problem des historischen Jesus', in, *Der historische Jesus und der kerygmatische Christus* (ed. H. Ristow and K. Matthiae, Berlin, 1961), p 18, cited by E. Käsemann, *EVB* **2,** 33; *NTQT*, p. 25.

ledged, since the accuracy of scripture is for the fundamentalist a dog-
matic belief, to be confirmed, but never established or undermined, by
historical evidence.

If there be no real loss, is there a real gain in the denial of eye-
witness content in the gospels? Bultmann would find a real gain in any
move which made Jesus less provable. There can be no real continuity
between the historical Jesus and the Christ of faith.[6] Historical evidence
is an insidious form of 'works' and justification is through faith alone.[7]
Faith is immune from the exigencies of any form of historical research.
But Bultmann would here claim a doubtful gain. For faith, while it
cannot depend on history, may not be insensitive to history. Historicity
and risk must go together.[8] Nor should faith wish to be immune from
historical or other threats. The critical historical method means 'to
let everything burn that will burn and without reservations await what
proves itself unburnable, genuine, true', and that 'many mistakes and
errors are made'.[9]

Nineham and Knox would also find gain rather than loss in any
account which limited historical acquaintance of Jesus and pushed
the believer closer to the church.[10] The gospels are first-hand documents of the church and only indirectly documents about Jesus. They
show what early Christian communities thought about Jesus. As
before, the gain is doubtful and the only certainty is that of definition.
There is a false confidence in the historical accessibility of the early
Christian communities. 'Whatever else the Church is, it is a historical
community, a cultural stream. . .flowing from the first century into our
own.' Yet 'the Church without ceasing. . .to be the Church, could not
deny, or even doubt, that God raised Jesus from the dead'.[11] The first
definition does not fit easily with the second. Does either of them
apply to the first and second century? The New Testament gives
evidence of at least six different ecclesiologies and different types of
communities.[12] It is therefore odd to suggest that what we meet directly
in the New Testament can be usefully described as 'the Church'.[13]

---

6 R. Bultmann, *Das Verhältnis der urchristlichen Christusbotschaft.*
7 R. Bultmann, *Jesus Christ and Mythology* (London, 1960), p. 84.
8 See R. W. Hepburn, *Christianity and Paradox* (London, 1957), pp. 91–127.
9 See G. Ebeling, 'The Significance of the Critical Historical Method',
   in, *Word and Faith* (London, 1963), p. 51.
10 See D. E. Nineham, *Historicity and Chronology in the NT* (London,
   1965), pp. 16–18.
11 J. Knox, *The Church and the Reality of Christ* (London, 1963),
   pp. 44 and 61.
12 E. Käsemann, *NTQT*, pp. 252ff., *EVB* **2**, 262ff.
13 John Knox, *The Church and the Reality of Christ*, maintains this position
   by sticking to his definitions and two forms of *ad hominem* argument:

However, at least one clear gain follows from the removal of any positivist proof for particular incidents and sayings. Freedom from casuistry based on sayings and incidents is assured, for casuistry needs literal accuracy. When asked for a Christian view of marriage, one cannot proceed by listing separate passages from the gospels. There is no valid ground for taking these as legal evidence of what Jesus or 'the Church' thought. Nor may we take incidents as precedents from the life of Jesus or 'the Church'. Both sayings and incidents lack the literal accuracy which would warrant them being used as legal prescriptions and precedents. One could argue that some community somewhere, at some time, thought this way, but that would not be enough to guarantee prescription and precedent. The removal of this kind of argument is a great gain.

In several other ways the discussion of the historical Jesus has made positive contributions to the understanding of Christian discipleship. It has under-lined the particularity of Jesus, his sovereignty over his followers, his immediacy and clarity and the identity of the crucified and risen Lord. In a word, the study of the historical Jesus confronts us with his lordship. Twenty years ago, a provocative essay[14] challenged premature solutions to the historical problems about Jesus. Historical scepticism had been exaggerated. We know little about the earthly Jesus; but there are some facts which will stand any test and which are important because the gospel cannot be anonymous. 'The Gospel is tied to him, who, both before and after Easter, revealed himself to his own as the Lord.'[15] He brought them to the God who is near and gave them the freedom of faith. The riddle of the historical Jesus is his particularity and the solution is the faith which confesses him as Lord. 'For to his particularity there corresponds the particularity of faith, for which the real history of Jesus is always happening afresh; it is

every student of the New Testament knows (p. 127), and if we don't we are either not reconciled to God or ignorant of how it happened (p. 120). Cf. the tautology of D. E. Nineham, *Eye-witness Testimony*, p. 255: 'Accordingly the gospels must be treated in the first instance as so many formulations of the early Church's growing tradition about the ministry of Jesus; the only thing for which they provide *direct* evidence is the beliefs about, and understanding of, that ministry in various parts of the early Church between the middle of the first and the early part of the second centuries.' The certainty here is based on a definition of the church in terms of NT communities; the reference to evidence obscures this point. An awareness of the acute problems faced by a 'a quest for the historical early church' is shown by F. G. Downing, *The Church and Jesus* (London, 1968), pp. 1–56.

[14] E. Käsemann, 'The Problem of the Historical Jesus', *ENT*, pp. 15–47; *EVB* I, 187–214.

[15] *Ibid. ENT*, p. 46; *EVB* I, 213.

now the history of the exalted Lord, but it does not cease to be the earthly history it once was, in which the call and claim of the Gospel are encountered.'[16]

In a second essay ten years later, the explosive effects of the first essay were considered.[17] Bultmann had continued to deny the relevance of the earthly Jesus to faith and kerygma. This denial was based on a definition which made the inaccessibility of the earthly Jesus a sufficient ground for his discontinuity with kerygma and faith. He was a Jew and not a Christian. Käsemann indicated that this Jew was 'as the common consciousness of Christendom asserts, the pioneer and perfecter of faith, the archetype of obedience, the new Adam, and, as such, not the presupposition but the centre of the New Testament'.[18]

The key point comes as the answer to the simple question, Why were the gospels written? They are a late form of proclaiming Jesus Christ. Yet they took a roughly biographical shape. Why was the earthly Jesus so important? His inaccessibility was a form of his lordship over his followers. Enthusiasts and others were quick to manipulate the message according to their taste and experience. The earthly Jesus pointed to the external and independent source of man's salvation. He could not be manipulated without remainder. The historical elements in the gospels are not enough to provide a biography; but they have great theological importance. 'They do not as such constitute the Gospel; but they do make it possible for the Gospel "to recall" him and so to incapsulate his history into the Gospel.'[19] It has always been necessary to recall the historical Jesus. So we have the puzzle that what is removed from existential encounter is of ultimate importance: the earthly Jesus 'served in primitive Christianity to demonstrate the autonomy of salvation, the priority of Christ in relation to his own, the "*extra nos*" of the Gospel message, the necessary exodus of the believer from his self-centredness.'[20]

With this sovereignty of Jesus goes the strong sense of his immediacy. Schweitzer continues to amaze his readers by concluding his negative account of the quest with the much quoted paragraph:

> He comes to us as One unknown, without a name, as of old, by the lake-side, he came to those men who knew him not. He speaks to us the same word: Follow thou me! and sets us to the tasks which he has to fulfil for our time. He commands. And to those who obey

---

[16] *Ibid.* ENT, p. 47; *EVB* 1, 214.
[17] 'Blind Alleys in the "Jesus of History" Controversy', *NTQT*, pp. 23–65; *EVB* 2, 31–68.
[18] *Ibid. NTQT*, p. 42; *EVB* 2, 48.
[19] *Ibid. NTQT*, p. 64; *EVB* 2, 67f.
[20] *Ibid. NTQT*, p. 63; *EVB* 2, 67.

him, whether they be wise or simple, he will reveal himself in the toils, the conflicts, the sufferings which they shall pass through in his fellowship, and, as an ineffable mystery, they shall learn in their own experience who he is.[21]

The same sense of immediacy is found in the most recent discussion. Jesus confronts us with a 'shift from narrative to invitation to share trust'.[22] He elicits trust.[23] It is wrong to isolate a convenient aspect of Jesus. 'No aspect of Jesus saves us, but the whole life touches our life as a whole.'[24] It is worth noting that Bultmann never ceased to maintain the immediacy which the believer finds in his encounter with his Lord.[25] Bultmann's rejection of the historical Jesus was largely motivated by a stress on the immediacy of faith.

The strange clarity of Jesus is a recurring theme. The gospels are like a splintered mirror which still reflects one face.[26] The clarity of the portrait is better than a precise inventory or a mechanical copy. 'There are paintings which seize the essentials better than photographs.'[27] A recent commentary on Mark makes a similar point. 'If we had a sound-film of the crucifixion of Jesus, we would have much better knowledge concerning a hundred details, but still we would not know what really happened in this death.'[28] The purpose of the narrative in Mark is 'to proclaim the One who encounters the hearer or reader today in the same fullness of power and seeks his faith.'[29] The doubts and contradictions of the different stories show that there is no timeless abstraction which can express the Word. It is a cause of wonder to all who work in this field that 'in the midst of the confusion, the original Christ-event still prevails'.[30]

Particularity, sovereignty, immediacy and clarity are all important in contemporary appreciation of the historical Jesus. They are all taken up in the central assertion of the identity of the crucified with the risen Lord who is on his way to take his throne. Ethics are important all the way. On the negative side, the earthly Jesus prevented enthusiasm or legalism from taking control. On the positive side there are several points to be made. First, the lordship and autonomy of

---

[21] A. Schweitzer, *The Quest of the Historical Jesus* (London, 1910), p. 401.
[22] L. E. Keck, *A Future for the Historical Jesus* (London, 1972), p. 134.
[23] *Ibid.* p. 192. [24] *Ibid.* p. 177.
[25] In his *Commentary on John*, his account of chapter 20 does this in an unforgettable way.
[26] E. Käsemann, *Der Ruf der Freiheit* (Tübingen, 1968), p. 36; *Jesus Means Freedom* (London, 1969), p. 22.
[27] *Ibid.*
[28] E. Schweizer, *The Good News according to Mark* (London, 1971), p. 22.
[29] *Ibid.* p. 21. [30] *Ibid.* p. 23.

Jesus indicate that the source of ethical endeavour takes its rise outside man. The shape of negative ethics is confirmed. Righteousness, discipleship, faith and love come from God. All is of grace. Trust in Jesus is not self-generated but is elicited. The initiative is with God, for

> that complex of word, deed and death called 'Jesus' is not the construct of the mind, nor a carefully nurtured product of a religious society determined to produce a perfect model. Precisely as a historical event, Jesus is a surprise to mankind; for though he was understood to be the expected one, he was not what was expected.[31]

God shows his grace in bringing and ratifying Jesus, and trust in Jesus is simply man's response, 'his lifelong "Yes" to what God has done in this life'.[32]

Secondly, the identity of the crucified and risen Lord preserves the one thing necessary for the disciple. He is a follower rather than an imitator, but the one thing about his Lord that he must know is the cross. He follows Jesus by taking up the cross. So in Phil. 2 the believer is called to think as Christ thought when he humbled himself and became obedient to the cross. Here is the central mystery of the gospel and it is the one point where the disciple is left in no ethical doubt. What lives on in the community of faith should be the love which came in the crucified Lord.

Finally, the future of the historical Jesus is primarily of ethical interest. It is remarkable that this emerges in the earliest and the most recent accounts we have examined. Schweitzer was to act out in his own life the need for discipleship to obey Christ in 'the tasks he has to fulfil for our time'. Only in such obedience and in the toils and sufferings it brings can Jesus be known by the wise and simple alike. Today, Keck insists, 'the chief theological questions are more moral than ontic and epistemological'.[33] In the face of human exploitation, poverty and suffering, the Christian cannot concentrate on the questions of ontology and epistemology. God's existence and our knowledge of his existence are of little interest when there is doubt concerning his moral integrity. When theology is oriented towards God's moral integrity, 'faith and ethics become two sides of the same coin'. The historical Jesus points to a future which is ethical. 'If the integrity of God is affirmed on the basis of Jesus, then the fundamental mode of Christian existence is not fulfilment of frustrated potential so much as discipleship or participation in rectification.' Discipleship and the Jesus of history help to overcome the 'massive and pervasive internalization of faith'.[34] So the Jesus of history gains, through critical investigation, a more powerful

---

[31] Keck,, *A Future for the Historical Jesus*, p. 192.
[32] *Ibid.*   [33] *Ibid.* p. 263.   [34] *Ibid.* p. 264.

ethical role than he could ever have through literalism and casuistry.

Uncertainty still remains and here, as before, the pursuit of certainty is the enemy of the pursuit of truth.[35] There will still be distortions of the historical Jesus, for each culture and generation has its limitations;[36] but the lordship of Jesus works through these limitations and his historical inaccessibility is one sign of this lordship to which disciple-ship answers with practical, ethical obedience. Faith will still be pre-carious; but the immediacy of Jesus and the strange clarity of his presence persist. The intensity of the fathers is matched by the experi-ence of critical scholars from Erasmus on:[37] 'These gospels give you back the living image of the sacred mind of Christ. They present Christ in his own person speaking, healing, dying, rising again. In a word, they so give the whole presence of Christ that you would see him less clearly if you beheld him face to face with your eyes.' *'Denique totum ita praesentem reddunt, ut minus visurus sis si coram oculis conspicias.'*[38]

FAITH AND PHILOSOPHY

Why do we find non-Christian ethical terms in early Christian writing? Extravagant claims have been made for the derivation of Christian ethics from Stoicism. Paul has been 'defended' on this charge.[1] There is a quick answer that ethical terms never have the same meaning in different contexts. Meaning is discoverable from usage, as Plato in the *Phaedrus*,[2] and Wittgenstein, on every hand, insisted. A term like

[35] To gain security, Nineham used definition and *ad hominem* argument: 'If some such view is tenable, we should have no further problem about the insecurity of a faith based on an historical event, for about this total event no sane man can, or ever will be able to, entertain the slightest doubt', *Historicity and Chronology*, p. 17. Sane men can and will entertain doubts concerning this total event, especially as a basis of faith.

[36] See pictorial evidence in 'Das Christusbild in seinen Wandlungen', by Hanna Jursch, in H. Ristow and K. Matthiae (ed.), *Der historische Jesus und der kerygmatische Christus*, pp. 675–710.

[37] Erasmus, 'Novum Testamentum, Praefatio, Paraclesis, id est adhortatio ad Christianae philosophiae studium', *Opera Omnia*, vi (Lugduni Batavorum, MDCCV, Edition of Joannes Clericus, reprinted 1962, Hildesheim).

[38] The logical problems associated with this kind of knowledge are similar to those associated with the knowledge of other minds. See N. Macleish, *The Nature of Religious Knowledge* (Edinburgh, 1938), and A. Plantinga, *God and Other Minds* (New York, 1967), pp. 187ff.

[1] J. N. Sevenster, *Paul and Seneca* (Leiden, 1961).

[2] *Phaedrus* 275f.

apatheia does not hold a constant meaning within the variety of Stoic writings. Christians, who used old terms in the framework of new arguments and new concepts, cannot be required to answer for their terms on the basis of non-Christian usage.

There is a threefold necessity laid on Christians and others to use ethical terms of independent origin. The necessity is linguistic, historical and logical. The linguistic necessity lies in the limited number of words of approbation and disapproval in any language. In English, it would be hard to talk ethics without using the words: good, right, fitting, proper, duty. Some words could be dropped but some must be retained to provide a point of identification for new values. In the process of using terms associated with other systems some violence will occur. Violence can occur both in borrower and borrowed. Violence was done to the classical tradition whose terms Christians reshaped and reinterpreted; and it has been argued that, without such treatment, the classical tradition could not have survived.[3] The word *apatheia* is used by Clement as consistent with *agapē* of the most intense kind. The same term is used by John, who still insists that Paul feared, 'For what perseverance was there if he did not fear?', and by Augustine, who regarded the absence of right affections as *stupor* and a curse. The strict Stoic view, as set down by Chrysippus, regarded all emotions as errors of reason and therefore bad. This orthodoxy was compromised by Poseidonios who distinguished rational from irrational powers of the soul; the *apatheia* of Chrysippus had only been possible when the soul was free from the body. But nothing like the Christian compromise could ever be justified on classical grounds.

Violence is done in return to the Christian view at isolated points by the unargued transfer of inconsistent associations. The antagonism between body and soul, which had been built into the idea of *apatheia*, was rejected by Clement; but he could not avoid exalting the spiritual at the expense of the physical. Jesus was truly human, but not a 'normal man'. He did not need to eat and drink; but he did so for appearance' sake.[4] Clement writes also, 'The body is only a husk, which is wrapped around us for our earthly journey, so that we may be able to enter this common place of correction.'[5] In this case the violence is clear but limited and the idea is built into Clement's system in a detailed and effective way. *Apatheia* brings the true gnostic closer to the divine likeness and finds perfection in *aphtharsia* which is nothing less than participation in the life of God.[6] It is an ethical quality

---

[3] R. Jolivet, *Essai sur les rapports entre la pensée grecque et la pensée chrétienne* (Paris, 1955), p. 198.   [4] *Strom.* 3.6.49; *Strom.* 6.9.71.2.
[5] *Quis Dives Salvetur*, 33.6, cf. *Strom.* 5.11.67.1–4.
[6] T. Rüther, *Die sittliche Forderung der Apatheia* (Freiburg, 1949), p. 102.

and to be distinguished from the natural freedom from passion which heretics claimed.[7]

To the linguistic necessity for the use of classical ethics must be added the historical necessity. We all have a 'given historicity', and 'I have no way of beginning religiously outside of my history, in abstraction from my society.'[8] Most contemporaries of Clement were Stoic or Platonist. When converted, they became either Christian Stoics or Christian Platonists. Christians have frequently erred on the side of defensiveness against related systems of behaviour. They would understand their own position better if they saw how close they were to other systems.[9] In particular, Christianity has affinities with both Jewish and Stoic ethics and the fathers were sound in the acceptance of these universal ethics of response. When the church turns inwards and sees the activity of God only within its own limits, it has lost the universal width of the ethic of Jesus. God's city is a universal community into which Christians find their way through Jesus.[10]

In the third place, there is a logical necessity for the use of non-Christian ethics. No one is a complete beginner in ethical argument and the logical structure of this highly social part of thinking is built out of discussion and interaction with several systems.[11] In the early church the structure which came to dominate was that of Platonism, mixed with a strong element of Stoicism. This necessity is sometimes acknowledged.[12] Frequently, idealism has been present without acknowledgement, because it was part of the intellectual background of the early decades of this century.[13] Every account of Christian ethics has depended on some form or forms of philosophical ethics. A recent survey of Christian ethics covers contemporary material.[14] Contributions to this subject are classified under three ethical motifs: deliberative (rational decision), prescriptive (moral injunction) or relational

[7] *Ibid.* p. 104.
[8] H. R. Niebuhr, *The Responsible Self* (New York, 1963), p. 112.
[9] *Ibid.* p. 150, 'Christianity represents a qualification of human practical existence or at least of Western moral life...rather than a genus of human moral existence.' This is a strange overstatement which shows no awareness of that great part of Christianity which could never be called 'Western'.
[10] *Ibid.* p. 178.
[11] Cf. A. C. Ewing, *Ethics* (London, 1953), p. 1.
[12] E.g. Paul Ramsey, *Basic Christian Ethics* (London, 1950), p. xiii; 'contemporary Christian ethics must make common cause with the ethics of philosophical idealism'.
[13] R. Newton Flew, *The Idea of Perfection in Christian Theology* (Oxford, 1934), p. 1.
[14] E. L. Long, *A Survey of Christian Ethics* (New York, 1967).

(response to divine initiative or to total context). The use of philosophical categories is restricted to the first motif. Yet this restriction can no longer be made credible, for all three motifs may be found in philosophical ethics. Prescriptivism is the dominant tendency in Hare and others, while existentialism is relational.

The most vigorous attempt to divide Christian ethics from philosophy offers paradoxically the final evidence for their necessary interaction. Philosophical ethics, it is declared, are inadequate and incompatible with Christian ethics, which are defined as 'the disciplined reflexion upon the question and its answer: What am I, as a believer in Jesus Christ and as a member of his Church, to do?'[15] The key word here is 'disciplined', and the question is whether philosophy is needed for disciplined thought. The reader's answer is easy when he reads the unintentionally comic jargon, 'so Calvin's "let us be whatever we are for each other" means the rejection of preferential differentiation and its displacement by organic interrelational differentiation as the true significance of koinonia'.[16] He will learn with some foreboding that it was too early in 1962 to say whether linguistic analysis was an 'Anglo-Saxon passion' or 'a major philosophical preoccupation of the twentieth century'.[17] After much explanation of the incompatibility of the two kinds of ethics and the insufficiency of philosophical ethics, it comes as a surprise to learn that the way ahead is possible through the help of Aristotle, Kant, William James and ethical humanism. So the most extended case for the exclusiveness of Christian ethics requires that such ethics should learn from philosophical sources. There is no thought of isolation.[18] Kant and William James inaugurate a way of ethics which shows the direction which needs to be taken.[19] We may therefore conclude that, however reluctantly, Christian ethics depends on some scheme or schemes of philosophical ethics for its formulation. This is a linguistic, historical and logical necessity. There is some choice to be made and it is better to be aware of our philosophical framework than to adopt one without examination. Within each historical context there are several possibilities. Our choice should be governed by the logical strength of each approach and its affinity to Christian concepts.

One work on Christian ethics went far beyond the kind of dependence which has been discussed. Ambrose's De Officiis took over from Cicero's work the title, plan and leading ideas. There were practical reasons: Christian ministers needed a handbook of moral instruction

[15] P. L. Lehmann, *Ethics in a Christian Context* (London, 1963), p. 45.
[16] *Ibid.* p. 66.   [17] *Ibid.* p. 225.
[18] *Ibid.* p. 282.   [19] *Ibid.* p. 281.

which could take the place of the non-Christian works in general use.
The work conveys an intensely personal Christian piety. 'Why do you
not go back to see Christ? Why do you not speak to him and listen to
his voice? We speak to him when we pray, we hear him when we read
the sacred oracles of God.'[20] The relation between the two works is
quite explicit; at the same time there is an explicit rejection of an
abstract framework and a preference for examples from the lives of the
fathers of old.[21] A mass of biblical material dominates the work.

Interpreters of Ambrose corroborate the conclusions we have reached
concerning the necessity of philosophical ethics and their adaptability
to Christian values. Ambrose criticises Cicero on particular points, omits
parts of Cicero and adds parts of his own.[22] The good man does not
think of his own rights which are part of Stoic teaching and never
balances his own interest against that of others. He is concerned for
others, not for himself. Life according to reason and the law of nature
is simply life in obedience to God. Christ is the pattern and the law
giver, to be loved and adored, trusted and depended on, as God. 'The
whole atmosphere is different. Coincidences of thought and language
must not lead us to ignore this. Even when the same precept is enun-
ciated by Ambrose and Cicero in practically the same words, it does
not signify the same thing.'[23]

What then are the possibilities which the contemporary Christian
may use in his ethical thinking? The intuitionism of Moore and Ross
would take too much time to defend. The emotivism of Stevenson,
with which many grew up, had some things to commend it.[24] Prescriptivism has been dominant until recently; but the criticisms of
Warnock are striking and to the point. This view, it is claimed, is too
barren and restrictive.

> In so far as the thesis is that moral discourse is in some way
> essentially (and not just causally) related to conduct, it is a
> completely impregnable platitude; but in so far as it attempts a

[20] *De Officiis*, 1.88.
[21] *Ibid.* 1.116.
[22] F. Homes Dudden, *The Life and Times of St. Ambrose* (Oxford,
    1935), 2, 502.
[23] *Ibid.* p. 554; cf. A. Paredi, *St. Ambrose, His Life and Times* (E.T.,
    Notre Dame, 1964), pp. 318f. Also cf. B. Maes, *La loi naturelle selon
    Ambroise de Milan* (Rome, 1967), p. 206, 'Une constatation s'est
    imposée: le contenu des vertus stoïciennes est profondément modifié
    par saint Ambroise.'
[24] It explained why bad men could not see good things. F. R. Tennant is
    reliably reported to have supported such an approach long before it was
    widely held.

serious assimilation of all moral judgements to imperatives, it seems to leave us once more with practically nothing to discuss.[25]

There is an urgent need to identify the subject matter of ethics and to see it as 'a subject in which there is still almost everything to be done'.[26]

As Clement and Augustine showed, and has been recently indicated, Platonism offers a scheme of ethics which can preserve Christians from their more obvious mistakes. Plato's approach to morals is similar to that of the New Testament in several ways. It begins with a strong anti-ethical strain. Socrates rejects conventional ethics. He is a destroyer of morals and a dangerous man. He perverts the youth. Yet he claims that this accusation springs from the fact that he knows that he knows nothing. Because he has discovered his ignorance of right and good, he must reject the conventional ethics and morals of his day. Plato's ethics are negative as are those of the New Testament. There is a transcendent form of the good to which man must take the upward path. There is only one thing that is good and it is a negation of the things which men regard as good. All definitions, all virtues, depend on the ultimate vision of the unique good. Yet at the same time as the stress on perfection, there is a continuing reference to the contingent which may participate in the transcendent good. He who has seen the vision of the good must descend to the world, and only when philosophers are kings can states find justice. The same accusation of newness or novelty was brought against Socrates and against Christians. The challenge to perfection is issued in the call to become like God, and it is joined from the beginning with a sense of man's contingency and limitations.

> Evils can never be done away with, for the good must always have its contrary; nor have they any place in the divine world but they must needs haunt this region of our mortal nature. That is why we should make all speed to take flight from this world to the other; and that means becoming like the divine so far as we can, and that again is to become righteous with the help of wisdom.

> There are two patterns, my friend, in the unchangeable nature of things, one of happiness, the other of godless misery – a truth to which their folly makes them utterly blind, unaware that in doing injustice they are growing less like one of these patterns and more like the other. The penalty that they pay is the life they lead, answering to the pattern they resemble.[27]

[25] G. J. Warnock, *Contemporary Moral Philosophy* (London, 1967), p. 74.
[26] *Ibid.* p. 77. [27] *Theaetetus* 176f.

My reasons for claiming that Platonism provides the best way for a Christian to do his ethics at the present time spring from the three propositions which are common to Plato and to the New Testament: (i) there is a sovereign good; (ii) man is subject to fallibility, contingency, choice, evil, corruption and death; (iii) nevertheless the claims of perfection and contingency can be reconciled by the participation of the particular in the unique divine perfection or by the word which joins the transcendent to the particular. Many objections may be brought. My contention is simply that the Christian has to make moral choices and to think ethically and that Platonism is the best way for him to do his ethics because it is sensitive to the peculiar ethics of the New Testament. This was the conclusion of the four diverse writers studied above, especially of Clement and Augustine. I shall support and explain my contention, by an exposition of the third chapter of Philippians,[28] in which the early fathers found Platonic themes. Using the most recent account of the Platonic tradition, I shall try to show how clearly the central ideas of Paul come through.

The closing parts of the letter to the Philippians state what Paul considers to be the motive of a Christian life, with a ruthless rejection of any other kind of life and a restless dissatisfaction which ends in the peace of God. There is only one good thing, and that is to know Christ. This is difficult to achieve and differs from most things which people consider good. Direction is what matters and life is like running a race. Paul has achieved the kinds of goodness which his enemies think important; but he moves them all from the credit to the debit side and puts the knowledge of Christ alone on the credit side. The difficulty of this procedure does not escape him, for he has not reached that knowledge of Christ which he takes to be the only good thing. Yet he underlines his decision by attacking those who follow the old values as dogs, workers of evil, with nothing but destruction ahead of them. Their god is their belly, and they find glory in their shame. They are concerned for earthly things. Then Paul turns to those who stand where he stands; he tells them to be glad, to keep on praying and not to be anxious, and he promises them God's peace.

The difficulty of this approach to ethics is clear. It is true to say that most contemporary moral thought would be against Paul here. So much the worse for contemporary thought, says the novelist and philosopher, Iris Murdoch, in a recent book.[29] Moral thought today is universally unambitious and optimistic. 'Unambitious optimism is of

---

[28] Clement's argument, *Stromateis* 2.22, would also help here. For an extended exposition of this chapter see my *The Philosophy of Clement of Alexandria* (Cambridge, 1957), chapter 7.

[29] I. Murdoch, *The Sovereignty of Good* (London, 1970).

course part of the Anglo-Saxon tradition; and it is also not surprising that a philosophy which analyses moral concepts on the basis of ordinary language should present a relaxed picture of a mediocre achievement.'[30] The kind of ethical discussion to which we have been accustomed deals with the language of ordinary people as they make moral choices. It analyses the way in which these choices are made, and defines ethics accordingly. It can hardly be anything but optimistic, since it takes as its goal and standard what has already been achieved. At the same time, Murdoch points out, existentialist discussion is just as unambitious and just as optimistic:

> An authentic mode of existence is presented as attainable by
> intelligence and force of will. The atmosphere is invigorating and
> tends to produce self-satisfaction in the reader, who feels himself
> to be a member of the élite, addressed by another one. Contempt
> for the ordinary human condition, together with a conviction of
> personal salvation, saves the writer from real pessimism.[31]

The gloom of people like Sartre is superficial, and conceals the elation which anyone may achieve when he acts according to his own will. The contrast between these viewpoints and Christianity is remarkable. On the other hand, not all the cards are stacked against the New Testament. Freud has given a picture of man as a fallen creature. His pessimism sees the *psychē* as a self-centred system largely determined by its past history, with ambiguous attachments and a fundamental sexual drive which man himself can neither understand nor control. Man cannot reach the kind of objectivity which moralists claim for him. We may therefore question from the beginning whether any man can choose in the way Sartre claims. In fact, Sartre admits that, when we deliberate, the decision is already made, and that our decisions come out of some pre-existent condition which he is also happy to call choice. British moral philosophers here claim that all talk of motives and intentions is difficult and that a man's actual choices indicate his moral life. All of which seems to ignore what Freud is talking about and the whole background to moral behaviour.

It is natural to ask a practical question: Is there any way in which selfish energies can be purified and redirected so that in moments of choice we have a better chance of acting rightly? This is where prayer comes in, prayer seen as attention to God, as a form of love, as a direction of man towards 'a single perfect transcendent non-representable and necessarily real object of attention'.[32] This is what God is: He is perfect, transcendent, he cannot be represented in any form before our

---

[30] *Ibid*. p. 50.   [31] *Ibid*.   [32] *Ibid*. p. 55.

eyes, and he exists in his own way. The focus of emotions on a particular goal and for a particular end by this kind of attention, is part of
human life. Human beings are attached to various ends, and as Paul
himself points out, the way in which we act depends a great deal upon
what we commonly think about (Phil. 4:8). 'There is nothing odd or
mystical about this, nor about the fact that our ability to act well
"when the time comes" depends partly, perhaps largely, upon the
quality of our habitual objects of attention.'[33] The God of peace, that is
the one God, the objective good, presents himself to those who look for
him in every place. We seem to be driven by a practical necessity to
focus on one supremely good thing, if the energies of our life are to be
directed along the right lines. But we could come to the conclusion
that goodness is a unity in another way. Moral decisions tend to make
us bring different kinds of goodness together. To say that courage is a
good thing, as Plato showed, requires the description of the best kind
of courage, as steadfast, calm, temperate, intelligent and loving. If we
want to define one kind of virtue we are forced to bring in other kinds
as well. So the case for one final kind of goodness is a strong one.

To say that only one thing is good takes us a long way to what Paul
is saying; but by itself it is clearly not enough. The two ideas which
need to be added are those of perfection and realism or certainty. 'Are
we not certain that there is a "true direction" towards better conduct,
that goodness "really matters", and does not that certainty about a
standard suggest an idea of permanence which cannot be reduced to
psychological or any other set of empirical terms?'[34] The notion of
perfection is important in any field of activity. If we are to judge any
human activity, we must have some idea of how that activity should be
performed in order to assess what we see before us. We assess an
achievement as more or less excellent according to our ideas of perfection or excellence. These ideas produce order in moral matters. 'The
idea of perfection moves, and possibly changes us, (as artist, worker,
agent) because it inspires love in the part of us that is most worthy. One
cannot feel unmixed love for a mediocre moral standard, any more
than one can for the work of a mediocre artist.'[35]

We may agree then, that there is one thing that is good and that it
is the idea of perfection. How do we know that this perfection is real?
How do we know that we can be certain about it? Here we might argue
very simply that our conception of God contains the certainty of its
own reality. 'God is an object of love which uniquely excludes doubt
and relativism.'[36] The perfect would not be perfect if it did not exist.
This is the kind of conviction on which moral discourse must be based.

[33] *Ibid.* p. 56.   [34] *Ibid.* p. 60.
[35] *Ibid.* p. 62.   [36] *Ibid.* p. 63.

It remains an act of faith, however, and we know that our redeemer lives, simply because he is our redeemer. What kind of argument can we put up for the existence of this perfection of which Paul and at least some moralists are bound to speak?

We turn for this point to the world of art. Art is concerned with a form of excellence and a form of perfection, and is opposed to fantasy. It is a form of realism. Rilke said of Cézanne that he did not paint 'I like it'; but he painted, 'There it is'. A great deal of art, visual and audible, is a matter of personal fantasy, and not a means of showing things as they are. But it is not hard to accept this as one definition of true art: that it breaks down personal fantasies and personal likes and presents us with what is. In the same way, goodness is necessary to exhibit fact. To act rightly involves a detachment from personal fantasies and an ability to choose according to reality. 'The authority of the good seems to us something necessary because the realism (ability to perceive reality) required for goodness is a kind of intellectual ability to perceive what is true, which is automatically at the same time a suppression of self.'[37] This is what Plato meant when he said that you could not see the good, but that in the presence of the good you were able to see other things as they are.

Now all of this is concerned to argue in an abbreviated way that what is good is one and perfect and real. There are some ambiguities which need to be cleared up, and it is possible that, even then, this train of argument would not convince. But whether it convinces or not, it does show that Paul, who wrote Philippians 3 and 4, was not dealing in strange authoritarian fantasy, but was confronting the stuff of moral life and human choices. There is in the end only one thing which is good, perfect and certain. This should be the frequent object of thought, because from it will spring the ability to avoid fantasy and illusion, to choose what is right, and to follow what is worth following. Paul does not stop here. He is not just arguing, he is declaring a gospel. The one perfect thing after which he grasps is the living Christ who has already grasped him. The goal to which he presses forward is a righteousness given by the grace of God and received by faith. The way which he treads is the way of the cross and resurrection, because Christ has died and brought the death of all that falsely claims to be good and is not, and because the cross of Christ is the one perfection by which the Christian is able to see things as they are, not in a distorted fragmentary way, but in the light of the resurrection. We may understand better why Paul is angry at those who want to offer something less than Christ, who want to bring Christ down to the level of one of many good

[37] *Ibid.* p. 66.

things. They have not seen his perfection. Paul's last word is a word of joy, because the object of infinite goodness and infinite love is the source of infinite goodness and infinite love to man.

Is this Platonic account simply an exercise in hermeneutics? As such it is intelligible, but how much has been lost in the process? Paul is here concerned to attack perfectionism of a Jewish and gnostic form. His opponents believe that the complete fulfilment of the law is possible and that they have achieved 'possession of eschatological promises in full, that is, the Spirit and spiritual experiences of such heavenly gifts as resurrection and freedom from suffering and death'.[38] Paul's argument against enthusiasm invariably turns to eschatology. This is the grand theme of the first letter to the Corinthians as well as the letter to the Philippians. 'But in the last resort and fundamentally, the anti-enthusiastic battle waged by the apostle is fought under the sign of apocalyptic.'[39] This does not mean that Hellenistic ideas are absent. Paul uses apocalyptic as much in Hellenistic as in Judaistic debate. The passage under discussion shows how hybrid most of the New Testament is. There is no doubt that the knowledge of which Paul speaks has Hellenistic rather than Hebrew overtones.[40] If a Platonic or existentialist exposition seems strangely hybrid, it is good to remember the initial varied character of the New Testament. The observation of different strands in any passage of scripture is the first step towards understanding it.[41]

Eschatology is at first sight weakened by a Platonic account. But Platonism can do better than existentialism at this point. It can also handle eschatology better than the idealism which still passes for Platonism with most theologians. When the antithesis between Plato and the bible is set out, it is normally done in terms of a Platonic

[38] H. Koester, 'The Purpose of the Polemic of a Pauline Fragment (Philippians iii)', *NTS* 8, 4 (1962), 331. Koester says, 'This perfectionistic doctrine of Law, however, was not simply moralistic, but constituted an integral part of an attitude that is best called "radicalized spiritualistic eschatology".'

[39] Käsemann, *EVB* 2, 126; ET *NTQT*, p. 132.

[40] This agrees with Dibelius' account in *An die Thessalonicher 1–11. An die Philipper* (3 ed., Tübingen, 1937), *ad loc.*, and not with Dupont, *Gnosis: la connaissance religieuse dans les epîtres de saint Paul* (Bruges and Paris, 1949), p. 415. The two views are discussed in F. W. Beare, *The Epistle to the Philippians* (London, 1959), pp. 112ff.

[41] As Käsemann has shown repeatedly. Cf. also his comment, 'It is logically unavoidable tensions, considered in a realistic manner, which create the possibility of understanding and life, true though it undoubtedly is that they can also be their destruction.' *ENT*, Preface to the English edition, p. 8.

idealism which is no longer acceptable to students of Plato.[42] Further, Paul's eschatology is not merely negative, reminding the enthusiast that the end is not yet, but primarily positive, assuring the believer that he is on the way, that he is genuinely linked to God by faith. Such incomplete but genuine apprehension is what Platonic participation and assimilation are about. This is why Clement[43] is able to identify the 'twofold end' of Plato (the unattained end and the way to it, or the goodness of the forms and the virtuous life) with the 'twofold hope' of Paul (God and obedience to him, hope expected and hope received, the fulfilment of faith and faith). Paul and Plato share the important theme that there is an ultimate goal which has present ethical significance.

The link between present faith and future fulfilment, or between participation and the Good, or between assimilation and God, is never accidental. They comprise one twofold end or twofold hope. The present way to the end is part of the end. This assurance is found in Plato and Paul. Clement quotes Romans 5 and 6 where Paul insists on what has been done for the believer rather than on how far he still has to go. Romans 6:22 points to present freedom from sin, service to God, fruit of holiness with the end of everlasting life. Romans 5:4, 5 speaks of patience, experience and hope which is not ashamed because of the Spirit who has been given and who has shed God's love abroad in men's hearts.

Some final comments point the way for further reflection. The affinity of the Philippians passage with Stoicism has been observed for some time; however the logic of the passage is Platonic rather than Stoic. There is a marked similarity between the above account and that of Gregory of Nyssa.[44] The similarity is not contrived and indicates a persistent strain of Pauline exposition. The sovereign good is linked with sovereign grace in Clement's twofold end and in Origen's exposition of 'There is none good but God'.[45] Justification is possible through faith in Christ, man's only righteousness. Since at this point we are at the centre of what Jesus and Paul taught, the Platonic affinity requires renewed attention. Even the idea that as man approaches God, he becomes more fully human, has both Christian and Platonic force. Of course, there have been kinds of Platonism which Christianity cannot use and neither is without tension or contradiction.

---

[42] See N. H. Snaith, *The Distinctive Ideas of the Old Testament* (London, 1944), and recently, J. Moltmann, 'Introducing the Theology of Hope', *Colloquium* (1973), p. 20. Compare such views with those of contemporary philosophers, I. Murdoch and I. M. Crombie, not to mention the work of the late F. M. Cornford.

[43] *Strom.* 2.22.131ff. [44] *Against Eunomius*, 8.5.

[45] *Comm. on Matt.* 15.10.

SITUATION ETHICS AND CHRISTIAN LOVE

'Love and do what you will.' The problems associated with situation ethics are not new. Similar issues were central in the attack of Pascal on the Jesuit Order in seventeenth-century France. To argue that it was right sometimes to steal or even to kill seemed reasonable to Jesuit casuistry but outrageous to Pascal.[1] Casuistry and situation ethics point to the openness of Christian ethics as well as to the fallibility of human calculation. The latter point has been ignored in contemporary exaggeration. The main points of situation ethics may be briefly stated. Love is the only intrinsic good and the ultimate norm of Christian behaviour. Decisions should be governed by the situations in which they are made, not by moral prescriptions. Apart from its inconsistency with the New Testament which has other norms than love,[2] the theory has further difficulties.

Obscurity arises from several factors. There is a lack of logical stringency which begins from the tautology, 'Only one "thing" is intrinsically good, namely love: nothing else at all', and 'Love wills the neighbour's good'.[3] The command to love is meaningless without some indication of what love will do;[4] indeed 'people's answers will be as different as their loves'.[5] Gestalt perception displaces argument.[6] Rapid, unexamined dismissal of rival views[7] and pretentious language[8] both suggest that the case could be better stated.

If there are no kinds of moral rules, then ethical reasoning is not possible. Some place for rules must be left in morals:

We are not all of us all the time moral aristocrats like Aristotle
(who, by the way, did not pretend to be moralising for the vulgar).
We are constantly pricked by desire or enraged by opposition; and
the best thing we can do is to sit on ourselves till we come round.
To that end rules are a great stand-by, and they are most serviceable

[1] Pascal, *Les lettres provinciales*, 6, 7, 13, 14.
[2] See above, Chapter 1, p. 35.
[3] J. Fletcher, *Situation Ethics* (London, 1966), pp. 57 and 103.
[4] Cf. A. MacIntyre, *Secularization and Moral Change* (London, 1967), p. 71f.
[5] D. Z. Phillips, in *Christian Ethics and Contemporary Philosophy*
(ed. I. T. Ramsey, London, 1966), p. 314.
[6] J. Fletcher, *Situation Ethics*, p. 141.
[7] E.g., *ibid.* p. 115, 'Sir David Ross tried to find a middle course between
Kant's legalism and Mill's utility. It was not a successful effort.'
[8] 'Credo ut iudicem' and 'ad nauseam' are consistently misspelt, e.g.,
pp. 48 and 124. See S. Potter, *Lifemanship* (Penguin Books, 1962), p. 22,
'To "language up" an opponent is. . .to confuse, irritate and depress by
the use of foreign words, fictitious or otherwise, either singly or in groups.'

when most inflexible: otherwise we shall make exceptions in our own favour.[9]

This is the point of the mediating distinction between 'act-agapism' and 'rule-agapism'.[10] The ultimate norm of love should be expressed in rules which will present personal interest and self-deception from deciding how to express love in particular cases. Finally, when love is separated from other ethical patterns, it involves an unreal estimate of man's sin, including his capacity for self-deception. *Quid est caritas? Magna raritas*, replied the poet. The abstract standard of love can justify the worst actions, as Augustine has shown.

Despite its internal inconsistency, situation ethics may best be seen as a form of act-utilitarianism. 'Let's say plainly that agapē is utility; love is well-being; the Christian who does not individualize or sentimentalize love *is* a utilitarian.'[11] The theory is concerned to bring about the greatest balance of good over evil in the universe. In accepting a utilitarian position it becomes open to a whole range of objections. Utilitarianism has been seriously crippled in recent debate. In the complexity of the modern world, the most encouraging feature is the increasing number of people who are prepared to say that there are some things which they would not do under any circumstances or for any end.[12]

In spite of these weaknesses, situation ethics can illuminate the analysis which we made earlier. Love is the ultimate concern of the Christian and love must produce particular acts rather than general rules. The command to love over-rides all other commands. So that while there is a place for moral rules, they may be destroyed by the one ultimate claim. There is an openness about Christian morality which situation ethics try to preserve. There is also a respect for the particular circumstances which form each situation. In several ways, situation ethics are not radical enough. The case against ultimate rules is supported by righteousness, discipleship and faith as well as love. In each instance the extremes of perfection and particularity destroy the security

[9] A. Boyce Gibson, in *Christian Ethics and Contemporary Philosophy* (ed. I T. Ramsey, London, 1966), p. 115.

[10] This distinction, framed by Frankena and used by Paul Ramsey, *Deeds and Rules in Christian Ethics* (1965), is parallel to the common distinction between act-utilitarianism and rule-utilitarianism.

[11] J. Fletcher, 'What's in a Rule: A Situationist's View', *Norm and Context in Christian Ethics*, p. 332, cited by G. Outka, *Agape, An Ethical Analysis* (Yale University Press, 1972), p. 86.

[12] See Bernard Williams, *Morality* (1973), pp. 111f. However see J. J. C. Smart and Bernard Williams, *Utilitarianism* (Cambridge, 1974), for sustained impressive argument on both sides.

of moral codes. Again, situation ethics show insufficient awareness of their own inadequacy, for 'no absolute claim can be fulfilled in any one context or at any one moment of time'.[13] Finally, too much is trusted to horizontal observation and not enough to divine inventiveness. Situations are not stable and observable in the way supposed by most examples offered.

> Love, concern, is the way of doing things which descends from God himself. Just for that reason, it cannot be pigeonholed. . .You cannot read the inventions of love off from the rules. It would be nice and easy if you could: it would also be unrewarding. You have to find out what to do. You need intelligence, judgement and imagination as well as loyalty and perseverance. No doubt situations are often similar, and then an appeal to precedent will be helpful. But, to the extent that they are not, love will have to find its own way through the bush.[14]

Necessary recognition of man's fallibility should neither blunt imagination nor deny novelty.

Is such love compatible with Platonism? Nygren's *Agape and Eros* denied this compatibility. While this denial has been refuted many times[15] there is enough truth in it to make it plausible. Marcion could not see anything comparable to the outgoing love of his strange God and few would deny that, on this point, Marcion was right. The crucial weakness of Nygren's case is that he omits Plato's account of the overflowing divine goodness in *Timaeus* 29E. Since this was the main point to which Christian Platonists like Justin[16] turned, his assessment can hardly be taken seriously. Other details support this conclusion. Plato insists that the gods are good and causes of good.[17] For Plato as for Aristotle,[18] goodness is active. In Plotinus love for the Good comes from the Good: 'the soul loves him, moved by him to love from the beginning';[19] and the soul, as it is raised by the giver of love, itself becomes love.[20] *Erōs* in Plato, Plotinus and Proclus, works for the good of the beloved, is creative, divine and placed by God in men, a uniting and saving force.[21] The love which Pseudo-Dionysius found in Proclus

---

[13] A. Boyce Gibson, *The Challenge of Perfection* (Melbourne, 1968), p. 22.
[14] *Ibid.* p. 20.
[15] See J. Burnaby, *Amor Dei* (London, 1938), and M. D'Arcy, *The Mind and Heart of Love* (New York, 1959).
[16] *1 Apol.* 10.2 and 59.1–5. See E. F. Osborn, *Justin Martyr* (1973), pp. 44–54.
[17] *Republic* 378f.   [18] *Nic. Eth.* 1168b–1169a.
[19] *Enneads*, vi.7.31.17–18.
[20] *Enneads*, vi.7.22.10.
[21] This paragraph is indebted to the useful statement of A. H. Armstrong, 'Platonic EROS and Christian AGAPE', *DR* (1961), pp. 105–21.

was a descending, cosmic love, active in providence. There is no Platonic incarnation; but there is an immanence which could be consistent with incarnation.[22]

[22] See J. M. Rist, 'Eros and Agape in Pseudo-Dionysius', *VC*, 20 (1966), 236, and A. H. Armstrong, 'The Platonic Tradition', *DR* (1952), pp. 18 and 22.

CONCLUSION

So much for the problems – what positive points emerge? Each pattern has grown and developed. An image or picture is creative and can open up new possibilities. A code of law is hard and dead, but a pattern or picture is never still. The wide variety of insight expressed by very different people confirms the openness and creativity of the four patterns which have been examined. With prolific development there remains remarkable constancy. Clement, Basil, John and Augustine belonged to different historical settings, and were strong in personal idiosyncrasies. Yet, beginning from the variety of the New Testament background, we may move to Alexandria, Asia Minor, Constantinople and North Africa, passing in our travels through four centuries. In such a movement we find that Christian morality is seen by these four people as well as by the New Testament largely in terms of righteousness, discipleship, faith, freedom and love. Few things are as insular as moral discourse, and few things change more rapidly. Yet here in the moral life of people called Christians there is surprising continuity. This gives new reason for speaking of Christian morality as an identifiable phenomenon.

The value of the notion of 'pattern' has been amply proved. Further investigation is needed to clarify the logic of such patterns. The relation between key ideas and related principles is something like that found between principles of natural law and their original axiom; but there is clearly more to be said of the imaginative or aesthetic element. There is very little explicit deduction. Further, how are patterns related to individual pictures like that of the path of justice, the following disciple, the carried cross, the athlete and the soldier? This kind of inquiry may be pursued elsewhere.

What are the main developments within each pattern? Paul's great mystery of the righteousness of God remains part of the gospel; but it is not the most frequent account of righteousness. The key concept is that of order, with which the New Testament is not greatly concerned.[1]

---

[1] The First Letter of Clement of Rome to the Corinthians, 20, makes explicit reference to the value of order for its own sake. See H. von Campenhausen, *Ecclesiastical Authority and Spiritual Power* (London, 1969), p. 87, for perceptive comment.

'Order', says Augustine, 'leads us to God.' There is a developing application of natural law. Philo had already identified the law of Moses with the natural law of the Stoics, and this law becomes important for Christians in discussions with pagans and in stating their own position. A natural law or order lies behind all things for each of the four writers we have considered. The weaknesses of this theory have been indicated. Within the pattern of righteousness there are other developments. The notion of a rule, or a way, recurs especially within the monastic movement. It is related to moderation, harmony and regulation which is part of the idea of order. Christian righteousness is practical. Christians are co-workers with God in his world, daily work is important, and there is no part of life without moral relevance. The rigorism of justice, as we see it especially in Basil, may be linked with either Greek or Hebrew origins or with the New Testament itself.

Discipleship dominates Christian ethics because discipleship is what makes them Christian. The following of Christ is always the first call on the Christian. There is a growing tendency towards intellectualism. The knowledge of God is life eternal. The love of truth is part of Christian discipleship. But in spite of the philosophical modulation from discipleship to assimilation, the notion remains an intensely personal one. Basil has a vehement desire to follow Christ, and Augustine knows that he, who made man, demands all of him. The intense demands of discipleship are accompanied by deepening personal communion. Long after the days of the New Testament, it is remarkable to hear Clement speak in such intimate terms of communion with Christ, to find Basil wounded with love, and John enduring to the end with the words 'Glory to God for all things'. Augustine turns to the psalms for confirmation of the nearness of God, 'It is good for me to hold fast to my God.' The common claim is that never to see the face of Christ would be worse than all the fires of hell.

Faith and freedom correct some of the dangers of righteous legalism. Faith is obstinately Christian, although Clement goes out of his way to prove that most of the Greeks had seen its necessity. Faith was what Christians had to argue for, and they argued well, except that faith became more intellectual in the process. Faith was linked to knowledge as much as to salvation. Nevertheless, from Clement through to Augustine there is a deepening awareness of man's humility before the God of grace, and of man's dependence on the infinite mercy of God. Faith is absolute freedom and absolute dependence. A distinction between free will and freedom is clarified as the years pass. Paul regarded man as responsible for his sin, and yet regarded him as the slave of that sin. The problems involved in this antithesis were made more urgent by the dualism and determinism of Gnostics and Mani-

chees. Free will grew in its importance for Christians; but freedom in
Augustine comes back to be entirely the gift of God's grace.

Love continues to crown the patterns of the Christian life. It becomes more mystical in fervent devotion to Christ. Yet the same love
grows more communal with the passing of the years. The church,
which is the one Christ loving himself, shows itself as a concrete reality.
Christian brotherhood goes beyond the classical ideal of friendship.
Practical expressions of Christian love are indicated in every writer.
Love becomes a rational thing tied to a view of the world. 'Love,'
says Augustine, 'but be careful what you love.' There is an order of
love to be observed. Love becomes more rigorous as it goes from
Clement through to Augustine. The rigour of Augustine has dangers
which are evident in his, 'love and do what you will'; a Christian may
in love persecute his fellow Christian.

May we therefore confidently reject the criticism with which we
began this study or is Christian morality 'incurably unintelligible'?
There is much that is initially obscure in what we have seen. While
the main patterns are clear, there is genuine confusion and contradiction. (Christians did not find moral judgement easier than pagans
whose ethics they had often appropriated.) More important, there is
ambiguity or polarity running through the whole of Christian ethics.
From the New Testament on, there is a strong positive emphasis on
the moral life. Christians must live better lives or the world will rightly
reject their faith. At the same time there is a negative emphasis which
insists that mere morality is a dangerous corruption. Negative ethics
persist throughout Christian history. There is no final resolution of
this problem. Great Christian thinkers are driven to irrational and
crude extremes when confronted by moralism which supplants or could
supplant the gospel. Paul describes legal righteousness as dung (Phil.
3:8) and tells fastidious Galatians to get castrated (Gal. 5:12). Augustine leaves plain invective to Jerome, but his response to Pelagius
remains an embarrassment. Still later, Luther's violence against
Erasmus repeats the offensive behaviour which Paul and Augustine
had shown.[2] Happily, the conflict between positive and negative ethics
is not peculiar to Christianity. Something like it is found in Plato whose
perfectly just man is negative in moral reputation. He enjoys the
worst reputation so that he may gain no advantage from his justice.[3]

This first conflict points to the deeper tension between perfection
and contingency. Here again, we are not far from Plato who argued
from particular cases to the form of the Good. The philosopher must be

[2] Luther, *Table Talk*, I, 797 *et passim*.
[3] *Republic* 361.

king; having seen the form of the Good he must return to the world of contingent things. The similarity with Christian devotion has long been noticed.[4] The other central tension, that of indicative and imperative or grace and law, has affinity with Platonism. For Plato there was one source of goodness and the good man drew from above that good which he expressed in a life of service. From Origen to the Cambridge Platonists the overflowing Good becomes the God of grace. An identification of these polarities and their comparison with similar tensions elsewhere is the first step to understanding. One may look for particular weaknesses. These are not easy to identify; appearances are strongly deceptive.

One particular weakness may be noted. The ethical ideal throughout this period was the martyr, 'Le martyre est le terme normal du voyage.'[5] He achieved likeness to God as far as man may. When the world became Christian, with such mediocre modifications, enthusiasm looked for other ways. None of these could be adequate to the earlier ideal and all indicated some ineptitude with the world. Monasticism combined enthusiasm with a legalism which made the world an enemy, simulating the martyr's position. Nowhere is this clearer than in the attitude to marriage and virginity, where the rival claims are never reconciled. More general weaknesses may be discerned. The central place which Basil gives to obedience is dangerous when the content of obedience is not defined. Again, the competitive streak in perfectionism is persistent. Christians were too anxious to prove that their ideal was better and more accessible than others; whatever pagan philosophers could do without they could also do without.

Yet, when we look at the four writers and their New Testament background, their attitude to the world is strongly positive. In Alexandria it was clearly possible to sin bravely each day of the year without any tedium of self-repetition. There were better places to start being a Christian; in later years many felt that to leave for the desert was the only sound option. But Clement put his ethics into the whole of daily life and discussed a mass of practical details. Basil saw the goal of the contemplative life in the pastoral care of men.[6] John never tired of reminding the monk of the world's need. He saw man's daily work as part of God's plan and design. Augustine maintained the

---

[4] A. E. Taylor, *Plato, the Man and his Work* (London, 1949), pp. 281f. and 295f.

[5] M. Spanneut, *Tertullien et les premiers moralistes africains* (Gembloux, 1969), p. 191.

[6] *Comm. on Isa.* 7. The authorship of this work is contested, but the theme is strong in Basil's milieu. See M. Harl, 'Les trois quarantaines de la vie de Moïse', *REG*, 80 (1967), 407–12.

autonomy of the secular and rejected the triumphalism of his day.[7]
All four were concerned to let the world be the world.

Each pattern has shown sensitivity to the demands of contingency and
perfection, and distortion when the tension between them failed.
Righteousness is neither legalism nor a doctrine of natural law. Discipleship is not ecclesiasticism or asceticism. Faith is neither creed nor
predestinarianism. Love is neither philanthropy nor antinomianism.
Yet each of these and other distortions have been found. Where an
ethic is serious about contingency and perfection it always runs the
risk of losing one for the other. There is no general rule for all cases
except the important principle that no rule can be more than half-
right. The demands of contingency or perfection cannot be generalised
and kept together. Perfectibility is not a present possibility.[8]

Each of the four patterns has grown and developed and yet has had
points where it threatened authentic Christian living. None of the
patterns can survive without respect for contingency and a sense of
perfection. While each picture has its dangers, there are built-in
correctives. Contingency and perfection make the Pharisee stop
swallowing camels and get after the greater righteousness. The apostle
must show his legitimacy by practical humility and his own devotion.
The believer faces the checks of adversity and the openness of freedom.
The antinomian learns that the cup of water is given to Christ. In
each case respect for the contingent and the challenge of perfection
are found.

For patterns and pictures may be dangerous. They can stultify as
well as create. When a man tries to resemble the picture he has made,
he faces 'one of the great paradoxes of morality, namely that in order
to become good it may be necessary to imagine oneself good, and yet
such imagining may also be the very thing which renders improvement
impossible, either because of surreptitious complacency or because of

[7] See R. A. Markus, *Saeculum: History and Society in the Theology of
St Augustine* (Cambridge, 1970), p. 133, where Augustine's thought is
described as a 'synthesis of three themes: first the secularisation of history,
in the sense that all history outside the scriptural canon was seen as
homogeneous and, in terms of ultimate significance, ambivalent; second,
the secularisation of the Roman Empire and of the state and social
institutions in general, in the sense that they had no immediate relation
to ultimate purposes; third, the secularisation of the Church in the sense
that its social existence was conceived in sharp antithesis to an
"otherworldly" Church such as was envisaged by a theology of the
Donatist type.'

[8] On the Christian rejection of perfectibility, see the useful outline in
John Passmore, *The Perfectibility of Man* (London, 1970), especially
pp. 68–93.

some deeper blasphemous infection which is set up when goodness is thought about in the wrong way'.[9] Respect for the contingent is always necessary. If the acting out of a picture becomes an end in itself, the Greek word for actor is appropriate: 'thou hypocrite!' Yet contingency may create problems for Christian ethics. If it invades the pattern to turn art into magic, it will require a literalism which is unattainable. The imitation of Christ cannot look to a literal account of the historical Jesus. Following and assimilation are personal things which go beyond mechanical mimicry. A literal account could not rule centuries and civilisations in the way the gospels have. That is not what respect for contingency means. It means, as Augustine put it, that love must, like fire, seize on the nearest thing and then extend to what is further away.

The challenge to perfection brings the patterns together in righteousness, discipleship, faith and love. Christianity is not the pursuit of the nice and the good. All of the writers we have considered found their powers of rhetoric strained by the task of describing Christian morals. Their approach to ethics must discredit a great deal of what has passed for valid analysis. They show the limitations of the urbanity and unconscious behaviourism of many ethical accounts. 'The "world" of *The Concept of Mind* is the world in which people play cricket, cook cakes, make simple decisions, remember their childhood and go to the circus; not the world in which they commit sins, fall in love, say prayers or join the Communist party.'[10] As William Blake wrote, 'Prudence is a rich ugly old maid, courted by incapacity', and 'The road of excess leads to the palace of wisdom.'[11]

A religion of promise and a theology of hope are needed. That is why Clement linked the Platonic *telos* with a Christian *elpis*.[12] The New Testament is concerned, not with easy perfectionism, but with hope in the future of Jesus Christ. His resurrection is an event which produces history and his word opens the horizon of the future. Because of what he has done, it is possible now to know and serve the promised future in creative discipleship and creative love.[13] It is for Clement

[9] Iris Murdoch, *The Nice and the Good* (London, 1968), p. 75. On the question of imitation, a final comment comes from T. E. Jessop, *Law and Love* (London, 1940), pp. 181ff., 'If. . .it is a mistake to copy the saints, it could be a disaster to copy Jesus. . .We honour and follow a genius, in morals and religion as in art, not by reproducing his external ways, but by catching his spirit and letting it work creatively in our own lives.'

[10] Iris Murdoch, *Sartre* (Cambridge, 1953), p. 35.

[11] W. Blake, *Marriage of Heaven and Hell: Proverbs of Hell;* for exposition of this theme, see A. Boyce Gibson, *The Challenge of Perfection* (Melbourne, 1968).

[12] *Strom.* 2.22. See my *The Philosophy of Clement of Alexandria*, pp. 84f.

[13] See J. Moltmann, *Theology of Hope* (London, 1967), chapters 3, 4, 5, especially p. 338.

an enterprise of noble daring to take one's way to God.[14] For Basil, man is 'ever to be pressing the soul on beyond its strength to do the will of God, having his glory as its object and desire'.[15] Faith is for John the exercise of a noble and youthful mind. The goal is *to phrikōdesteron*, the breathtaking, aweful end of becoming like God. Every man is to be perfect in Christ.[16] Augustine never moves from the simplicity of 'Blessed is he who has God' and the cry of every man, 'Late have I loved thee, O beauty so old and so new!'[17] The good news of Jesus Christ is that they who so hunger and thirst after righteousness shall be filled.

In the end only a theology of the cross will do; for hunger and thirst are more important than being filled. 'Perfect pilgrims, not yet perfect possessors.' 'But if you once say, "that is enough", you have already perished.'[18] Christian ethics, like art, can live only in the presence of its failure.[19] The meek inherit the earth and the poor in spirit possess God's kingdom. Those who share the world's suffering and need may know the liberty of the children of God. Only in the contingent cross is eternal glory seen; and it is seen on earth, for 'the glory of Jesus is that he makes his disciples on earth ready and able to carry the cross after him, while the glory of the church and of Christian living is to be counted worthy to praise the Crucified as God's wisdom and power, to look for salvation in him alone and to make life an act of worship under the sign of Golgotha.'[20] The cross is the chief of all good things, man's glory, his whole confidence and crown.[21]

So we end, where the New Testament began, with a sovereign goodness which reaches out to all men in the world. Such an end is always a beginning; for the divine goodness 'is a living and eternal act of free and undeserved love, an indeficient ocean of bounty, which can never be fathomed or by finite degrees be wholly received'.[22]

---

[14] *Ex.* 10.93.2.

[15] *S.R.* 211.

[16] *Hom. on Heb.* 22.1; cf. Aquinas' account of faith as 'the courage of the spirit'. *Hom. on Matt.* 18.4.

[17] *On the happy life*, 11; *Confessions*, 10.27.

[18] Augustine: 'Perfecti viatores, nondum perfecti possessores.' 'Si autem dixeris, Sufficit, et periisti'. *Sermon* 169.15.18. Cf. *On perfection in righteousness*, 8.19.

[19] Cf. Iris Murdoch, 'Against Dryness', *Encounter* XVI (1961), 20.

[20] E. Käsemann, *Paulinische Perspektiven* (Tübingen, 1969), pp. 106f.; ET, *Perspectives on Paul* (London, 1971), p. 59.

[21] John Chrysostom, *Hom. on Matt.* 54.5.

[22] Thomas Traherne, *Christian Ethics* (1675), chapter 11.

SELECT BIBLIOGRAPHY

TEXTS AND TRANSLATIONS

The most widely accessible series of texts are the *Patrologia Graeca* and the *Patrologia Latina* edited by J. P. Migne. In the former, Clement is found in volumes 8 and 9, Basil is found in volumes 29–52 and John Chrysostom in volumes 47–64. In the latter, Augustine is found in volumes 32–47. A text of Sextus is found in *The Sentences of Sextus*, H. Chadwick (Cambridge, 1959). Citations are from these texts except for Clement who is cited from the edition of O. Stählin, *Die griechischen christlichen Schriftsteller der ersten drei Jahrhunderte*, volumes 12, 15, 17 and 39 (Leipzig, 1905–36).

Selections of text with translations are found in the admirable series, *Sources Chrétiennes*, and to a lesser extent in the *Loeb Classical Library*. Translations into English are available for most of the texts cited, although the translations used are my own except in the case of the ascetic works of Basil where I have followed the translation of W. K. L. Clarke fairly closely. The most extensive and accessible translations are:

Wilson, W.: *Clement of Alexandria, Ante-Nicene Christian Library*, vols. 4, 12 and parts of 22 and 24, Edinburgh, 1882 and 1884.

Clarke, W. K. L.: *The Ascetic Works of Saint Basil*, translated with introduction and notes, London, 1925.

Jackson, B.: *Letters and Select Works, St. Basil, Nicene and Post-Nicene Fathers*, ed. P. Schaff, Second Series, vol. 8, reprinted Michigan, 1968.

Dods, Marcus: *The Works of Augustine*, edited and translated, 15 vols., Edinburgh, 1871–6.

Pusey, E. B. *et al.*, *A Library of the Fathers of the Holy Catholic Church*, Oxford, 1842– , *John Chrysostom*, vols. 18–39.

Various translators: *John Chrysostom, selected works, Nicene and Post-Nicene Fathers*, ed. P. Schaff, First Series, vols. 9–14, reprinted Michigan, 1956.

Various translators: *Augustine, selected works, Nicene and Post-Nicene Fathers*, ed. P. Schaff, First Series, vols. 1–8, reprinted Michigan, 1956.

COMMENT AND EXPOSITION

Allard, P., *S. Basile* (Coll. '*Les Saints*'), 7 ed., Paris, 1929.

Amand, D., *Fatalisme et liberté dans l'antiquité grecque*, Louvain, 1945.

—, *L'ascèse monastique de S. Basile*, Maredsous, 1948.

Amand de Mendieta, E., 'L'amplification d'un thème Socratique et Stoïcien', *Byzantion* (1966), pp. 353–81.

Archambault, P., 'Augustin et Camus', *RA* (1969), pp. 195–221.

Armstrong, A. H., *St. Augustine and Christian Platonism*, Villanova University Press, 1967.

—, 'Platonic EROS and Christian AGAPE', *DR* (1961), pp. 105–21.

—, 'The Platonic Tradition', *DR* (1952).

—, (ed.), *The Cambridge History of Later Greek and Early Medieval Philosophy*, 1967.

Baguette, C., 'Stoïcisme dans la formation d'Augustin', *REA* (1970), pp. 47–77.

Bardy, G., *Clément d'Alexandrie, Les moralistes chrétiens*, Paris, 1926.

—, 'La spiritualité de Clément d'Alexandrie', in *La vie spirituelle*, 1934, pp. 81–104 and 129–45.

Barrett, C. K., *A Commentary on the First Epistle to the Corinthians*, London, 1968.

—, *A Commentary on the Epistle to the Romans*, London, 1957.

—, *The Signs of an Apostle*, London, 1970.

Baur, C., *Der heilige Johannes Chrysostomus und seine Zeit* (2 vols.), Munich 1929, 1930. ET *John Chrysostom and his time*, London, 1959 and 1960.

—, 'Das Ideal der christlichen Vollkommenheit nach dem hl. J. Chrysostomus', in *Theologie und Glaube*, 6 (1914), 564–74.

—, 'Der Weg der Vollkommenheit nach dem hl. J. Chrysostomus', in *Theologie und Glaube*, 20 (1928), 26–41.

Bayet, A., *Le suicide et la morale*, Paris, 1922.

Beardslee, W. A., *Human Achievement and Divine Vocation*, London, 1961.

Békés, G., *De continua oratione Clementis Alexandrini doctrina* (*SA* 14), Rome, 1942.

Benito y Duran, A., 'Filosofía de San Basilio Magno', *Studia Patristica*, v, *TU*, Berlin, 1962.

Berrouard, M. F., 'Augustin et l'indissolubilité du mariage', *RA* (1968), pp. 139–55.

Betz, H. D., *Nachfolge und Nachahmung Jesu Christi im NT*, Tübingen, 1967.

Bigg, C., *The Christian Platonists of Alexandria*, Oxford, 1886.

Bornkamm, Barth and Held, *Tradition and Interpretation in Matthew*, London, 1963.

Boularand, E., *La venue de l'homme à la foi d'après S. Jean Chrysostome*, Rome, 1939.

Bourgeault, G., *Décalogue et morale chrétienne*, Paris–Montreal, 1971.

Bouttier, M., *Christianity according to St. Paul*, London, 1966.

Broudehoux, J. P., *Mariage et famille chez Clément d'Alexandrie*, Paris, 1970.

Bultmann, R., 'Das Problem der Ethik bei Paulus', *ZNW* (1924).

Burnaby, John, *Amor Dei, A study of St. Augustine's teaching on the love of God as the motive of Christian life*, London, 1938.

Buri, F., *Clemens Alexandrinus und die paulinische Freiheitsbegriff*, Zürich and Leipzig, 1939.

Chadwick, H., 'All Things to All Men', *NTS* (1955), 261–75.

—, *The Sentences of Sextus*, Cambridge, 1959.

—, *Early Christian Thought and the Classical Tradition*, Oxford, 1966.

Chrysostomica, Studi e ricerche intorno a S. Giovanni Chrisostomo a cura del Comitato per il XV, centenario della sua morte: 407–1907. Rome, 1908.

Clarke, M. T., *Augustine, Philosopher of Freedom*, New York, 1958.
Clarke, W. K. L., *The Ascetic Works of St. Basil*, translated with introduction and notes, London, 1925.
—, *St. Basil the Great. A Study in Monasticism*, Cambridge, 1913.
Coleman-Norton, P. R., 'St. Chrysostom and the Greek Philosophers', *Classical Philology* (1930), pp. 305–17.
Comeau, M., 'La vie intérieure du Chrétien', *RSR*, 20 (1930), 5–24, 125–49 and 481–505.
Cossu, G. M., 'Il motivo formale della carita in S. Basilio Magno', *Bollettino della Badia Greca di Grottaferrata* (1960).
Courcelle, P., *Recherches sur les Confessions de Saint Augustin*, Paris, 1950, 2nd ed., 1968.
Courtonne, Y., *S. Basile et l'hellénisme*, Paris, 1934.
Cupitt, D., *Crisis of Moral Authority*, London, 1972.
Daloz, L., *Le travail selon St. Jean Chrysostome*, Paris, 1959.
D'Arcy, E., *Human Acts*, Oxford, 1963.
Davies, W. D., *The Setting of the Sermon on the Mount*, Cambridge, 1964.
Dehnard, H., *Das Problem der Abhängigkeit des Basilius von Plotin*, Berlin, 1964.
Delhaye, P., *Permanence du droit naturel*, Paris, 1960.
Dihle, A., 'Demut' in *RAC*, 6, 646–796.
Dirking, A., 'Die Bedeutung des Wortes Apathie beim heiligen Basilius dem Grossen,' *Theologische Quartalschrift*, 134 (1954), 202–12.
Donahue, J. R., 'Stoic indifferents and Christian indifference in Clement of Alexandria', *Traditio*, 19 (1963), 438–47.
Dumortier, J., 'La culture profane de S. Jean Chrysostome', in *Mélanges de science religieuse*, 10 (1953), 53–62.
—, 'Les idées morales de S. Jean Chrysostome', in *MSR*, 12 (1955), 27–36.
Ebeling, G., *The Nature of Faith*, London, 1961, ET of *Das Wesen des christlichen Glaubens*, Tübingen, 1959.
Elser, 'Der hl. Chrysostomus und die Philosophie', in *Theologische Quartalschrift*, Tübingen, 1894, 550–76.
Enslin, M. J., *The Ethics of Paul*, New York, 1930.
d'Entrèves, A. P., *Natural Law*, 2nd ed., London, 1970.
Ernesti, K., *Die Ethik des Titus Flavius Clemens von Alexandreia*, Paderborn, 1900.
Evans, R. F., *Pelagius: Inquiries and Reappraisals*, London, 1968.
Faller, O., 'Griechische Vergottung und christliche Vergöttlichung', *Gregorian* VI (1925).
Festugière, A. J., *Antioche païenne et chrétienne. Libanius, Chrysostome et les moines de Syrie*, Paris, 1959.
Fletcher, J., *Moral Responsibility*, London, 1967.
Flückiger, F., *Geschichte des Naturrechtes*, Zürich, 1964.
Folliet, G., 'Aux origines de l'ascétisme et du cénobitisme africain', *SA* 46 (Rome, 1961).
Foot, P. (ed.), *Theories of Ethics*, Oxford, 1967.
Freeman, K., *The Paths of Justice*, London, 1954.
Funk, F. X., *Klemens von Alexandrien über Familie und Eigentum*, *Kirchengeschichtliche Abhandlungen und Untersuchungen* II, Paderborn, 1899.

Furnish, V. R., *The Love Command in the New Testament*, New York, 1972.
—, *Theology and Ethics in Paul*, Nashville, 1962.
Gibson, A. Boyce, *The Challenge of Perfection*, Melbourne, 1968.
—, *Theism and Empiricism*, London, 1970.
Giet, S., *Les idées sociales de S. Basile*, Paris, 1941.
—, 'Le rigorisme de S. Basile', *Revue des sciences religieuses*, 23 (1949), 333–42.
—, *Sasimes*, Paris, 1941.
Gilson, E., *The Christian Philosophy of Saint Augustine*, London, 1961.
Gosselin, R., *La morale de S. Augustin*, Paris, 1925.
Gribomont, J., *L'Origénisme de S. Basile, L'homme devant Dieu, Mélanges offerts à H. de Lubac*, Paris, 1963.
—, 'Les règles morales de S. Basile et le NT', *Studia Patristica* II (Berlin, 1957), 416–26.
Halliburton, R. J., 'Fact and Fiction in the Life of Augustine', *RA* (1968).
Hand, V., *Augustin und das klassisch-römische Selbstverständnis*, Hamburg, 1970.
Hare, R. M., *Freedom and Reason*, Oxford, 1963.
—, *The Language of Morals*, 2 ed. Oxford, 1961.
Harl, M., 'Les trois quarantaines de la vie de Moïse', *REG*, 80 (1967), 407–412.
Hausherr, I., 'Les grands courants de la spiritualité orientale', *Orientalia Christiana Periodica* I (1935).
Hengel, M., *Nachfolge und Charisma*, Berlin, 1968.
Heussi, K., *Der Ursprung des Mönchtums*, Tübingen, 1936.
Holl, K., *Enthusiasmus und Bussgewalt beim griechischen Mönchtum*, Leipzig, 1898.
—, *Ueber das griechische Mönchtum, Ges. Aufsätze* II, Tübingen, 1928.
Holte, R., *Béatitude et sagesse, S. Augustin et le problème de la fin de l'homme dans la philosophie ancienne*, Paris, 1962.
Houlden, J. L., *Ethics and the New Testament*, Penguin Books, 1973.
Huby, P., *Greek Ethics*, Oxford, 1967.
Humbertclaude, P., *La doctrine ascétique de s. Basile de Césarée*, Paris, 1932.
Jessop, T. E., *Law and Love*, London, 1940.
Jolivet, R., *Essai sur les rapports entre la pensée grecque et la pensée chrétienne*, Paris, 1955.
Joly, R., *Le vocabulaire chrétien de l'amour, est-il original?*, Brussels, 1968.
Jüngel, E., *Paulus und Jesus*, Tübingen, 1964.
Käsemann, E., *An die Römer*, Tübingen, 1973.
—, *Die Legitimität des Apostels*, Darmstadt, 1956.
—, *Exegetische Versuche und Besinnungen*, 2 vols., Göttingen, 1960 and 1966; ET *Essays on New Testament Themes*, London, 1964; *New Testament Questions of Today*, London, 1969.
—, *Der Ruf der Freiheit*, Tübingen, 1968; ET *Jesus Means Freedom*, London, 1969.
—, *Jesu letzter Wille nach Johannes 17*, Tübingen, 1966; ET *The Testament of Jesus*, London, 1968.
—, *Paulinische Perspektiven*, Tübingen, 1969; ET *Perspectives on Paul*, London, 1971.
Keeling, M., *Morals in a Free Society*, London, 1967.

Kramer, W., *Christ, Lord, Son of God*, London, 1966; ET of *Christos Kyrios Gottessohn*, Zürich, 1963.

Laird, J., *An Enquiry into Moral Notions*, London, 1935.

Laun, F., 'Die beiden Regeln des Basilius, ihre Echtheit und Entstehung', in *Zeitschrift für Kirchengeschichte* 44 (1925), 1–61.

Leduc, F., 'Le thème de la vaine gloire chez S. Jean Chrysostome', *POC* (1969).

Legrand, P. E., *S. Jean Chrysostome, Les moralistes chrétiens*, 2 ed., Paris, 1924.

Lilla, S., *Clement of Alexandria*, Oxford, 1971.

Lindsay, A. D., *The Moral Teaching of Jesus*, London, 1937.

Macleish, N., *The Knowledge of God*, Edinburgh, 1938.

Malingrey, A. M., *Philosophia*, Paris, 1961.

Manson, T. W., *Ethics and the Gospel*, London, 1960.

Markus, R. A., *Saeculum: History and Society in the Theology of St Augustine*, Cambridge, 1970.

Marrou, H. I., 'Humanisme et christianisme chez Clément d'Alexandrie d'après le Pédagogue', in *Entretiens sur l'antiquité classique*, III, *Recherches sur la tradition platonicienne*, Fondation Hardt, Geneva, 1955.

Maur, I. a.d., *Mönchtum und Glaubensverkündigung in den Schriften des hl. Johannes Chrysostomus*, Freiburg/Schw., 1959.

Mausbach, J., *Die Ethik des heiligen Augustinus*, 2 vols., Freiburg/Br., 1929.

Méhat, A., *Étude sur les Stromates de Clément d'Alexandrie*, Paris, 1966.

Merlin, N., *S. Augustin et les dogmes du péché originel et de la grâce*, Paris, 1931.

Mersch, E., 'Deux traits de la doctrine spirituelle de S. Augustin', *Nouvelle Revue* 57 (1930), 391–410.

Meyer, L., 'Liberté et moralisme chrétien dans la doctrine spirituelle de S. Jean Chrysostome', in *RSR*, 23 (1923), 283–305.

—, 'Perfection chrétienne et vie solitaire dans la pensée de S. Jean Chrysostome', in *Revue d'ascétique et de mystique*, 14 (1933), 232–62.

—, *S. Jean Chrysostome, maître de perfection chrétienne*, Paris, 1933.

Morison, E. F., *St. Basil and his Rule. A Study in Early Monasticism*, Oxford, 1912.

Moule, C. F. D., 'Obligation in the Ethic of Paul', in *Christian History and Interpretation, For John Knox*, ed. Farmer, Moule and Niebuhr, Cambridge, 1967.

—, *The Birth of the New Testament*, London, 1962.

Murdoch, I., *Sartre*, Cambridge, 1953.

—, 'Metaphysics and Ethics', in *The Nature of Metaphysics*, ed. D. F. Pears, London, 1957.

—, 'Vision and Choice in Morality', in *Christian Ethics and Contemporary Philosophy*, ed. I. T. Ramsey, London, 1966.

—, 'The Idea of Perfection', *Yale Review*, LIII (Spring 1964), 342–80.

—, *The Nice and the Good*, London, 1968.

—, *The Sovereignty of Good*, London, 1970.

Neander, J. A. W., *Der hl. Johannes Chrystostomus*, 2 vols., 3 ed., Berlin, 1858; ET London, 1845.

Niebuhr, R., *An Interpretation of Christian Ethics*, London, 1936.

Nineham, D. E., *Historicity and Chronology in the NT*, London, 1965.

Nothomb, D. M., 'Charité et unité. Doctrine de S. Basile le grand sur la charité envers le prochain', *POC*, 4 (1954), 309–21 and 5 (1955), 3–13.

O'Connell, R. J. *St. Augustine's Early Theory of Man*, Harvard, 1968.

O'Connor, D. J., *Aquinas and Natural Law*, London, 1967.

O'Meara, J. J., 'Augustine and Neoplatonism', *RA* (1958), pp. 91ff.

Oppenheimer, H., *The Character of Christian Morality*, London, 1965.

Osborn, E. F., 'Ethical Perspectives in the New Testament', *Australian Biblical Review*, xvi (1968), 1–14.

—, *Justin Martyr*, Tübingen, 1973.

—, *The Philosophy of Clement of Alexandria*, Cambridge, 1957.

Outka, G., *Agape, An Ethical Analysis*, New Haven and London, 1972.

— and Ramsey, P., *Norm and Context in Christian Ethics*, London, 1969.

Pascal, B., *Les provinciales*, ed. H. F. Stewart, Manchester, 1920.

Passmore, J., *The Perfectibility of Man*, London, 1970.

Pfitzner, V. C., *Paul and the Agon Motif*, Leiden, 1967.

Preisker, O., *Das Ethos des Urchristentums*, Gütersloh, 1949.

Preiss, Th., 'La mystique de l'imitation du Christ et de l'unité chez Ignace d'Antioche', *RHPR* (1938), pp. 197–241.

Prunet, O., *La morale de Clément d'Alexandrie*, Paris, 1966.

Puech, A., *S. Jean Chrysostome et les moeurs de son temps*, Paris, 1891.

Quatember, F., *Die christliche Lebenshaltung des Klemens von Alexandreia nach seinem Pädagogus*, Wien, 1946.

Ramsey, I. T., (ed.), *Christian Ethics and Contemporary Philosophy*, London, 1966.

Rimml, R., 'Das Furchtproblem in der Lehre des hl. Augustin', *Zeitschrift für katholische Theologie*, 45 (1921), 50–65.

Rist, J. M., 'Eros and Agape in Pseudo-Dionysius', *VC*, 20 (1966).

Rivière, J., *S. Basile, évêque de Césarée, Les moralistes chrétiens*, Paris, 1925.

Rondet, H., 'La théologie de la grâce dans la correspondance de S. Augustin', *RA*, 1958.

Rüther, T., *Die Lehre von der Erbsünde bei Clemens von Alexandrien*, Freiburg/Br., 1922.

—, *Die sittliche Forderung der Apatheia in den beiden ersten christlichen Jahrhunderten und bei Klemens von Alexandrien*, Freiburg/Br., 1949.

Sage, A., 'La contemplation dans les communautés de vie fraternelle', *RA* (1971).

—, 'La règle de S. Augustin', *REA* (1968).

Schaffner, O., *Christliche Demut*, Würzburg, 1959.

Scholl, E., *Die Lehre des hl. Basilius von der Gnade*, Freiburg, 1881.

Schulz, A., *Nachfolge und Nachahmung*, München, 1962.

Schulz, S., *Die Stunde der Botschaft*, Hamburg, 1967.

Schweizer, E., *Lordship and Discipleship*; ET, London, 1960.

Scott, C. A. Anderson, *New Testament Ethics*, Cambridge, 1930.

Sevenster, J. N., *Paul and Seneca*, Leiden, 1961.

Smart, J. J. C., and Williams, Bernard, *Utilitarianism, For and Against*, Cambridge, 1973.

Spanneut, M., *Tertullien et les premiers moralistes africains*, Gembloux, 1969.

Spidlik, T., *La sophiologie de S. Basile, Orientalia Christiana Analecta* 162 (Rome, 1961).

Stiglmayr, J., 'Zur Aszese des heiligen Chrysostomus', in *ZAM* (1929), 29–48.

Stockmeier, P., *Theologie und Kult des Kreuzes bei Johannes Chrysostomus*, Trier, 1966.
Strathmann, H., *Geschichte der frühchristlichen Askese*, Leipzig, 1914.
Telfer, W., 'The trustworthiness of Palladius', *JTS*, 38 (1937), 379–82.
Ternus, J., 'Paulinische, Philonische, Augustinische Anthropologie', *Scholastik* II (1963).
Thonnard, F. J., 'La morale conjugale selon S. Augustin', *REA* (1969), pp. 113–31.
—, 'La notion de concupiscence en philosophie augustinienne', *RA* (1965), pp. 95–105.
—, 'La notion de liberté en philosophie augustinienne', *REA* (1970), pp. 242–70.
Troeltsch, E., *Augustin, die christliche Antike und das Mittelalter*, München u. Berlin, 1915.
Vandenberghe, B. H., 'La théologie du travail de S. Jean Chrysostome', *Revista Española de teología*, 16 (1956), 475–95.
Verbeke, G., 'Augustin et la stoïcisme', *RA* (1958), pp. 81f.
Verheijen, L., *La règle de S. Augustin*, 2 vols., Paris, 1967.
Viller, M., 'Le martyr et l'ascèse', *RAM*, VI (1925), 105–42.
—, 'Martyre et perfection', *RAM* VI (1925), 3–25.
—, and Rahner, K., *Aszese und Mystik in der Väterzeit*, Freiburg/Br., 1939.
Vischer, L., *Basilius der Grosse, Untersuchungen zu einem Kirchenvater des. 4. Jahrhunderts*, Basel, 1953.
Völker, W., *Das Vollkommenheitsideal des Origenes*, Tübingen, 1931.
—, *Der wahre Gnostiker nach Clemens Alexandrinus*, Berlin and Leipzig, 1952.
von Campenhausen, H., *Tradition and Life in the Church*, London, 1968.
von Wright, G. H., *The Varieties of Goodness*, London, 1963.
Wagner, W., *Der Christ und die Welt nach Clemens von Alexandrein*, Göttingen, 1903.
Warnock, G. J., *Contemporary Moral Philosophy*, London, 1967.
Watson, N. M., Review article, 'The Meaning of Righteousness in Paul', *NTS*, 20, 2 (1974), 217–28.
Wilder, A. M., 'Equivalents of Natural Law in the Teaching of Jesus', *JR* (*1946*), pp. 125–35.
Williams, B., *Morality*, Penguin Books, 1973.
Woods, G. F., *A Defence of Theological Ethics*, Cambridge, 1966.
Ziesler, J. A., *Christian Asceticism*, London, 1973.
—, *The Meaning of Righteousness in Paul*, Cambridge, 1972.
Zumkeller, A., *Das Mönchtum des heiligen Augustinus*, Würzburg, 1968.

INDEX OF PASSAGES CITED

A. THE OLD TESTAMENT

B. THE NEW TESTAMENT

C. CLASSICAL, JEWISH AND EARLY CHRISTIAN WRITINGS

INDEX OF MODERN AUTHORS

SUBJECT INDEX